Creative Industries and Economic Evolution

NEW HORIZONS IN INSTITUTIONAL AND EVOLUTIONARY ECONOMICS

Series Editor: Geoffrey M. Hodgson
Research Professor, University of Hertfordshire Business School, UK

Economics today is at a crossroads. New ideas and approaches are challenging the largely static and equilibrium-oriented models that used to dominate mainstream economics. The study of economic institutions – long neglected in the economics textbooks – has returned to the forefront of theoretical and empirical investigation.

This challenging and interdisciplinary series publishes leading works at the forefront of institutional and evolutionary theory and focuses on cutting-edge analyses of modern socio-economic systems. The aim is to understand both the institutional structures of modern economies and the processes of economic evolution and development. Contributions will be from all forms of evolutionary and institutional economics, as well as from Post-Keynesian, Austrian and other schools. The overriding aim is to understand the processes of institutional transformation and economic change.

Titles in the series include:

An Economic Analysis of Innovation
Extending the Concept of National Innovation Systems
Markus Balzat

Evolutionary Economics and Environmental Policy
Survival of the Greenest
Jeroen C.J.M. van den Bergh, Albert Faber, Annemarth M. Idenburg and Frans H. Oosterhuis

Property Rights, Consumption and the Market Process
David Emanuel Andersson

The Evolution of Path Dependence
Edited by Lars Magnusson and Jan Ottosson

Economics, Culture and Social Theory
William A. Jackson

Deep Complexity and the Social Sciences
Experience, Modelling and Operationality
Robert Delorme

Creative Industries and Economic Evolution
Jason Potts

Creative Industries and Economic Evolution

Jason Potts

Senior Lecturer in Economics, University of Queensland and Principal Research Fellow, Queensland University of Technology, Australia

Edward Elgar

Cheltenham, UK • Northampton, MA, USA

Published by
Edward Elgar Publishing Limited
The Lypiatts
15 Lansdown Road
Cheltenham
Glos GL50 2JA
UK

Edward Elgar Publishing, Inc.
William Pratt House
9 Dewey Court
Northampton
Massachusetts 01060
USA

A catalogue record for this book
is available from the British Library

Library of Congress Control Number: 2010939248

ISBN 978 1 84720 662 6 (cased)

Typeset by Servis Filmsetting Ltd, Stockport, Cheshire
Printed and bound by MPG Books Group, UK

Contents

Tables

Acknowledgements

This is the part where I thank everyone else for writing this book for me. Nice to be able to do that but here I really must, not at the bidding of false modesty but more to head off possible law-suits: six chapters were jointly written with colleagues ranging over cultural and media studies, ethnography, complexity theory, regional geography and behavioural economics. Who knows how litigious they might be? My thanks to Stuart Cunningham, John Hartley, John Banks, Paul Ormerod, Michael Keane and Peter Earl, all of whom contributed substantially to various ideas in this book and enabled a breadth and depth of perspective that would have been impossible for me working alone. (They are also excused from any speculations they do not wish to take credit for.) Thanks also to Lucy Montgomery, Jean Burgess, Axel Bruns, Hasan Bahkshi, and others at the ARC Centre of Excellence in Creative Industries and Innovation (the CCI) at Queensland University of Technology who have discussed and debated the ideas herein. This book was written across several universities, so an institutional acknowledgement is also due to Imperial College Business School (London), the Vice-Chancellor's Office at City University (London), and the support of the National Endowment for Technology, Science and the Arts (London). Thanks also to the publishers of *Agenda, New Media and Society, Journal of Cultural Economics, Policy*, and *International Journal of Cultural Policy* for kind permission to reproduce (in substantially edited form) parts of Chapters 3, 5, 6, 8 and 12.

1. Introduction

1.1 DYNAMIC VALUE AND THE ECONOMICS OF CULTURE

This book offers a new way of looking at the arts, culture and the creative industries from the perspective of evolutionary economics. It offers a 'new' cultural economics, or better: an *evolutionary economics of creative industries*.

The evolutionary economic approach to cultural and creative industries is new because it largely abandons the dominant neoclassical market-failure model of welfare and subsidy that otherwise underpins modern cultural economics. An excellent survey of this is Throsby (1994). Instead, it offers a market-process model of innovation dynamics and economic and cultural co-evolution. This is not a new approach (Grampp 1989, Cowen 1998, 2002, Peacock 1993, 2006, Cowen and Kaplan 2004, among others) but more a new consolidation. I propose here a general framework to refocus the economic analysis of arts and culture away from market-welfare arguments and cultural protectionism and instead towards open-market arguments based on consumer and producer uptake of new ideas, innovation dynamics, and industrial evolution. This focus on evolutionary economic dynamics of arts and culture leads us to trace different economic mechanisms – specifically, the contribution of the creative economy to the innovation system. In turn, this leads to very different policy models. So this is a book about the economics of arts and culture but done so from the perspective of economic evolution.

Let me be clear about my intentions from the start. I do believe that the arts, culture and creativity are all good things (that is, they are 'goods') and that we should seek to have more of them. It's that last bit – the 'more of them' – that is the economics part because there are several ways you can do that. One is to find market failure and then correct it in a Pigovian manner, for example with subsidy. This is market support in theory, but in practice works as an incomes policy. From the evolutionary economics perspective, the problem with this model is that it actually fails here, just as elsewhere in the economic order, due to the stultifying effect it has on entrepreneurship and innovation. It's the 'things unseen' – *ála* Bastiat

– the frustrated dynamics that are the problem. So we need a better model, a better way of unleashing the forces of a creative economy.

The model I propose – the evolutionary economics of the creative industries – is based on the theory of innovation in the context of market-based economic evolution. Central to this model is a focus on what the arts, cultural and creative industries do best, as they have throughout history: namely they drive, facilitate and engender the origination, adoption and retention of new ideas (the innovation process) into the socio-cultural and economic system. From this perspective, the prime economic value of the arts, cultural and creative sectors is not heritage or entertainment, or the like. Rather, these are spillovers from the deeper contribution of this sector to the processes of economic dynamics. The arts, cultural and creative industries sectors are economically significant and interesting because as part of the innovation system they are a mechanism of economic evolution. That's the line I argue in this book.

This will advance a 'dynamic value' argument based in the theory of economic evolution: that's the underlying economics. This does not diminish or sully the many positive externalities of the arts, cultural and creative industries sector to personal or national identity, to community cohesion or humanistic integrity, or even to social justice. But these are not the most interesting thing about the arts, cultural and creative economy from the evolutionary economic perspective: for that we must look to the role of arts, culture and the creative industries in terms of their contribution to the process of economic evolution. I will venture to explain how the creative industries are in important ways on par with science and technology, also a significant force of economic evolution. The difference is that whereas science and technology deals mostly with the manipulation and development of new material forms and the economic opportunities this creates (Arthur 2009), the arts, cultural and creative sectors deal with the human interface, with the new ways of being and thinking and interacting, and with, in effect, the human side of change. In other words, they operate on the demand side of economic evolution, whereas science and technology operate mostly on the supply side. This should not be construed as 'hard' (technology and engineering) versus 'soft' (arts and play): that is a category error. Rather, we need only recognize that all innovation processes and trajectories – the processes that drive all economic growth and development as an evolutionary process of 'creative destruction' – involve people originating and adopting new ideas, learning to do new things and experimenting with variations, and seeking to embed these new ideas into new habits, routines, and even identities (Chapter 7). That is often done in a highly social context (Chapters 8 and 14). The arts, cultural and creative industries all contribute to the innovation processes that shape economic evolution (Chapter 9). That is why this book focuses on the dynamic value of the creative industries (which is not everywhere the same as their intrinsic value, cultural value or market value).

For too long this has not been the predominant view of the arts and cultural sectors. From the perspectives of popular public policy (Throsby 2001, 2006), political economy (Du Gay and Pryke 2002, Hesmondhalgh 2002) and much of cultural economics (Towse ed. 1997, 2003), the production of arts, culture and creativity is often slanted toward a view that they are somehow special, possibly separate, sometimes ineffable; too important in any case to be left entirely to the market. This gives rise to the modern (since the 1950s at the latest) protectionist instinct in cultural policy that, in turn, has led to the many various endeavours to shelter and protect this 'exceptional' sector behind walls of cultural-elite administered public funding bodies or by other regulatory and institutional means.

So this will also be an anti-protectionist book, but not from a market efficiency perspective. My argument will be closer to a gains-from-trade line, in the classic Adam Smith (*Wealth of Nations*) and Tyler Cowen (2002) sense, but it is ultimately about evolutionary dynamics. The market failure and subsequently protectionist approach is flawed, I believe, because it is built on a fundamental misconception of the economic value of the arts and cultural sector. In short, it values it as an asset (a cultural asset) to be preserved and maintained and possibly shielded from the market. Yet in doing so it overlooks the role of the arts, cultural and creative industries in the dynamic process of evolutionary change. This requires a different perspective, namely, not a view of this sector that sees just a bunch of cultural workers, assets or even treasures, but instead a view that has at its focus the 'human capital' of creativity, novelty generation, new interpretations and meanings, and all of the creative skills and abilities that enable humans to continually change and adapt to changing ecological, social, technological and economic environments. That's what this book is about.

1.2 CREATIVITY RISING

The rise of the concept of the 'creative class', the 'creative industries' and the 'creative economy', both as academic and policy focus, has occurred only recently. Through the 1970s and 1980s the industrial development orthodoxy was argued to be essentially driven by large-scale corporate R&D-based models of innovation and national innovation systems (Nelson ed. 1993, Rothwell 1994). Economists and technocrats thus favoured strong industry and innovation policy directed at high technology and emerging technology sectors, often in conjunction with government assistance (such as MITI in Japan, ITRI in Taiwan, or partnerships with military contractors such as in the US, or with government research, such as CSIRO in Australia). Economists had long pointed to the significance of human capital in the economic growth process (Schultz 1961, Romer 1990a), but this focused on the importance of investment in education, particularly higher education. Within this model, human capital contributed to the innovation system that powered economic growth and development; the arts and culture contributed little, basically nothing. The arts and cultural industries were viewed as just another industry – media and entertainment, say – or as a sector to be preserved in order to maintain cultural assets and capabilities. This was done so that citizens or future generations might perhaps enjoy and value them, but in essence it relied on non-economic justifications; for cultural reasons mostly, but social and political reasons too. Appended to this was invariably a Keynesian 'good for the economy' argument of spending multipliers, tourism and urban development; but no mention of innovation.

During the 1990s a new line of argument began to emerge – first in Australia (in a much ridiculed 'Creative Nation' report of 1994) and more fully in the UK (DCMS 1998) – that refocussed the notion of treating the arts and cultural sector as a net drain on the economy (though one worth having due to positive cultural externalities), and instead sought to connect it to economic growth and innovation policy (for example, Hartley and Cunningham 2001). This was advanced by a motley group of economists and urban geographers, drawn from the study of economic growth, human capital, urban development and innovation. They offered a very different perspective that emphasized the role of cultural investment in creating the conditions under which innovation and growth can thrive. This approach came to focus on a wider set of industries than the core arts and cultural industries (heritage, craft, visual and performing arts, and so on), extending it to the more commercial domains of fashion, design, new media, video games, and the like. The 'economics of creative industries' framework thus emerged through a focus on the growth and development benefits of creative industries at multiple levels, from entrepreneurship, urban regeneration, regional development and national economic growth (Hartley et 2005, Work Foundation 2007). I will seek here to further develop this 'innovation and growth' line of argument by unpacking it into a framework of evolutionary economics (Dopfer 2005, Dopfer and Potts 2008).

Evolutionary economics centres on the study of economic growth and development. But it differs from 'new growth theory' (Paul Romer, Robert Lucas et al.) by placing less emphasis on human capital, ideas and technology spillovers *per se*, and more on the role of entrepreneurship, innovation trajectories, and the market process of Schumpeterian creative destruction. These are certainly not mutually exclusive domains and there is much theoretical overlap. But because the evolutionary approach focuses on the disequilibrium processes of an innovation trajectory, it allows us to elucidate the role of the creative industries in the dynamics of economic evolution. Specifically, it connects the creative industries to different phases of an innovation trajectory and to the organizations, social networks and institutions that facilitate this process. It seeks to explain how the creative industries are an integral part of the innovation system (Handke 2006, Bakhshi et al. 2008, Potts 2009b). Whatever their cultural value or static economic value, the creative industries are from the evolutionary economic perspective also a much underappreciated part of the explanation of long-run economic growth and development.

This may seem a curious thesis. For how can it be that industries devoted to seemingly superficial domains of media, fashion, craft, design, performing arts, advertising, architecture, heritage, music, film and television, games, publishing and interactive software can possibly contribute to the deep and serious pathways of economic growth and development? At first sight, the creative industries are not progenitors of the standard causes of economic growth in developing new technology, in capital deepening, in operational efficiency, in business model innovation, or in institutional evolution. Yet look closer and it becomes apparent that many of the people and businesses in this sector are intimately involved in all of these things.[1] The creative industries are deeply engaged in the experimental use of new technologies, in developing new content and applications, and in creating new business models. They are broadly engaged in the coordination of new technologies to new lifestyles, new meanings and new ways of being, which in turn is the basis of new business opportunities. The creative industries are not seminal forces of material economic growth, but they are commonly germinal in their role in coordinating the individual and social structure of novelty and in resetting the definition of normal.

To be clear, I am not arguing the trivially obvious point that the cultural and creative industries produce economic value. Of course they do: they are part of what people like (that is, they produce goods), and so there is production and consumption on the order of 3–8 per cent of GDP in most developed nations, which is a lot. Nor am I arguing that they are of unappreciated economic significance, which was more or less the line advanced by creative industries champions such as the UK's DCMS when pointing to their contribution to jobs and value added in most OECD economies. I take these points as given and, to be frank, largely uninteresting. (Note for example that you could make the same argument about the 'destructive industries' (demolition, waste processing, recycling, and so on): they too are economically significant and probably underappreciated.) But I want to argue a stronger and perhaps more contentious point, namely that the creative industries are important and significant in the evolutionary process of economic growth and development due to their hitherto underappreciated role in the *facilitation and* re-coordination of economic change. Creative industries are important mechanisms in the process of economic evolution through their role in the origination, adoption and retention of new ideas.

This may seem counter-intuitive. We know that economic growth and development is driven by innovation as new ideas are developed and diffused through the economic order. Yet this is not as orderly a process as if new ideas were somehow piled on top of old ideas. Instead, economic growth is an evolutionary process of 'creative destruction' (as explained by both Karl Marx and Joseph Schumpeter) in which the knowledge-base of agents, firms, industries and nations are transformed from within. This will often involve significant disruption of previous activities along with new connections and patterns of trade, production and consumption. Economic evolution involves people changing what they do, changing who they are, how they live, and even what they think; the creative industries are key providers of the mechanisms and resources for this process of adaptation.

Economic growth requires continuous re-coordination of the economic order[2] and the principal mechanism to achieve this is the market system. Yet coordination through price signals is only one (albeit the central one) of many coordination processes at work in an evolving economic order. Other mechanisms include hierarchy and power relations (as in a firm or organization), networks, and a broad class of social mechanisms of shared signs, symbols, stories and other messages (Hermann-Pillath 2010). It is this latter set of functions in relation to the dynamics of 'messages, identity and meaning-making' that, I hypothesize, plays a fundamental role in an evolving economy by socially processing innovations to re-coordinate the economic order (a theme examined in Chapter 14). The creative industries contribute to the social technologies of the innovation system.

Admittedly, this may seem abstract. With the exception of advertising and possibly architecture it is far from obvious that the creative industries are consciously and deliberately engaged in this function to advance the dynamic efficiency of market capitalism. Indeed, in the cases of the subversive arts, music, fashion, and again architecture, the opposite may seem closer to the truth. Yet consider how economic growth generates increased surplus that will be in part consumed through increased arts and culture (messages and meaning), which in turn feeds back to renewed sources of economic growth as the messages and meaning-making in effect processes the new technologies such that they become socially embedded, opening new opportunities for value creation. This process may well be indirect, possibly in the extreme, making it difficult to analytically trace and examine. But a world of continual change in the underlying ideas that compose the economic order is sustainable only to the extent that mechanisms operate to continually re-coordinate the personal identity, social organization and institutions that ultimately compose the economic order.

Economic growth, in other words, involves more than just the existence of new (technological) ideas, or the broad adoption of new ideas, but fully requires that these new ideas lead to changed behaviours, habits and routines, changed personal identities and social organization, and to a renewed sense of what is normal, all of which is the outcome of the sorts of services provided by the creative industries. This requires more than just research, development, production and distribution. It also requires new ways of thinking that lead to new ways of living (as examined in Chapter 7 on identity dynamics): it is here that the creative industries, however indirectly, play their role in the process of ongoing economic evolution.

This dynamic emergent conception is a long way from the conventional economic and policy treatment of the cultural economy. The long-standing orthodoxy is that these humanities-soaked cultural industries are simple beneficiaries of the wealth-creating and societal-transforming power of the science, technology and engineering-based growth of knowledge processes as the main drivers of economic growth since the industrial revolution. They are certainly not, in this canon, responsible for any aspect of such growth and development. They are grudging and begrudged beneficiaries of technology-led growth, not generators.

The arts and cultural aspects of the economy do of course produce value *qua* value – but it is artistic and cultural value that adds to cultural wealth, not economic wealth. These economic domains are, it is commonly supposed, properly viewed as objects of cultural policy not economic policy. But my central thesis is that this view is wrong because it misrepresents the extent and indeed existence of the many essential services involved in the process of adaptation to novelty and the facilitation of change that by definition underpins economic evolution.

I will not much argue here that the economic value of the creative industries derives from their seminal 'creative' contributions as generators of new ideas. I will not argue the insipid line that creative industries produce creativity. The creative industries are probably no more or less creative in this sense than, say, the engineering or agricultural industries, both of which also deal in the origination of new ideas. I stress this because I think a singularly unhelpful misunderstanding has crept into much thinking and theorizing about the economic role of the creative industries that in effect treats them as the suppliers of creativity,[3] as a literal reading of the term 'creative industries' would imply. But I do not argue this. Rather, from the evolutionary perspective, the economic value of the creative industries accrues not from their supply of originating ideas (although of course there will be some of this) but more importantly from their role in the subsequent adoption and retention phases of the innovation process.

1.3   CREATIVE INDUSTRIES

Two overarching analytic ideas are joined in this book: creative industries and economic evolution. The concept of economic evolution is long-standing and broadly understood by many economists and social scientists, referring to the application of evolutionary thinking to the study of economic structure and dynamics. Yet the concept of creative industries is more recent (*circa* 1998 not 1898) and outside of a small group of cultural academics, regional geographers and certain policy circles the notion of creative industries is still somewhat novel and often ambiguous. Worse, the concept has overtly political rather than disinterested academic origins. So, we ought to briefly embark on a survey of this concept and its analytical and socio-political context, as well as its connection to evolutionary economics.

The concept of creative industries was first mooted in Australia in the early 1990s in the context of a radical reformation proposal for arts and cultural policy funding mechanisms and justifications. It is nowadays associated with a bunch of breakthrough monographs by a largely unconnected group of scholars of the creative economy (for example, Caves 2000, Howkins 2001, Florida 2002). Yet the concept of creative industries I use in this book originates in 1998, with the release by the UK Government's Department of Culture, Media and Sport (DCMS) of its first 'Creative industries mapping document'. This was based on the idea that a set of new growth industries in the post-industrial UK economy could be usefully grouped into 13 (later 11) sectors to be collectively labeled the creative industries. They were all artistically and creatively driven producers of intellectual property (IP), such that in the creative industries: creativity is the input and IP is the output.[4]

Details of this new industrial sector classification need not concern us immediately, although it has been much copied and criticized (often simultaneously). The central point was its underlying premise – that the arts are a powerful but largely unrecognized source of economic regeneration as drivers of innovation. Deftly and unabashedly, the concept of creative industries shifted arts economics in a single throw from mostly Pigovian/ Keynesian welfare-theoretic foundations to a very different economic argument in Schumpeterian innovation-theoretic foundations. In consequence, a new economic way of thinking began to descend upon the economics of arts and culture in terms of open complex innovation systems, an insight recognized in some quarters as a potential line of progress. The underlying idea (as articulated by Richard Florida, Danny Quah, Charles Leadbeater and John Howkins, among many others) was that the next big 'resource boom' was in being smart and creative and then selling that to others.

The impetus for creative industries came from public policy experience of regional economies experiencing simultaneous economic decline through loss of traditional manufacturing, along with 'new economy' regeneration that was in part through creative industries growth. The tides of globalization that eroded the old economy base of modern cities also, it turned out, opened new channels through which the creative industries flowed with new ideas, business models and markets (Roodhouse 2006). The rise of the creative industries has also been pushed by the significant changes in recent decades in digital information and communications technologies and the growth of new media (Jenkins 2006a).

I will explore in this book the evolutionary economic logic of this new source of growth and development, why it is happening, and what it means for cultural and economic analysis. The answer is roughly this: the creative industries are not a fortuitous happenstance emerging just in time to save declining industrial regions, but the systematic outcome of economic liberalization and globalization that has produced, among other things, real growth (that is, falling relative costs of ICT, and so on) and also much reduced real costs of education and leisure, leading to higher levels of cultural and creative consumption. As modern economies become increasingly wealthy, they also become smarter and better leisured, or at least better at blurring the line between work and leisure, than at any time in human history. The rise of the creative industries follows. Academic and policy interest follows soon after. And that's about where we are up to now, it seems. The focus of this book is somewhere over that horizon and specifically with what this means for: (1) our general understanding of the process of economic evolution; (2) our general understanding of the process of cultural evolution; and (3) the interaction of the two, especially with respect to institutions and policy. The rise of the creative industries should be no less surprising than the rise of communication and transport industries, for example, or even financial services, as instances of enabling mechanisms that are part of the same process of the growth of knowledge and the continual remaking of the space of economic opportunities to create and consume value.

1.4   CREATIVE INDUSTRIES AND NEW ECONOMIC POLICY

Ideas have consequences and the DCMS re-conception of the creative industries as a source of competitive advantage, economic growth and regional revitalization had an electric effect on many a regional policy manifesto. Civic leaders now had an audited and compelling 'good for the economy' argument to promote cultural amenities, inner city development, and local arts and media industry support, and so on. These programs, often previously on the books as liabilities, as for example with heritage maintenance, festivals or bike paths, were now re-calibrated as growth drivers of evolutionary significance. No longer, went the new story, did a region have to be serious and hard-working to be vital and growing (Currid 2007). Post-industrial economic logic instead required a region to have great cafes, theatres, and wi-fi for all, which is politically a much easier sell than a new oil refinery or container port. Mining, refining and manufacturing would now be done elsewhere, perhaps in Brazil or China, freeing post-industrial nations to concentrate on their comparative advantage in building a new economy of services and experience goods (Andersson and Andersson 2006, Sundbo and Darmer 2008). These were the rewards of going post-industrial, even post-modern. The creative industries thus became an attractive proposition to those who could exploit such comparative advantage.

A new economic reality thus emerged in terms of a knowledge-based or 'weightless economy' (Leadbeater 2000, Quah 1999). The creative industries thus became a central element in the 'new economy' where ultimate scarcity would increasingly shift from physical resources to human creativity in defining the limits on economic growth. In the new economic order, it was explained, machines (or perhaps China) will do the work, leaving people time to think – a sentiment not heard since the 1940s. On the strength of a 'what's good for the creative arts is good for the (new) economy' argument, a small number of social sciences and humanities academics, along with numerous industry interest groups, quickly adopted the new industrial classification of the creative industries. Like Pinocchio, the creative industries had become a 'real' industry: something that actual people did, that serious scholars studied, and that effective policy targeted.

But the concept offers something further, namely an interesting bridge between a pairing that has not historically travelled well together: humanities scholars in general but cultural studies in particular, and economists. Reframing the creative arts and industries as 'good for economic growth' has afforded humanities-style research into these domains a new legitimacy; indeed, urgency. But first they had to cross the bridge. The most striking feature of this new bridge (which we at the CCI call 'cultural science') is how smoothly it bypasses the vast and unruly political economy territories of analytic Marxism and the utopian notions of economic equality and social justice that had otherwise metastasized in the humanities and much social science. These had previously resulted in an overtly critical rather than constructive content and a reflex suspicion of economic competition and growth, along with the diminution of the value (and values) of science and technology. These almost reflexive positions had the consequence of marginalizing cultural studies, and indeed the broader humanities, from any serious economic policy discussion. So, via the bridge of Schumpeterian economic growth, academic concern with new media, fashion, consumer co-creation and the construction of meaning was ultimately, though with difficulty, re-conceptualized as the study of a significant driver of economic growth. A new language of innovation systems, complex feedback dynamics and knowledge-based economies has begun to flow through and recharge (or infect and colonize, depending upon perspective) the humanities and social sciences, pulling them into an interesting and potentially fruitful new alliance with the economists.

Industry groups were also quick to mobilize, correctly sensing a new opportunity for support in terms of an investment model ministering to regulatory, infrastructure and skills requirements, or to renewed pleas for direct subsidy by citing new evidence of (now dynamic) significance. It was here, however, that the initial vagueness became apparent in detail of what the creative industries actually comprised, and specifically how the value they created was produced and manifest. Something was new and different, but it was hard to say exactly what. Consider the interest group Focus on Creative Industries:

> Whilst FOCI welcomes the recognition of the strong economic contribution made by the creative industries in terms of wealth creation and employment, we would also keenly stress that this sector is very different from traditional industries. They deal in value and values, signs and symbols; they are multi-skilled and fluid; they move between niches and create hybrids; they are multi-national and they thrive on the margins of economic activity; they mix up making money and making meaning. The challenge of the creative industries is the challenge of a new form of economic understanding – they are not 'catching up' with serious, mainstream industries, they are setting the templates which these industries will follow.[5]

The new creative industries view thus inverted the standard cultural economics line on productivity deficits and market failure that positioned the cultural economy as a net welfare recipient, something transcendentally worthy, but inherently unprofitable (Potts and Cunningham 2008).

Instead, the new view of arts and culture sought to reposition the creative industries front and centre in the new growth of the new economy.

The economic contribution of the creative industries is thus not its output of cultural products or content *per se*, or even its role in generating employment, regional growth or exports. Rather, it contributes to the origination, adoption and retention of new technologies, as well as offering and developing new pathways for the growth of knowledge and human potential, which in turn offers new economic opportunities. The creative industries are part of the market economy, regularly supplying information commodities and experience goods. But they are also part of the mechanism by which economic systems evolve through their role in the origination, adoption and retention of new ideas. If this evolutionary hypothesis is correct, then we would expect that they would contribute to the co-evolution of political, legal, cultural and social systems. From this perspective, the economics of the arts and culture is thus presently undergoing an 'evolutionary' turn. From its traditional welfare-theoretic basis in the neoclassical economics of market failure, and its standard policy prescriptions in Keynesian economics (obliquely conditioned by Marxian economics) it is now moving inexorably towards the open-system evolutionary perspectives of the likes of Schumpeter and Hayek.

Economists have long appreciated that creativity matters (see Chapter 4). Creativity as practical imagination, as Joseph Schumpeter explained, is the generator of the evolutionary process of entrepreneurship and innovation that ultimately drives economic growth. The upshot is the beginnings of a radical remake of the economics of the socio-cultural domain in terms of the evolutionary economics of the creative economy, and of a deeper understanding of the role of creativity and its emergent industries in the process of economic evolution. The creative industries contribute through the many ways by which new ideas are adopted and adapted into new use, and socially and culturally embedded for ongoing use. They make change individually and socially possible, without which economic evolution could not occur.

1.5   THE MICRO–MESO–MACRO FRAMEWORK OF EVOLUTIONARY ECONOMICS

Given this book is themed and organized about evolutionary economics and the process of economic evolution, it will perhaps be useful to outline what that actually is.

First, evolution is a process that occurs in all open systems. It is a process of variation and differential replication (that is, selection) of some 'knowledge unit', whether genetic information, a meme or idea, or generally a *rule*. In biology these are genetic rules. In cultural-economic evolutionary theory these are generic rules. A rule is a procedure for operations. In economics, these are the 'rules for' transactions and transformations of both production and consumption variously known as preferences, technologies, capabilities, knowledge, meanings, understandings, and so on, as the 'generic rules' that underpin and steer all human action in the cultural and economic domain. These generic rules are, from the evolutionary perspective, what the cultural and economic systems are ultimately made of and ultimately what evolves in the process of economic evolution.

Dopfer and Potts (2008) propose that a general analytic framework for evolutionary analysis in the social sciences – namely those that deal with human being, interaction and the growth of knowledge – can be conceptualized in terms of a generic analysis composed of micro, meso and macro analytic domains. Micro (the agent) and macro (the aggregate whole) are well known analytic constructions. What is new is *meso*, which refers to the rule (the unit of evolution) and its carrier population – which is the *meso unit* – and also to the process by which it got there, which we call a *meso trajectory*.

The elementary unit of economic evolution is the individual human agent as a 'rule carrier'. This evolutionary conception of agency uses rules for operations but also originates, adopts and retains novel generic rules, along with the dynamic capabilities to do so, themselves also rules (Dopfer 2004). The economic agent is thus both a rule-consumer and a rule-producer. The origins of value, by this account, do not accrue from the mere existence of a new idea or novel rule, but from the new operations it enables the agent to perform. This is the emergent value the rule creates and the agent realizes. Evolutionary microeconomics conforms to the neoclassical doctrine of methodological individualism by locating the unit of explanation in the generic and operant properties of the individual agent. However, it differs on two essential points: (1) rules change; and (2) there is a population of agents. This has micro, meso and macro dimensions.

In evolutionary microeconomics the individual agent is modelled as a complex system of generic rules. These rules can and do change in the course of imagination, adaptation and learning, shifting the agent's identity. Furthermore, the process by which they change is not an exogenous or complicating notion, but the prime focus of generic microeconomic analysis. In turn, evolutionary meso-economics addresses the rule itself and its 'carrier population' of micro agents and other carriers. The dynamic model is the rule trajectory describing how a rule is innovated in one carrier and then subsequently adopted and retained by many. A meso trajectory, then, is the basic process of economic evolution. Of course, a meso trajectory is thus composed of micro trajectories of the individual process of adoption and retention in each carrier (this is evolutionary microeconomics). Evolutionary meso-economics is the study of the trajectory of the population of rule carriers.

This furnishes an analytical framework to study qualitative change in the composition and structure of a rule, as well as the population structure of all rules in the economic system. This in turn underpins an open-system developmental theory of economic coordination and change by furnishing the conceptual building-blocks for an evolutionary macroeconomic analysis. By this stage, however, we are no longer specifically concerned with economic agents or their operations (actions by rules), but with the meso unit itself – a generic rule, its population and its trajectory – as the unit of analysis. Macro is thus the study of the dynamic coordination of all meso units as a generic order. It further follows that the coordination of the macro system can be de-composed into two levels: (1) the deep coordination of how all rules fit together; and (2) the surface coordination of how all carrier populations fit together. Evolutionary macro-dynamics is the study of how deep and surface coordination is de-coordinated and re-coordinated in consequence of a meso trajectory.

The 'generic' or meso approach to evolutionary economics makes no direct connection between micro and macro analysis. You can't aggregate micro to arrive at macro. Instead, there is an aggregative relation between micro and meso, where the sum of carriers of a rule form a meso unit composed of a carrier population, which then forms an element of the macro structure of the economic order. The macro whole, the economic order, is thus a complex evolving system of meso units, just as the micro agent is a complex developmental system of particular generic rules. But meso is not invariant. Instead, we come to macro not via aggregation of micro but via the complex emergence and self-organization of meso populations and structures.

The thinking behind this book, as with its organization, proceeds as an evolutionary analysis of the cultural and creative economy seen through the lens of the micro–meso–macro framework. Evolutionary analysis, of course, applies to the study of all open systems. Physical and life systems are one such major class, socio-cultural systems are another. An evolutionary analysis of culture is well under way as developing from the life sciences (for example Boyd 2009, Dutton 2009, Runciman 2009). Cultural studies, and indeed the humanities in general, have never properly developed an analytic basis for this. Yet many interesting and important aspects of cultural and humanities analysis can be usefully recast in the evolutionary framework, and, via the bridge to evolutionary economics, that is what this book seeks to further contribute to.

1.6 OVERVIEW

This book is largely a compendium of papers – some published, some not – written over the past four years at the ARC Centre of Excellence for Creative Industries and Innovation (the CCI) at Queensland University of Technology in Brisbane, Australia. These are not just reprinted here. I have endeavoured substantially to re-write and reduce them to an essence that when assembled as a book tells a coherent story of the many aspects of an evolutionary approach to the economics of the creative industries as a study of the innovation process from the cultural science perspective.

Chapter 2 provides an overview of the differences between cultural economics and the new evolutionary economics of the creative industries. Chapter 3 offers a different analytic perspective on the cultural and creative economy by analysing the creative industries' representation on rich lists, and particularly young rich lists. Chapter 4 examines the economics of creativity with a view to shifting this toward an evolutionary economics of creativity. Chapter 5 examines a curious but stylized observation on creative response, namely the tendency to overshoot under competitive conditions. Chapter 6 examines the concept of signalling games in creative industries' labour markets and production, which differs from the standard Veblenian analysis on the demand side. Chapter 7 is about identity dynamics, which is the recognition that economic evolution, as a process, involves change in individual and eventually collective identity. Chapter 8 introduces the concept of 'social network markets', which is the analytic view of the creative industries from the evolution market-based perspective rather than an industrial perspective. Chapter 9 then introduces the concept of the creative industries over a meso trajectory, examining how they relate to each phase of the innovation process. Chapter 10 offers a new perspective on the connection between fashion and economic dynamics, in effect arguing that fashion accelerates the turnover of new goods and thus refreshes opportunities for consumer entrepreneurship. Chapter 11 examines the institutional foundations of the creative economy from the perspective of the evolution of the market economy and its institutions. Chapter 12 then proposes four macro models of dynamic interaction between the creative industries and the rest of the economy, finding that dynamic evolutionary models fit the data best. Chapter 13 examines the prominent issue of the spatial agglomeration of creative industries, arguing that this is also for dynamic reasons. Chapter 14 elaborates an extension of the social network market concept to the particular domain of novelty bundling markets, highlighting both how consumer entrepreneurship evolves and the powerful explanatory logic of economic sociology. Chapter 15 proposes that creative industries policy may be more relevant, not less, to the considerations of economic development. Chapter 16 concludes by extending the creative industries model of economic evolution into a new research program of cultural science.

NOTES

1. Much recent work by the UK's National Endowment for Science Technology and the Arts (NESTA) has sought to explore precisely this thesis (Bakhshi et al. 2008).
2. Note that this connects the Schumpeterian arguments for innovation processes to Austrian or Hayekian understandings of an 'economic order'. See Hayek (1973), Dopfer and Potts (2008).
3. Admittedly, this is a key assumption in one of the CCI's recent analytic exports: the 'creative trident' methodology.
4. This nascent industrial classification 'creative industries' was defined by the DCMS (1998) as the set of 'industries which have their origin in individual creativity, skill and talent and which have a potential for wealth and job creation through the generation and exploitation of intellectual property.'
5. See http://www.mmu.ac.uk/h-ss/mipc/foci/mission.htm.

2. Cultural economics vs economics of creative industries

Prolegomena

Starting at the CCI in 2006, my first order of business was to elucidate the difference between cultural economics – the standard economic line in arts and cultural domains – and an evolutionary 'economics of creative industries'. This unpublished chapter is what I arrived at. I felt then and still do now that this distinction is crucial because upon it turn very different analytic world views, problem domains and solution concepts. Both are 'economics of . . .' but they differ between analysis of closed-system allocation problems (cultural economics) versus open-system coordination and change problems (economics of creative industries). This explains why evolutionary (not neoclassical) economics is the proper foundation for analysis of the creative industries.

2.1 CULTURAL ECONOMICS AND THE EVOLUTIONARY CHALLENGE

Like many modern things, the economics of arts and culture – cultural economics – properly arrived only in the 1960s. There had been previous gestational steps (for example Veblen 1899, cf. Ruskin 1880[1]). But cultural economics (or better, Cultural Economics, *JEL*: Z1) arrived with the seminal application of Keynesian and neoclassical concepts and tools to analysis of the production and consumption of cultural commodities in a market economy.[2] This was motivated by: (1) the problematic economic viability of this (culturally and politically valued) sector, and (2) the manifest disjunction between high cultural value and low economic value. From these axioms, cultural economics developed about the standard applied microeconomic and econometric analytical set pieces of, in prime instance: the structure of consumer demand; the extent of market failure; the inefficiencies of industrial organization; the difficulties of factor markets; and the perennial challenges of cultural policy from the economic perspective.[3]

The central theme of cultural economics derives from 1920–30s welfare economics as expounded by Arthur Pigou (Peacock 1969). At the micro level, this is formulated in terms of applied neoclassical economics (for example the work of William Baumol). At the macro level, cultural economics is formulated as 'cultural Keynesianism' of elite cultural 'pump-priming' for social-good multiplier effects via public expenditure on goods with known positive externalities (Pinnock 2006). The 'neoclassical synthesis' in economics of the mid-20th century thus counseled reallocation mechanisms to achieve 'Pareto optima' in microeconomic analysis (that is correcting for market failure), and its macroeconomic analysis counseled public expenditure to smooth the vicissitudes of the market order (that is, correcting for aggregate demand failure). Cultural economics thus offered an economic analysis based on market-failure and welfare-theoretic policy solutions to the problem of production and consumption of cultural commodities in a competitive market order.

Cultural economics then runs through standard analytic set-pieces, broadly finding the following:

- Cultural products are inherently monopolies
- Consumer tastes must be educated
- Producer incomes are low and variable
- Arts markets have 'lemons' problems
- Non-profit organizations are rife
- Cultural markets have unstable equilibria
- Media markets tend to monopoly
- The 'cost disease' is widespread
- Demand curves often lie below cost curves
- Price discrimination is problematic
- Productivity growth is inherently limited
- Labour is oversupplied, and careers are inherently risky
- Rent capture is endemic
- The true value of cultural products is higher than market value

This list is far from exhaustive yet it captures the basic analytic premises and concerns of the cultural economics view of the inherent limitations of market systems in coordinating the production and consumption of cultural commodities.[4] Cultural economics analytically defines these problems and seeks to measure or estimate their impact. Properly handled, this analysis is used to advise policy in the direction of mechanisms to restore a welfare-maximizing equilibrium; variously by re-aligning incentives or by Pareto-optimal reallocation of resources into and within the cultural economy. This analytic framework effectively commits cultural economics to a closed-system equilibrium analysis and specifically to welfare theory (as opposed to growth theory) as the appropriate way to evaluate arts and cultural economic contexts and situations. It is good for what it nominally aims to achieve, namely an efficiency/welfare economic analysis of the production and consumption of cultural goods. But it fails precisely at the point of enquiring into dynamic significance. It says nothing, and is axiomatically designed to say nothing, about the role of the cultural (and creative) industries in the process of economic change and evolution.

So, there is a basic problem with the cultural economics model from the perspective of evolutionary economics. Specifically, there is little sense of the dynamic value of market mechanisms to coordinate new information on changes in constraints or opportunities. This is a classic Hayekian economic concern, namely local knowledge. In an open system, markets are coordination mechanisms to facilitate structural change and adaptation (Potts 2001). In a closed system, however, markets are only viewed as an allocation mechanism. This is why, in the welfare-theoretic framework, it is natural to correct their failures by overlaying a planning system of re-allocation. This requires expertise to evaluate what prices really should be, an expertise, it should be noted, that is then supplied by elite planners in the cultural production system. In the closed system view, there is a 'one best way' the cultural system should work. Where the market fails to achieve that end, such a model presumes that planning and redistribution should then prevail (for the counter-argument, see Cowen 2006).

Yet if economies and cultures are both continuously transforming (that is, evolving) from within through complex co-evolutionary interactions, then the role of markets and market institutions becomes central and, moreover, not easily second-guessed. A well-functioning market system is a complex open system sustained by a continuous flow of information and ideas. Such a system may not be allocatively efficient at any particular point in time in terms of a Pareto optimum. But from this open-system evolutionary perspective, that is not the primary value of the market system. Instead, the dynamic value of a market system is to continually facilitate and promote enterprise competition that allows the cultural order and the economic order to adapt and change, and perhaps in surprising new ways (Jones 1995, 2006; Kirzner 1997; Cowen 2002; Dopfer and Potts 2008).

In the standard cultural economics model, economic systems and cultural systems are naturally in equilibrium; indeed, they are modeled as essentially separate. Yet, if the natural state of the economy (or culture) is not stasis but instead that evolutionary change is normal then we arrive at a rather different analytic perspective on the nature and contribution of the cultural economy. Specifically, the evolutionary economic perspective on the cultural and creative economy offers a definite role with respect to 'generic' change. For example:

- they monitor and analyse change and communicate that to people (for example publishing);
- they sculpt new products and facilitate their adoption (for example design);
- they smooth institutional adjustment to technical and cultural change (for example media);
- they create new generic spaces for new operational possibilities (for example architecture);
- they develop new uses for new technologies (for example video games, film);
- they facilitate their embedding (television and film), and so on.

These dynamic or evolutionary functions are only manifest and indeed are only necessary in a world of endemic and endogenous change (see Chapter 9). In economic equilibrium, much of the creative industries would not exist except perhaps for performing arts and museums to reflect and refract the fading light of a static culture. By this account the *raison d'être* of creative industries is economic and cultural change, which implies that economic and cultural systems should both be understood as open co-evolving complex systems.

2.2   SIX DIFFERENCES BETWEEN CE AND ECI

Let me now seek to unpack the distinction between cultural economics (CE) and the economics of creative industries (ECI). I sketch six dimensions: (1) analytic foundations; (2) agents and preferences; (3) markets; (4) coordinating institutions; (5) technology; and (6) income, growth and cultural co-evolution.

2.2.1   Analytic Foundations

A key distinction between cultural economics and the economics of creative industries turns on analytical foundations with respect to the market order. Cultural economics is based upon a static equilibrium perspective, associated with both neoclassical economics (and analytic Marxism), in which all resources, technologies, preferences and opportunities are in effect predefined. The market then operates as a mechanism to allocate these given resources over known opportunities to their optimal use. Yet sometimes this doesn't work and we have 'market failure', which offers scope for social welfare-improving redistributive intervention.

The economics of creative industries is based on evolutionary, Schumpeterian and Austrian economics, all ostensibly studies of open systems in which markets produce coordination not optimal allocation. The ECI hypothesis is that creative industries produce dynamic coordination. The entrepreneur and the artist, in this view, are never far apart; both are agents of change and re-coordination. Artists may seek to introduce cultural or economic change, as do entrepreneurs. There are social entrepreneurs and there are commercial artists; there is private design of public spaces and public design of private commodities. Private philanthropy can be entrepreneurial in promoting public art and culture. The wealth of commerce feeds art, and the wealth of art feeds commerce. Culture and economy co-evolve.

The creative industries perspective highlights the continuous and complex interaction between artistic and commercial realms and how this drives evolution in both (Caves 2000; Cowen 1998, 2002; Potts 2009b). The cultural economics perspective on the other hand seeks to reinforce such distinctions, for example in a pointed separation of high culture from low or commercial culture, or of the high transcendental motives of the artist from the low pecuniary motives of the entrepreneur. Art is for higher moral and civic purposes, constituting an implicit public good (subject to market failure) and thus a proper subject of economic analysis. The creative industries perspective does not debate this, but sees it as missing the point: namely, that artists and entrepreneurs are both engaged in innovation, both living in the same über-space of novelty and change amidst ongoing and general growth of knowledge processes (Hayek 1945, Loasby 1999).

A further aspect concerns the role of the expert in the cultural economic order. Experts and expert evaluations are central to cultural economics because where there is (analytically identified) market failure in effective price signals, then some other mechanism (or agent) must direct the flow of resources; hence, the cultural expert. Cultural economics mostly accepts this arrangement, finding few inherent problems in its execution beyond the importance of finding good experts (Throsby 2001, Haan et al. 2005). The creative industries approach, however, while recognizing the enormous difficulty of evaluating novel artistic and cultural products, is inherently skeptical of this mechanism, preferring instead a market solution. Thus the ECI solution is more market opportunities, not fewer. This is achieved by strategically fostering intermediate evaluative competitive organizations and institutions. The venture capital market in high-technology sectors is a suitable example, and many galleries and large media companies perform a similar coordination and evaluation role. The creative industries perspective, therefore, is that the market mechanism itself will provide for experts (by way of consumer demand incentive) and they need not be selected by political mechanisms. The evaluation of quality is something that market mechanisms systematically do better than government planning because they better elicit and make use of distributed information processing and local knowledge (Hayek 1945).

A fundamental difference between CE and ECI thus lies in the analytic conception of the market mechanism or market process, a difference that traces whether analysis is framed as allocation problems in a closed system (CE) or coordination problems in an open system (ECI). Indeed, I contend that most conceptual differences between CE and ECI trace to this origin. Consider the following somewhat crude generalizations:

- ECI conforms broadly to an open system conception of 'cultural Schumpeterianism' (Garnham 2005; Chapter 11 below) in which growth and change is the central concern; whereas CE hews to the closed system view of 'cultural Keynesianism' where maintenance of aggregate demand is central.
- ECI has a broadly optimistic view of cultural change, new media, and so on, and the possibility of further novelty, as consistent with an open system experimental perspective. CE, however, tends toward pessimism about the prospects of the new, preferring maintenance of cultural heritage. ECI tends to a lesser role for government intervention, whereas CE tends to a more significant role.
- The CE research program focuses on analysis of optimal intervention to redistribute resources to maximize social welfare, creating value in a closed system. The ECI research program is less concerned with allocation problems and market failure but more with prospects for the creative industries in driving cultural and economic growth through openness and enterprise.
- The CE perspective is essentially conservative. It seeks to preserve what is currently good against the waves of creative destruction brought by competitive markets. The ECI perspective is basically radical, in that it values openness, access and the 'continual revolution' of the current system by new ideas that add value. Creative industries produce change, and the study of creative industries is the study of endemic and perpetual competitive evolutionary change.

The economics of creative industries is thus firmly in the camp of open and therefore evolutionary systems analysis. It views both economic systems and socio-cultural systems as open systems and seeks to understand how they mutually coordinate. Cultural economics is theoretically based about closed system analysis concerned with the efficiency of known quantities at a point in time (Mas-Colell 1999).

2.2.2   Agents, Preferences and Creativity

Cultural economics and the economics of creative industries make different assumptions about the economic agent as analytically situated in a closed system (CE) versus an open system (ECI). In a closed system, an agent is essentially just a preference map and with little independent 'agency' (or identity or imagination, and so on; see Potts 2000, Herrman-Pillath 2010). The central analytic concern is to elucidate those preferences and to figure their consequences against the current map of resources. The economic agent is integral to the demand function, but the real agency resides with the 'social planner' who seeks to see all such individual preferences and to then integrate them into a social welfare-maximizing re-allocation.

In an open system, however, agency involves more than optimization in commodity space or maximization in social welfare space, but is concerned with the acquisition of new ideas, information and knowledge, and broadly with the ongoing process of adaptation to an ever-changing environment (Schubert, forthcoming). Creativity and imaginative problem-solving are, in the ECI view of agency, a means to the end of adaptation for *all* agents. In cultural economics, agents receive culture from markets according to their preferences. But in the economics of creative industries, agents generate culture and re-coordinate this through market mechanisms. This is a subtle but important difference.

The cultural economics focus on the preferences of agents and how these preferences relate to demand for cultural products extends to the notion that preferences may require education or support. It allows and indeed turns on the notion that agents may have the wrong preferences. This is particularly so with respect to 'high-cultural' production such as ballet, museums or classical music (Throsby and Withers 1979). The implicit model is that a minimum scale of economically viable production of 'good' cultural goods is only viable if a corresponding set of preferences exists. The cultural Keynesian model sought to confine resource allocation decisions to an elite with the 'right preferences', but a more democratic alternative is obtained by educating 'the masses' toward better preferences, from which they will derive higher utility. (This is a common thesis in the political economy of the humanities too.) There are many direct and indirect ways to achieve this, ranging from direct education to the subsidy of access.

This view of agency is not inconsistent with economic theory; in other circles it is simply known as marketing. From the ECI perspective the economic agent not only demands creativity and cultural products but also, and perhaps more importantly, supplies them. ECI does not focus on analysis of preferences and measures to change them for the better, but rather presumes that preferences are mostly endogenous (Earl and Potts 2004) and acquired in market-like situations more commonly than by top-down imposition. Instead, ECI focuses on the agent's capabilities for and use of creativity under the broader heading of problem-solving and in the provision of 'solutions' (as creative outputs) that may be adopted by others.

This difference can be abstracted in two distinct conceptions of the economic agent. Cultural economics is based on *Homo oeconomicus*: defined by a universal rational choice behavioural rule, a given set of preferences, and a resource endowment. The economics of creative industries, however, is better represented by what Dopfer (2004) and Dopfer and Potts (2008) call *Homo sapiens oeconomicus*: a model based on an acquired suite of rules for cultural and creative operations and generic capabilities and also a suite of higher-order rules for the origination, adoption and retention of novel ideas. It is the capability of these higher-order rules, or knowledge about how to generate and use knowledge, that enables *Homo sapiens oeconomicus* to adapt to a changing environment with innovative solutions. Creativity is thus not an additional feature of the human agent, but the primitive upon which situational rationality is built. Where CE privileges rationality and preferences, ECI privileges the capability to originate novel solutions and to adopt and retain them as the essential behaviour of the economic agent in an open system.

2.2.3   Markets

The difference between CE and ECI in respect of market analysis is straightforward: cultural economics is centered on the prospect and efficiency implications of market failure; whereas the economics of creative industries is centered on the efficacy of existing markets in processing novelty and the prospect of new markets associated with the coordination of new opportunities, which is to say with the efficacy of the market process. CE focuses on existing markets and what's wrong with them. ECI focuses on how new markets emerge, along with other new or adapted institutions.

From the evolutionary, Austrian and public choice perspective, the concept of market failure is argued to be flawed as a foundation for analysis and policy. Any possibility of diagnosed market failure and prescribed government intervention thus needs to be set against the prospect of government failure that public choice economists consider to be the more important concern. Austrian economists argue somewhat differently, noting that markets are always failing (that is, are in perpetual disequilibrium), but that that itself creates opportunities for entrepreneurs to correct these errors: this is the market-process line (Kirzner 1997). Evolutionary economists broadly accept both arguments.

Yet central to CE is the assertion that markets sometimes (perhaps always) produce 'the wrong prices' due to information imperfections, imperfect competition, and externalities. In turn, ECI tends to argue that market prices reflect useful information about where value lies. Furthermore, and as discussed in Chapter 6, market structures continuously evolve as new markets emerge or as the institutional forms of the markets change (this is the evolutionary/institutional argument). The debate is not about degrees of market failure – an implicit perspective in CE (Brooks 2001) – but about the role and limitations of market-based coordination of creative output.

The study of creative industries markets in ECI emphasizes the value of open markets in providing a measure and space to continuously evaluate new ideas. Markets provide the institutional infrastructure for conjectures of value to be converted into real 'bids' and 'asks'. Yet the CE perspective is more focused on the recidivism of the market system to attribute appropriate value to otherwise expertly valued quality. It is sometimes argued, for example, that the market is an information-aggregation mechanism that is essentially populist rather than elite (Keat 2000). The market is said to mistake 'market value' for 'true value' and thus to require correction.

New value is created through the openness to new opportunities, implying that some market positions (and the firms and workers who occupy these market niches) will be challenged. From the evolutionary economic perspective, this is entirely normal. Specifically, arts and cultural markets will have 'power-law' outcomes as a consequence of market competition (De Vany 2004). Indeed, when markets function well, this is what we should expect as a consequence of competitive rivalry on all scales. From the CE perspective, however, markets will systematically fail to arrive at what is best and good for the arts and culture.[5] Yet in ECI, markets are a 'social technology' by which new ideas may enter and transform the extant economic and cultural system.

A further difference concerns the treatment of market structure. In CE, as in neoclassical economics, all that is not perfect competition is imperfect competition, the worst form of which is a monopoly. Imperfect competition is a generic instance of market failure to be corrected with public action via regulation or redistributive intervention. Needless to say, the cultural industries are rife with monopoly and imperfect competition, as for example in the media and communications industries, which are in consequence commonly at least partially (and sometimes wholly) in the public sector, or failing that are heavily regulated.

From the open system perspective, however, monopoly and imperfect competition are not universally bad: what matters is the scope for competitive rivalry.[6] A market trajectory, from the introduction of a novel idea through its innovation into a mature industry, may be highly competitive and rivalrous over its evolutionary development yet may never at any point meet any of the criteria of perfect competition. It may begin and end as a monopoly but yet have been highly competitive throughout the process (Dopfer and Potts 2008). Rather than viewing monopoly as something government rightly sets out to regulate or control, evolutionary and Austrian economists tend to regard government actions and interventions as a specific *cause* of monopoly and competitive weakness. They tend toward a view of cultural policy regarding markets as ideally more about fostering new markets by furnishing institutional support (Cowen 2006, Cunningham and Potts 2010) and are less concerned with problems of predation in mature markets that effective competition policy institutions should address in any case. The policy implications of ECI thus tend toward a view of cultural policy as a subset of innovation policy (Cunningham 2004, 2006; Potts 2009b), and of innovation policy as a subset of competition policy.

2.2.4 Coordinating Institutions

Systematic differences exist between CE and ECI in analysis of coordinating organizations and institutions. Cultural economics, by and large, has little to say about the structure of coordination of knowledge and activities (as compared to the allocation of resources) because its central focus is on cultural commodities, or cultural resources, rather than analysis of coordination mechanisms. The result is infrequent concern or critique of existing organizational forms or institutions. There are numerous exceptions to this, but I'm painting with a broad brush here to highlight systematic differences in analytic focus.

It is widely observed, for instance, that the cultural industries have a large proportion of not-for-profit and quasi-governmental organizations. Yet in CE, analysis of alternative organizational or institutional forms is uncommon (cf. Cowen 2006). Similarly, most funding arrangements in cultural industries involve institutions built around negotiated coalitions of lobby groups, experts and government agencies. These often contain strong rent-seeking and rent-capture elements. Yet there is a marked reluctance in CE to propose and analyse alternative market-based funding arrangements. Once again, CE is broadly conservative with regard to analysis of coordinating institutions and analysis of coordinating mechanisms much beyond top-down negotiated arrangements, such as for example a 'national cultural policy' (Throsby 2006). CE thus tends toward a skeptical view of coordination arising spontaneously and an overriding presumption that without high-level intervention this culturally important industry will decay.[7]

A further aspect of CE, not shared by ECI, is a strong focus on national boundaries with respect to protection or identification of an industry. This shows up with respect to concern about, for example, the Australian film industry and threats from other nations' film industries, as the implicit mercantilist terms of the debate. The economics of creative industries, however, focuses more on self-organization of the industry and the market reach of the firms within it (Cowen 2002). ECI has little reason to suppose that culture or creativity has any overriding national provenance. But it does give rise to a rather different set of primary concerns centered on such self-organization processes. This unfolds, for example, with respect to regional development and specialization (DCMS 2001), the growth of cities (Landry 2000, Florida 2002), and the importance of geography and clustering (Scott 2006, Lazzeretti et al. 2008), and with the continually shifting boundaries of market and non-market coordinating institutions (Banks and Potts 2010). ECI is also focused on new forms of organization and coordination: for example on phenomena such as the growing importance of network forms of coordination (Castells 1996); the new coordination possibilities created by the internet and other ICT, and new digital media in general (Shirky 2008). The ECI perspective is less nationalistic in its industry thinking than CE and moreover embraces 'globalization' for the opportunities it provides for market growth and specialization.

CE policy, in turn, is mostly about the economics of markets in which markets have already done their dynamic coordination work (cf. Potts 2001). In contrast, ECI is mostly about analysis of new and emerging markets in consequence of entrepreneurship and innovation, that is, where that work is yet to be done. Here we are dealing with the emergence of coordination and the formation of new institutions. This is why the ECI approach tends to be more aware of coordination problems than CE, making ECI more open to novel coordination solutions and less beholden to extant institutional forms. This is unsurprising, as CE deals mostly with mature industries and embedded institutions in which analysis of coordination is premised on the proposition that coordination has already failed in some way, rather than on how it might yet work. The ECI agenda therefore is less with analysis of existing market imperfections and more with the problem of missing markets or market institutions (with which government can help).

2.2.5 Technology

Cultural economics and the economics of creative industries have different analytical attitudes to, and preferred policy treatment of, technology and the implications of technological change. In essence, CE is pessimistic. It finds technological advance everywhere but in the arts and culture (Baumol and Bowen 1966). In turn, ECI is optimistic in its view of new technology, and especially digital ICT as a driver of the creative industries. The classic statement of this is Baumol's 'cost disease' model, where most economic sectors experience technological progress and productivity growth but not the cultural sector. In consequence, real wages and other input costs in the cultural industries will rise owing to growth of productivity in other sectors, yet revenue will not. This is of course a variation on the declining terms-of-trade argument in development and international economics. It is a standard justification for permanent subsidy of the arts sectors to sustain them, for in the absence of subsidy they will succumb (Baumol et al. 1989). Yet empirical analysis of whether this actually happens is at best mixed (Cowen 1996) and at worst finds that the theory is wrong (Cowen 2002).

The literature of cultural economics has little to say on the implications of new technology. It tends to regard its main impact as a threat to jobs and existing arrangements (Kesenne 1994). However, the ECI approach challenges this presumption under the broader study of innovation in the service sector.[8] Productivity gains do occur in the service sector, and especially in the creative industries, often by process innovations involving new technologies that can improve organization, communication, representation, delivery, and so on. From this perspective, there is less reason to suppose that the 'cost disease' is particularly troubling to the creative industries (Cowen and Kaplan 2004).

The ECI approach also emphasizes the role of the creative industries in finding new uses for new technologies (Hartley 2009a in the context of 'digital literacies'), as well as for their role in the adoption and retention of new technologies through the origination and facilitation of services (Potts and Mandeville 2007, Potts 2009a). This would include, for example, the effect of design on aesthetics and function in the uptake of new technologies (Postrel 2005) and other social and cultural aspects of their embedding. An example is digital animation and video games, which has pushed the frontiers of computing and software to develop new production models, and even product genres. This 'innovation-pull' accelerates the use of such technologies in other industries. The creative industries are highly technologically dependent (for example broadcasting, software, publishing, architecture) and the scale and scope of each is afforded by available technologies that are routinely tested to their limits here, as well as pushed to new developments.

2.2.6   Income, Culture and Progress

Another difference between CE and ECI concerns the treatment of income and the relation of the cultural and creative economy to the processes of economic growth and development. In CE, there is little connection between a progressive culture and economic growth.[9] These are separate analytic domains. Instead, analytic concern with income is focused on dysfunctions in cultural industries' labour markets, or on variance of income distribution. ECI, however, seeks to connect income dynamics with the process of economic growth and development (see Chapter 3). ECI analysis centers on an enterprise economy where income derives from the creation and use of knowledge and where economic growth derives from the growth of knowledge.[10] This views creativity as a source of new income and economic growth, and not just an input into cultural production.

ECI is thus a source of economic progress through cultural and economic adaptation and co-evolution. The ECI research program seeks to explain the relationship between the growth of the economic system and the growth of arts, media and culture.[11] There has been a considerable effort devoted to analysis of the industrial dynamics of cluster development, particularly so at the level of regions and cities. This has drawn a strong spatial element into analysis (Florida 2002, 2005). Yet we are still a long way from macro growth models with creative industries as a factor.[12] In contrast, the relation between the cultural economy and economic growth has no part of the research program of CE, except for the implications of international trade in cultural commodities that along UNESCO lines are often perceived as exploitation or at least in need of regulation.

The CE perspective broadly conforms to the static culture/society model. The ECI perspective instead views culture/society as continually engaged in evolution and specifically as co-evolution with the market economic system. The ECI perspective places much greater emphasis on forces that regenerate new cultural elements and worries less about those aspects that are lost in the process (Cowen and Tabarrok 2000). The CE perspective is more concerned with the cost of lost or threatened elements and what might be done to mitigate such evolutionary competitive forces. CE is less concerned with the forces generating new cultural elements or the institutions of this 'creative destruction' process. ECI, on the other hand, is concerned with little else.

2.3 CONCLUSIONS

Economic analysis of the arts, cultural and creative industries is thus composed in terms of two distinct frameworks: CE and ECI. These draw on different arguments in economic theory and emphasize different economic aspects. The first is *cultural economics*, an applied branch of neoclassical microeconomic theory. This concerns the study of market failure in arts and cultural markets, whether as inputs or outputs. Standard policy recommendations tend to be public interventions to correct the market failure.

There are many other analytic frameworks in economics that have been directed toward analysis of arts and culture – including Austrian economics, public choice theory, behavioural and institutional economics, complexity economics and Schumpeterian economics. I have gathered these under the rubric of the (evolutionary) *economics of the creative industries*. They all share a suite of common departures from the standard cultural economic model in terms of open-system analysis and can be gathered toward a unified 'new economics' of arts, culture and creativity. All focus on the problems of dynamics and coordination in an open complex system and thus emphasize different things: entrepreneurship rather than intervention; market processes rather than market failure; innovation processes rather than conservation; adaptive behaviour and learning rather than given preferences; technological opportunities rather than technological threats; coordination problems rather than allocation problems; institutional dynamics rather than coalition structures; income dynamics rather than income inequities; globalization as an opportunity not a threat; cultural–economic co-evolution rather than separation, and so on.

These raise different questions, underpinned by different analytic frameworks. They need not produce strictly competing hypotheses. Typically, this occurs along the line of ECI seeking to unleash market or entrepreneurial forces and CE seeking to constrain and redirect them toward social optima. But the deeper difference lies with a conception of what the arts, culture and creativity are ultimately for: what purpose and function and role do they play in relation to the economic order? This is a difficult question but it can be answered in an abstract sense as the fundamental difference between CE and ECI. In cultural economics, the arts and culture and human creativity are ends in themselves. Their value accrues ultimately to those who produce and consume art and culture, as based on their preferences. This is certainly not wrong; indeed, it is the logical place to start. But it misses the context of art, culture and creativity in relation to novelty, change and adaptation to new circumstances or opportunities. This is what the economics of creative industries seeks to develop.

Contrast this with the economics of science and technology, for example. On the one hand we may equivalently argue that science is an end in itself, a systematic method for the discovery of the deep truth of nature. Some people – namely scientists – have a preference for this over other pursuits, giving rise to a 'science economy' (cf. a 'cultural economy'). Yet we have no trouble seeing past that personal preference (as producers or consumers of 'science') to the dynamic benefits of science and the personal and economic opportunities these entrepreneurially constructed new ideas create. We can immediately focus on the spillovers and positive externalities and see the connection to economic dynamics of the 'science economy'; indeed, this is the basis of new growth theory in economics. But in the arts and cultural sector we have tended toward the opposite, focusing only on the inherent benefits and preferences of arts and cultural producers and consumers and ignoring wider spillovers and externalities on economic dynamics – for example, classifying them as (measurable) non-economic benefits. The ECI approach seeks to refocus economic analysis precisely on these dynamic benefits, interactions and feedback mechanisms that dynamically connect cultural and economic systems. That is why it is fundamentally different from the CE approach: in essence, its focus is with the innovation dynamics not the welfare statics.

*   *   *

The next six chapters deal with some of these dynamic mechanisms. Chapter 3 examines the evidence for creative entrepreneurship by examining the creative content of young rich lists. Chapter 4 examines the evolutionary economics of creativity, connecting it to adaptive problem solving in a changing world. Chapter 5 explores a particular dynamic in creative competition, namely the tendency to overshoot markets, resulting in what we call the 'creative instability hypothesis'. Chapter 6 examines 'signaling games' and 'multiple games' in creative industries' labour markets, offering a new theory on both investment in creative education and on the economics of consumer co-creation. Chapter 7 explores identity dynamics, endogenous preferences and the role of fashion in the process of cultural and economic dynamics. Chapter 8 presents an interpretation of the creative industries in terms of 'social network markets'. These are all starting points toward a map of the evolutionary microeconomics of the dynamic mechanisms of the creative industries.

NOTES

1. John Ruskin (along with Matthew Arnold) instigated a radical rupture between 'culture' (aesthetics) and 'civilization' (economy) that has bedevilled subsequent attempts to arrive at an economics of culture. I thank John Hartley for drawing my attention to this.
2. Galbraith (1960), Robbins (1963), Baumol and Bowen (1966). See also the 2005 vol. 37(3) special issue of the journal *History of Political Economy*.
3. Good overviews of this literature are Throsby and Withers (1979), Throsby (1994, 2001), Blaug (2001), Blaug ed. (1976), Heilbrun and Gray (2001) and Towse ed. (1997, 2003).
4. In review, see Baumol and Bowen (1966), Blaug ed. (1976), Throsby (1994, 2001), Towse ed. (1997, 2003), Caves (2000), Frey (2000), Heilbrun and Gray (2001), De Vany (2004).
5. Note this leads to a focus on different markets. Cultural economics tends to focus on 'high art', such as performance art and museums or art as an investment good, whereas ECI tends to focus on new art, commercial and technological art, such as new digital media and games for example.
6. Including the 'contestability' of markets, see for example Baumol (1982).
7. cf. Throsby (2001) and Mas-Colell (1999) with Grammp (1989), Frey and Pommerehne (1989), and Frey (2000).
8. See for example Gallouj (2002), Tether (2003), Tidd and Hull (2003), Tether and Metcalfe (2004), Vang and Zellner (2005).
9. This includes rightful skepticism about the value of input–output economic impact studies for various components of cultural industries (Seaman 1987).
10. Aghion and Howitt (1992), Loasby (1999), Lipsey et al. (2006).
11. In the *Treatise on Money*, Keynes (1930) argued that the growth of wealth would flow through to the growth of culture. This seems a sensible and historically observable phenomenon (for example Roman culture and art, Ming culture and art, Florentine culture and art, late 17th century Dutch art, mid-20th century American art, and so on).
12. Yet growth models with 'knowledge sectors' have become mainstream (Aghion and Howitt 1992).

3. Young, creative and extremely rich

Prolegomena

This chapter is an edited version of Potts (2006): 'How creative are the super-rich?' *Agenda*, 13(4): 339–50. It argues that the rise of the creative industries also shows up in 'rich lists'. This is a sign of their contribution to economic evolution.

3.1 INTRODUCTION

What sort of evidence do we have for these hypothesized evolutionary changes in the creative economy? The standard measures of the creative economy are the so-called 'creative industries mapping documents' – first produced by the UK's DCMS in 1998 then widely replicated in other regions and nations. These industrial surveys routinely find that the creative industries are indeed a significant and a growing part of the economy. This framework has subsequently been applied to creative employment, also finding significance and growth (Higgs et al. 2008). Taken together, these aggregate statistics are consistent with the 'rise of the creative economy' thesis argued by the likes of Richard Florida, Charles Leadbeater, John Howkins et al. that underpins modern creative industries policy (Cunningham 2006).

Yet beyond journalistic calibrations and population statistics there are also more subtle ways to test the hypothesis of evolutionary dynamics in the arts, cultural and creative sector using smaller and more extreme data sets. Specifically, evolutionary and innovation economics predicts that we should observe the creation of significant wealth and income by the pioneers and leaders of this (or any) emerging, growing, evolving sector. Think Henry Ford in automotive manufacture, or the Google boys in search. These are not like the monopoly rents that accrue in mature industries but are due to 'Schumpeterian profits' earned by new value created, rather than existing rents extracted (Dopfer and Potts 2008: 47–50). It follows, and especially in the creative domain (Galenson 2007,

2009), that we would also expect the age profile of this group to be skewed toward young talented entrepreneurial risk-takers.

For the past few decades financial magazines in many countries have collated so-called 'rich lists'. These contain information about the source of wealth by industry, along with biographical information, including age. This offers a mostly untapped data source on the extreme tails of wealth in respective industries. Unlike DCMS population data for example, the study of the tails of distributions offers a different perspective by illuminating the leading edge of economic evolution characterized by entrepreneurial profits that can be considerable.

Traditionally, the study of the tails of income in the cultural and creative sector has focused on the other extreme: namely the 'starving artist'. Yet while this may have been a real phenomenon in past centuries, it is mostly a myth, in modern times, because in a market economy those starving artists have ample recourse to other, usually secondary, jobs and sources of income (Throsby and Hollister 2003). But the successful in this industry domain have not been much studied because, simply, why bother? There are no public policy implications at the end of it; it conflicts with the standard cultural policy line of positive externalities and subsidy; and, at best, it demonstrates only the extent of winner-take-all dynamics in this sector, as Rosen (1981) and De Vany (2004) show.

But this wealthy extreme is interesting from the evolutionary economic perspective because it offers a simple hypothesis test: if these sectors are growing and evolving economically, then we should observe a disproportionate share of young creatives on the rich lists. So, I investigated it, publishing the resultant paper in *Agenda*, an Australian policy and economics journal (Potts 2006). The paper generated a surprising amount of media attention, including my only citation in UNCTAD's 2008 *Creative Economy Report* (?!). I suspect this attention was not because of the innovative data or method but because the conclusion – which was basically that yes, there is evidence of a disproportionate share of the young and creative on rich lists – resonated with an increasingly popular sense that the creative industries are indeed drivers of the modern economy and that the best and brightest of talented and entrepreneurial youth need not be discouraged by starving artist mythology. Hiding in plain sight was evidence that the artistic, cultural and creative sector was a domain where fortunes could be made through an effective mix of creativity and entrepreneurship. That was something I was certainly never told in school (see also Boyd 2003).

3.2 YOUNG CREATIVES IN THE NEW ECONOMY

My *Agenda* paper sought to analyse the contribution of the creative industries to the ranks of the extreme tail of wealth using rich list data from Australia (2004–06), along with several other countries. The basic finding was that while the creative industries represent only a small share of aggregate income – on the order of 5 per cent – and an even smaller share of the largest national and global companies, they are disproportionately represented as generators of extreme personal wealth over all age groups – about 10 per cent. Yet the main finding of my study was that this was far more so for the young rich creatives, who approximated one-third of the young rich (defined as those under 40, whereas the median age of rich lists is typically in the 60s). Young fortunes are the stand-out feature of the creative industries and a tangible sign of their evolutionary economic significance in both an open economy and an open society.

By seeking to unpack the sectoral composition of the upper extreme of new personal wealth, we may better understand the dynamic economic, cultural and policy significance of the creative industries as a driver of economic growth and transformation. Yet the creative industries are tricky to analyse, as they cut across standard industrial classifications. Within the service sector, aggregate labour productivity for example is difficult to measure, and with the exception of huge media companies, creative industries' companies tend to be small and fast changing in structure and size. So it's hard to tell what's really going on at the level of industrial dynamics (Caves 2000, Castañer and Campos 2002). Furthermore, the creative industries tend to be concentrated in major global cities due to the benefits of the proximity of creative talent and elite consumers, making them significant drivers of urban development.[1] Challengingly, creative industries' products are not so much mass-produced as mass-accessed (often at low marginal cost) as their outputs are by definition *sui generis*. Still, by providing a window into the Schumpeterian profits in an economy as reward to successful novelty, rich list data and analysis may help us to better understand how individual creativity can be harnessed to generate new sources of economic value and wealth.

Modern economics offers two explanations of extreme personal wealth. The standard explanation accrues from rents to talent and skill or the rents accruing to power, exclusion, or other market imperfections. Extreme wealth is thus explained in the same model as poverty, namely market failure. In evolutionary economics, however, vast wealth is analysed as the result of (Schumpeterian or evolutionary) profit that accrues to the introduction of a valuable new generic idea into an open economic system as a return to entrepreneurship and innovation. Extreme wealth is a function of the extent of the market; when a good new idea is adopted on a global scale, these profits can be very large.

Rich list data indicate that most extreme personal wealth is due to profit from entrepreneurship, not from inheritance or power, or the like.[2] Although entrepreneurship and innovation occurs throughout the economy on all scales, it has also long been known that it tends to cluster in places, sectors and times about particular new technologies. Examples include railways and steel in the late 19th century; radio in the 1930s; mass-production manufacturing in the 1950s; microelectronics in the 1960s; finance and banking in the 1980s; and digital technologies in the present epoch. These clusters of entrepreneurial activity resulted in a changed relative size and organization of industries, in new firms, and were often accompanied by the creation of significant new personal wealth to the entrepreneurs who led that process.

Economic evolution is commonly analysed in terms of differential growth rates of firms or industries, but it may also be analysed through the differential accumulation of profit as personal wealth. Yet despite their ubiquity in the business press, where they originate, rich lists have been little used in economic analysis much beyond the work of John Siegfried et al., who used rich list data to identify the origins of extreme wealth and to connect this to the study of the market process.[3] Siegfried et al. found that such fortunes are broadly distributed across the economy, but with ever shifting concentrations. In the 1800s, for example, vast Australian fortunes were concentrated among pastoralists and merchants. By the 1950s these fortunes were disproportionately concentrated in manufacturing, and by the 1990s the concentration had shifted to financial services.[4] This is *prima facie* evidence for economic evolution as a process of structural transformation through the emergence and growth of new industries as well as (by inference) the decline in significance of other industries. A further finding was that three-quarters of large fortunes originate in highly competitive industries. Siegfried et al. (1995: 285) attribute this to the normal working of the competitive process, noting that:

> A good number of the great fortunes in the world have accrued to individuals who first recognized an opportunity. Many of the competitive entrepreneurial fortunes fit the Schumpeterian characterisation of competition as a process of creative destruction, with new products replacing old ones. These are essentially disequilibrium fortunes.

Analysis of rich lists thus offers a useful data source for the study of the frontiers of the creative destruction process of economic growth and evolution.

Several rich lists were analysed from Australia, New Zealand, the UK and USA. Rich lists are compiled by business magazines through subcontracted research organizations and are sufficiently complete for comparative analysis.[5] The main problem is sectoral attribution: in essence 'creative industries' is a new and unsettled classification that does not conform neatly to SIC codes, nor the truncated classifications that rich-list compilers tend to use. So I had to make some adjustments by direct inspection rather than using the classifications provided.

3.3   FOLLOW THE MONEY

The creative industries' share of GDP, of the largest companies, of all personal fortunes and of the young rich is summarized in Table 3.1.

The share of creative industries as a proportion of the economy provides our benchmark for comparing the proportion of creative industries in the rich lists. These estimates are between 2 and 8 per cent, with differences due to relative sizes of creative industries and different definitions. For Australia, the 4.5 per cent figure represents the DCMS classification by sector, whereas the 6 per cent figure includes the creative industries themselves and creative workers embedded in other sectors, as with the UK figure.

Consider large companies. In the global Forbes 2000 there were 75 creative industries firms in the top 2000 (3.5 per cent), 51 of which were media companies, 19 in software and just five in design, fashion, publishing and games. The creative industries are not significantly represented in the world's biggest businesses. The same pattern holds in Australian firms. In 2006 just seven private creative industries companies were in the top 500, and of the top 500 public companies only 30 were in creative industries, half of which were media companies.

Of the 200 richest Australians in 2006, creative industries contributed a 9 per cent share. The same 9 per cent figure came out of New Zealand,

Table 3.1   Creative industry shares (%)

Country	Economy	Largest Firms	All Rich	Young Rich
Australia	4.5–6.0	3.7	9	35
NZ	3.1	–	9	–
UK	7.9	–	13	36
USA	2.4–8.0	–	14	–
World	4	3.5	25	39

although skewed toward entertainment and the arts. Of the 500 richest Britons, the creative industries accounted for 13 per cent. This high figure is somewhat differently composed to both the Australian, global and US distribution, with a significant portion of individual musicians, actors and entertainers, as well as a single advertising fortune. Many publishing and fashion fortunes are evident in this list (one in three), but relatively few software and technology fortunes (one in ten). Of the richest Americans, 14 per cent originate in the creative industries. This distribution is heavily skewed toward the top 100 of which 24 are creative industries' fortunes. This broadly reflects the enormous cultural and media empires and exports associated with Hollywood, as well as television stars and the significant presence of young software billionaires. Interestingly, the global rich list of the top 100 personal fortunes (*Forbes*), entry to which begins at US$6 billion, finds about one in four in creative industries (although mostly comprised of software and media fortunes). Over the top 500 this count falls to 15 per cent as multigenerational 'old economy' fortunes reassert. Still, this plainly signals the global significance of the creative industries to the composition of the new economic order.

3.4   CREATIVE INDUSTRIES AND YOUNG RICH

Recently, rich list providers have begun to track a separate list of 'young rich', aged 40 and under. The young list has a lower minimum wealth and ends well below the top of the open list. Yet these lists share important similarities but for a notable difference accruing to the distribution across industries: specifically, the young rich are much more drawn from the creative industries than their older brethren.

First, consider the world's billionaires aged 40 and under according to *Forbes*. There were 46, of which 19 inherited wealth, leaving 27 self-made. Of these, eight were young Russians obtaining fortunes in metals and oil. Of the remainder, finance, retail, online gambling, transport and manu-facturing absorbed another nine. But the remaining ten all came from the creative industries: 39 per cent of the total self-made wealth of the world's young billionaires originated in the creative industries. Beyond hopes of spectacular inheritance or Russian primary industries, the creative indus-tries are the best launching platform to a fast billion or so (the next best are gambling and finance).

The Australian young rich list compiles only self-made wealth, finding an expected number of young athletes and property developers (about one in four). But also 9 per cent were entertainers, 10 per cent developed new software, 11 per cent were in fashion or design and 6 per cent were in new media. Overall, 37 per cent made their fortune in the creative industries. The UK's *Sunday Times* young rich list for 2006 was compiled with a cut-off of age 30, and so has fewer trading companies (and a notable absence of software and technology) and a preponderance of music, fashion and film wealth. Once again creative industries represented a 36 per cent share of top 100 wealth.

The economic significance of the creative industries by aggregate employment and income is on the order of 5 per cent. As a source of extreme personal wealth across all comers this figure rises to about 10 per cent. These fortunes overwhelmingly originated in competitive industries associated with the development of new market niches. This view from the tail clearly indicates that the creative industries are significant generators of new wealth. Yet the most striking observation is the much greater significance of the creative industries to 'young wealth'. More than one in three young Australian and UK fortunes originated in the creative industries compared with one in ten for the 'adult' lists. Something interesting is going on here.

3.5   WHAT DOES THIS MEAN?

Why is this happening, and why now? In Chapter 11 I argue that this can be explained as the outworking of globalization and institutional changes. But also note that the barriers to entry in the creative industries are lower than in other sectors, as most of the capital required is carried as talent or 'human capital'. Combined with the ubiquity of digital technologies, this enables creative industries entrepreneurs and artists to tap into global markets with greater ease and effectiveness now than in the past. Indeed, most of the Australian young creative industries' rich appear to have made their fortune in global not local markets. This pattern is observed in other countries that share an institutional framework that promotes creative enterprise on a level playing field (Cowen 2002).

The difference in age profiles in the concentration of creative fortunes highlights an important observation on the modern origins of new wealth. Once, great fortunes came from resources, primary industries and manufacturing. But a recent and profound shift in the creation of value has occurred that shifts the locus of value toward information and services (Quah 1999, Leadbeater 2000, Florida 2002). The creative industries' fortunes are increasingly in the space of media, fashion, software and design as providers of 'content' and intangibles. We already know that the creative industries sector is growing faster in aggregate than the economy-wide average (as part of the general rise of the service sector). Yet we can add the further observation that the extremes of wealth in this sector are leading this advance through the design of new businesses to connect new technologies to new markets. This is the 'creative edge' of the evolutionary transformation of the economic order.

Analysis of economic change from the sectoral perspective commonly takes 'economic significance' to mean an aggregate of the output that a particular industry generates. This is applied to mature industries and new industries alike in order to appropriately focus public policy attention. Big or prominent industries get more attention; small or diffuse industries get less. This is a sensible method for calibrating industry, trade or competition policy to an economy in equilibrium. Yet it can be seriously misleading when applied to a context where new industries are emerging and extant industries are changing (Baumol 2002). The study of economic change thus should focus on what is happening in the tails of the distribution because that's where the leading (and trailing) edges reside.

The study of the extreme rich in the context of creative industries highlights a classification problem that bedevils cultural, media, industry and competition policy; namely, the social value of creativity. There is a well-worn argument that, viewed as cultural industries, creative endeavours warrant public subsidy (see Chapter 2). Yet re-conceptualized as creative industries, we find here an escalator to personal wealth. Did the creative industries generate so many young rich because of effective policy planning, or in spite of it? Australia's creative rich, for example, certainly may have benefited from public support of, and merit-based access to, acting academies and universities. Yet the relative ease of starting companies, hiring staff and protecting intellectual property is probably also not insignificant to the creation of media and software fortunes.

There is little evidence for a catalytic role played by industry or cultural policy in generating these fortunes. Indeed, it can be reasonably argued that the recent rise of creative enterprise as a legitimate source of economic value and significant personal wealth has taken policy makers in these domains somewhat by surprise (Cunningham 2006). The public policy attention focused on the creative industries arose largely due to monitoring of average or aggregate measures, such as employment or trade figures, that are necessarily *post hoc* and attain significance only after the early phases of industrial evolution have passed (Ross 2009). Still, closer monitoring of relative growth rates and new fortunes might have helped policy makers keep pace with industrial transformation. It is certainly not the purpose of government in a liberal democracy to render great fortunes for a handful of individuals, but it is surely the job of policy to set the conditions for wealth creation through enterprise as widely as possible. Still, political economists are too often prone to view rich lists as static emblems of the social injustice of a market economy. But rich lists are interesting not because of the power structures they ostensibly represent – for they are transitory, disequilibrium phenomena – but rather for the forward insight into the evolution of industries and markets that the emergence of new (individual profit-based) fortunes reveals. The creative industries, in this view, are not the perpetual subsidy cases of the much maligned cultural industries, but a new and vibrant sector characterized by significant opportunities for rapid and global growth.

Rich lists thus offer useful data sources on economic dynamics and industrial evolution. They are mostly composed of entrepreneurs making great fortunes at the leading edge of a new idea or economic opportunity. The younger they are, the more we can view this as a harbinger of things to come. My analysis of rich lists over a brief period (2004–06) and over a few countries (all highly developed) nevertheless indicated a striking conclusion: the creative industries are indeed economically significant in aggregate (as the DCMS and others have said), but they are far more so at the entrepreneurial cutting edge of modern economic innovation. One in three new young fortunes originate in this sector, which is remarkable for a sector that has a one-in-twenty measure of economic significance.

NOTES

1. As for example in the work of Richard Florida, Elisabeth Currid, Paul Romer, and others.
2. The ratio is typically well over two-thirds, and has been growing markedly since about the early 1980s.
3. Siegfried and Roberts (1991); Siegfried and Round (1994); Hazledine and Seigfried (1997).
4. Siegfried et al. (1995).
5. Siegfried and Round (1994), Stilwell and Ansari (2003).

4. Evolutionary economics of creativity

Prolegomena

This chapter is an edited version of an unpublished paper written in 2008 that sought to unpack the broader literature on the economics of creativity and to reconstruct it by distinguishing between operational and generic creativity, as a core analytic distinction in evolutionary economics.

4.1 INTRODUCTION

Creativity is a primary resource of all nations because, like rationality, it is an endowment of all people. And while we may certainly argue about the exact distribution over people and nations, clearly it is the case that some people are more 'creative' than others (Boden 1990, Csikszentmihalyi 1996), yet in practise only some nations, regions or people are able to extract significant economic benefits from creativity. Why is this?

As outlined in Chapters 1 and 2, there has been a recent turn in economics to focus on the creative industries. Interest in this sector is due to its apparent importance in the growth processes of post-industrial nations.[1] However, the industrial supply-side focus on creativity in terms of firms, jobs, exports, industries, agglomeration and the role of the public sector has largely proceeded without micro foundations in an economic theory of creativity. Instead, it has proceeded in terms of standard microeconomic analysis of variously: (1) transaction costs (Caves 2000); (2) welfare economics (Baumol and Bowen 1966, Throsby 1994, 2001, Towse ed. 2003); (3) trade theory (Cowen 1998, 2002); (4) increasing returns (De Vany 2004); and (5) the economics of agglomeration and clusters (DCMS 2001, Florida 2002). These models have yielded significant analytic insight and have proven amenable to the development of arts, cultural and creative industries policy. The absence of foundations in a microeconomics of creativity has not thereby hindered the economic analysis of creative industries, nor the supporting role it plays in cultural and media studies, urban geography or sociology. Instead, the theory of creativity research remains largely centred in cognitive, behavioural and social psychology that then extends outward to education theory, organization theory and other applied domains. That economics might be relevant to understanding creativity is a decidedly minority opinion, although it does have some precedent (for example Winter 1975, Throsby 2001, Magee 2005, Galenson 2007, 2009, Witt 2009a, 2009b).[2] Yet these are for the most part partial models not systematic frameworks. The micro foundations of creativity and its economic effect are thus principally supposed to be of a psychological or socio-cultural nature, not an economic one.

Yet I want to challenge that presumption with a set of 'first principles' of an evolutionary economic analysis of creativity. Rather than starting with a set of creative industries and then analysing their economic properties in search of a creative essence, I instead start with creativity as a human and economic behaviour and then consider how this affects the economic and socio-political system. This is developed in terms of an analytic distinction between generic and operant creativity, which I propose as a possible foundation of the evolutionary economics of creativity.

4.2   WHAT IS CREATIVITY?

A folk definition of creativity is 'seeing the same thing as everybody else, but thinking of something different'. Creativity is a mental or cognitive process (seeing and thinking), in relation to what might subsequently exist and then seeking to make it so (doing) (Csikszentmihalyi 1996). Creativity is thus a sub-set of 'adaptive intelligence' proceeding from imagination through the realization of novel objective forms, solutions or products (Boden 1990, 1994). Creativity is subjective cognition and experimental action that results in objective difference: it is the creation of something where previously there was nothing (Sternberg 1999). The effect of creativity is that the world is made qualitatively different, whether locally or globally, or in small or large measure. Creativity generates variety and variety transforms people, organizations, cultures, societies and economies. Creativity is the origin of human and economic growth and also of socio-cultural and political development and evolution. It is enormously important; but still, what is it?

Creativity is not synonymous with search or discovery. That creativity is 'just search' is a common thesis among natural scientists. The problem with this model is ontological, as it effectively denies the very notion of creativity at the outset to replace it with random motion (in a space) coupled with post hoc selection for high value movements (in that space). In search and optimization models, creativity is not an aspect of agency but rather the result of dynamics over a set of random gambits or a drift process with selection. This is an elegant model and indeed underpins the theory of biological evolution (Campbell 1960). But it is ultimately inappropriate in economics because it fails to account for the higher-order conjectural processes at work in human creativity that rely on the creation of 'models of the world' as the space in which creativity operates before being (entrepreneurially) translated into real world contexts.

Instead, an evolutionary theory of agent-based foundations would argue that creativity is an action of micro agents seeking to make new connections through a process of 'playing' with how things are related (Potts 2000, Earl 2003, Dodgson et al. 2005). This begins with an ability to see things from a different perspective and to develop a new organization of familiar components that creates a space of new opportunities. Creative acts change the space of what exists, resulting in new generic information through the process of making new connections.

The economics of creativity has several analytic dimensions. First, creativity is a process that proceeds from subjective ideas (in the mind) to objective forms (in the world). It is a subject–object interaction and neither an entirely subjective nor an entirely objective phenomenon. This dynamic interaction of both subject and object makes creativity difficult to classify analytically, as standard subjective frameworks will miss the objective aspect, and vice versa. The economics of creativity thus requires a unified subject–object analytical framework (see Dopfer and Potts 2008).

Second, creativity occurs at multiple levels, from everyday 'routine' creativity to paradigm-shifting creativity and all points between. There is no such thing as 'average' creativity. In the language of complexity theory, creativity is 'scale-free'. The absence of a standardized unit of creativity is problematic for theoretical and empirical analysis, yet creativity can occur at all scales because new connections (Potts 2000, Earl and Wakeley 2010) can be made at all possible scales.

Third, creativity involves both novelty and appropriateness. Novelty may be new to the individual or global novelty new to the world. Appropriateness implies qualities of fitness, utility or value, such that creative ideas must fit with or add value to the existing world, which thus acts as a selection mechanism. Creativity is thus not just a variety-generating mechanism – as with biological mutations – but involves novelty that is appropriate, and therefore valuable, to a particular problem domain.

Fourth, creativity can be in form or content. In a particular medium or process creativity seeks to manipulate that form to a creative end. Creativity can also relate to the conceptual content to transform the ideas or meaning of that content. These modalities are further compounded as creativity may relate to a creative process,[3] creative people, creative organizations,[4] creative artifacts, outputs or services.

Fifth, there are multiple overlapping categories of creativity. Creativity may be expressive, productive, theoretical, inventive, innovative, assimilative, accommodative, personal or public. Creativity may result from serendipity, analogical reasoning, or deliberative process. It may occur as improvisation in real time or as an organized process over a period of time. It may be due to divergent thinking tending away from what is already known, or from convergent thinking as selective evaluation of connections between known possibilities. Furthermore, divergent and convergent creative mechanisms may be at work within the same creative process.

Sixth, creativity is an aspect of general intelligence. There are many common notions of creativity as 'intuition beyond rationality', or even associated with madness and outside scientific investigation (Rothenberg 1990). Yet creativity is best analytically approached as a mechanism of general intelligence referring to sets of elementary neuronal functions with a high association of reliability to facilitate the process of creation, design, invention and imagination of new concepts or ideas. Creativity should therefore be positively correlated with both general intelligence and particular subject knowledge. Furthermore, creativity is subject to many special treatments in neuroscience, cognitive science, behavioural and social psychology, artificial intelligence, design studies, organizational and management theory, education theory, arts and literature, history and philosophy. These domains have mostly resisted any attempt to synthesize a general theory (cf. Sternberg 1999), but taking them together points to the possible integrative value of an evolutionary economics of creativity.

4.3 WHY DOES CREATIVITY EXIST?

Consider two speculative but evolutionary theories of creativity. These address creativity first as an evolved adaptation to a changing economic environment and second as a signalling mechanism in a competitive social environment.

4.3.1 Adaptive Creativity

From the evolutionary perspective, creativity can be modelled as an adaptation to a world of ongoing change, with creativity as an instinct (Lumsden 1999). We know this because, to a first approximation, all humans are creative and there are no examples of human societies that do not make art or have culture (Dutton 2009). So, there must be a common genetic inheritance, else there would be exceptions. In turn, difference in forms and expressions of creativity across humans can then be explained by different environmental circumstances. From the evolutionary perspective creativity is a mental process as part of human genetic inheritance that develops through environmental interactions. Like all adaptations, these evolved capabilities were honed by powerful selective forces operating over long stretches of time. This is why creativity can be studied so effectively from an evolutionary perspective (Simonton 1999).

An evolutionary model of creativity is thus that of a mechanism of human adaptation to a changing environment. Creativity is not an adaptation *per se* but a higher-order adaptation to enable adaptation. It is only 'expressed' or 'operationalized' in a dynamic environment, giving it discontinuous functional value. The instinct for creativity has value only in environmental circumstances requiring changed behaviour or new solutions. The extent to which such circumstances manifest and the strength of their effect is expected to condition the selective advantage of creativity proportionate to the extent of change in the socio-cultural and economic environment. The more dynamic the environment, the more highly valued creativity should thus be.

The human species has evolved from a nomadic existence as consistent with a complex distribution of (economic) resources in the ancestral environment (Potts 2003). Humans have also lived in social groups with language-based coordination for at least 40,000 years (Pinker 1997). Creativity has been with us, as cave paintings and prehistoric artefacts testify (Findlay and Lumsden 1988, Mithen 1996, Orians 2001, Dutton 2009), through the long journey of the human species and its travails in an ever changing environment (Konner 2010). Creativity is thus an evolved economic adaptation to a changing resource environment long before DCMS (1998) rediscovered this atavistic economic endowment. A general theory of creativity would thus imply that creativity exists as a mental adaptation to a complex and changing environment. This is a plausible foundation for a theory of the economics of creative industries in a rapidly evolving and globalized economic system.

4.3.2   Strategic Creativity

A somewhat different argument about the evolutionary origins of creativity can be made by considering the competitive social environment of the human species. This makes a sexual selection argument in which creativity is a form of signalling of innate qualities of intelligence, but also a dominance behaviour of not adopting others' ideas but instead creating and adopting your own ideas in a social context with the prospect that others might also adopt them, thus leading to higher status with pay-offs in sexual competition (Miller 2009). These suggest further micro-foundations of evolutionary creativity economics.

Specifically, this implies a strategic theory of creativity via feedback between agents with differential costs and benefits to proposing and adopting new ideas in a competitive social network where other agents are also differentially proposing and adopting new ideas. The economics are the opportunity cost of adopting your own idea versus someone else's. In this model creativity is a socialized form of aggression and dominance for sexual competition (Miller and Haselton 2002). The evolution of creativity in humans would thus be argued to be a product of strategic competition in social groups, with creativity operating as a signalling mechanism of difficult to observe qualities, such as intelligence, foresight and rationality in relation to communicable models of the world. Such a competitive selection process is likely to lead to overinvestment, resulting in the highly creative nature of the human species and also its prolonged development (Spence 1973, Miller 2000, Konner 2010).

In this strategic model, creativity is a cognitive and behavioural species of signalling through the competitive market space of attention. It is the proposition of a new idea into a space of other agents who also have new ideas: the coordination problem is who adopts whose ideas. Institutions will in turn emerge to regulate this interaction. The result is both the growth of knowledge – via differential adoption of ideas – and the emergence of socio-cultural institutions to regulate this behaviour. Creativity in this view is an adapted instinct in all humans.[5] Creativity may be an outcome of social competition that originated from proposing new ideas to a social group as a strategic behaviour with pay-offs in terms of social status and access to higher-quality mates.

4.4 CREATIVITY AND ECONOMIC ANALYSIS

Creativity, like rationality, is not a free good. It has both costs and benefits and the actual supply of and demand for creativity will depend on the incentives, technologies and institutions of a particular socio-cultural economic environment. Creativity – or more broadly invention, novelty generation, origination and imagination – is of manifest significance to economic dynamics. Still, compared to the extent of creativity research in psychology for example, economists have largely eschewed the topic. There seem to be at least four reasons why.

4.4.1 Why Do Economists Ignore Creativity?

First, creativity is presumed as the very definition of something outside and beyond economic analysis. This supposes that creativity is a 'free good', something economic agents have in abundance and without scarcity. Furthermore, following the erstwhile psychology line of research on the links between madness and creativity, creativity can be construed as not entirely rational, placing it beyond microeconomic analysis. Yet neither the abundance or madness thesis is at all consistent with modern creativity research. Creativity is not free; it involves cognitive and behavioural costs. Nor is creativity irrational; it is an aspect of intelligent behaviour in a dynamic environment. Both point to the prospect of an economics of creativity. Second, creativity is often argued to have little economic consequence, as the value of creativity only comes with its subsequent implementation, adoption and innovation as led by entrepreneurs.[6] This is not wrong from a static perspective. But a theory of innovation-led growth and evolution that neglects to account for the conditions by which this process originates can only ever be a partial theory. Third, difficulties with measurement of creativity render it a dubious subject for an empirically oriented science. Simply put: if standardized units or measures of creativity do not exist, either in input or output, then economic models of creativity cannot be developed or deployed. Fourth, it is widely supposed that creativity is already analytically covered by the economics of information, specifically as the space of new ideas to be processed by market systems. Yet the economics of information is not a theory of novelty. It offers no explanation of why or how new ideas succeed or fail.

Nevertheless, creativity has entered economic analysis in several ways. The central line follows Joseph Schumpeter's conception of entrepreneurship and the role of novelty generation as the first phase of the process of innovation. Schumpeter pointedly distinguished between invention and innovation, with the role of the entrepreneur associated with the making of innovation, which occurs as a novel idea is adopted for use. Invention and the creativity underlying it is not, strictly considered, part of the process of economic evolution, but rather a precondition. Similarly, Kirzner (1973) argued that entrepreneurship was characterized by 'alertness' to opportunities. Business or entrepreneurial creativity does not then consist of creating ideas, but of alertness and then acting to marshal resources to realize them.[7] Another approach is Romer's (1990b) 'economics of ideas' which argues that unlike physical objects, which are inherently scarce, the space of new ideas is potentially infinite and constrained only by the number of people working at creating and discovering them. Further, each new combination of elements creates a new element for further recombination, manifesting increasing returns. Like Kirzner, Romer's approach models creativity as a form of alertness, effort or investment that yields new ideas and opportunities.

While none of these approaches offers a fully fledged 'economics of creativity' they do endeavour to analyse the processes by which creativity as novelty generation is transformed into value. This suggests a foundation for analysis of the behaviours and institutions that facilitate creativity. There have been several key developments here. First, in seeking to reconcile Schumpeterian macroeconomics with behavioural microeconomics, Winter (1975) proposed a theory of novelty generation based on routines, involving the 'combinatorics of routines' and 'copying errors' arising from imitation of routines (Becker et al. 2006). This Darwinian conception of novelty generation is widely used in analysis of organizational innovation. Yet this model is ontologically problematic when what is being created is genuine novelty, rendering selection theory, which is a search and optimization model, technically inapplicable (Gabora 2005: 84). Evolutionary selection theory is many things, but it is not a theory of evolutionary creativity.

A different line was taken by Magee (2005) on the economics of invention in terms of the cognitive mechanism of 'analogical transfer', which many researchers believe central to creativity analysis. Magee examines the psychology of creativity underpinning the analogical transfer mechanism. He develops a framework for analogical learning decomposed into two factors: experience and creative efficiency. Experience is considered in terms of personal, firm, and network experience in which increased experience contributes to the specialized knowledge that makes invention possible. Creative efficiency proceeds through 'the ability of individuals groups and organizations to turn experiences into learning and new ideas' (Magee 2005: 41) in terms of cognitive, knowledge, motivational and organizational efficiency. The value of Magee's approach is the decomposition into two in principle observable processes.

David Throsby's (2001, 2006) work on artistic production functions is also important in unpacking the economics of creativity for the insight into the opportunity costs involved. Throsby analysed the trade-offs artists made to pursue creative careers. This afforded estimates of the utility functions underlying creativity as production. He found that creativity, as work, is a normal good with diminishing marginal utility. In other words, we are willing to pay to be creative, but what we are willing to pay is a function of opportunity cost.

An interesting refinement is Galenson's (2007) analysis on the lifetime production of creative geniuses. Galenson identified two distinct forms of 'creative genius' – young conceptual innovators who do their best work while young as deductive conceptual leaps (for example Picasso, Warhol, Eliot, Welles: see Galenson 2009); and experimental innovators who do their best work when mature through continual experimentation and refinement (for example Cezanne, Pollock, Frost, Hitchcock). (Note this reinforces Magee's separate mechanism of experience in creative production.) By emphasizing that cognitive, behavioural and social technologies underlie the process of innovation as much as physical technology, Galenson's econometric discovery of two distinct 'production technologies' among great artists focuses economic analysis of creativity on two otherwise neglected aspects, namely the demographic profile of a population of economic agents and the differential importance of accumulated and practised craft expertise.

These micro theories of economic aspects of creativity are complemented by meso and macro theories associated with the institutional structures that facilitate economic creativity. There has been a flurry of such work, starting with Caves (2000) who used transaction cost theory to analyse the coordination economics of the creative industries. Others, led by Florida (2002), have sought to identify the post-industrial significance of the creative class as an occupational segment of the economy, or more broadly the concept of a creative economy (Howkins 2001). Currid (2007) has developed this line in terms of a particular city (New York) in respect of how its creative resources facilitate broader economic development. Since the DCSM (1998) report, there has been extensive policy interest in the macroeconomic significance and regional development impact of the creative industries, particularly in regional development policy circles. These lines of industrial and spatial analysis are not based on a microeconomics of creativity. Rather, they investigate the organizational and institutional characteristics of places or situations that give rise to creative output and value creation. This offers a cultural geography or organizational culture analysis of creativity (Potts et al. 2009b), not a microeconomics of creativity. As such, we have still at best only partial theories of the economics of creativity.

4.4.2   Creativity and Opportunity Cost

All humans have some degree of endowment of creative capability, but the economic effect of this resource depends upon other choices relating to specialization, experience, and connections made with other agents. Creativity has manifest generic and social benefits, but it also has opportunity costs for individuals. The concept of operational creativity thus relates to the specific organizational and material conditions in which the supply of creativity is a function of the relative scarcities and prices of creative output, and over which the demand for creativity depends upon the material conditions of an economy. There are multiple levels of operational analysis of creative opportunity cost.

First, creativity is the origination of a new idea that is (by definition) self-adopted. This implies the opportunity cost of not adopting someone else's ideas, as in the strategic theory of creativity above. Therefore, a latent cost of creativity is thus not adopting other people's ideas but instead acting as if the adoption process is self-centric. That is good if your ideas are better, but less so if not. Creativity is thus a form of entrepreneurial conjecture about the quality and value of your own ideas (Shackle 1972) with attendant opportunity costs and benefits.

Second, creativity is a behaviour in time, implying a choice at the margin about whether to continue being creative (investing time, effort and resources), and thus consuming current utility plus potential future pay-off, or to work under the leadership of someone else's creativity for more stable income and environment (Throsby 2006). This trade-off depends upon the material and economic conditions that pertain in a local context. In consequence, the supply of creativity will be dependent upon this individual calculus in a particular social and market context. The opportunity costs of creativity will thus depend on the expected variance in outcome of creative endeavour compared to the lower variance (and possibly higher expected return) from adopting others' creativity. This ratio of variance is a possible measure of the opportunity cost of creative endeavour.

Third, creativity consumes resources. Thus the supply of creativity will be a function of available resources and relative costs. On one hand, economic growth and technological change has made the means of production (for example PCs, internet, books, and so on) increasingly affordable. The cost of creative inputs has fallen significantly during past decades (Hutter 2008). Combined with high and rising education levels and surplus time, this has led to a flourishing of supposedly non-market production and innovation (Benkler 2006, Leadbeater 2008, Shirky 2010). Globalization has made many previously marginal creative outputs now commercially viable and has created a multitude of new niches for creative output (Cowen 2002). This in turn has powered the rise of the creative industries through the growth of demand, shifting the calculus of opportunity costs associated with creative endeavour. The rise of the creative industries may thus be explicable in individual opportunity cost terms as much as industrial policy terms. In turn, the value of creative skills and endeavour, and the socio-cultural and political spillovers this engenders, may also have a dynamic opportunity cost explanation.

An economics of creativity should thus seek to differentiate between the generic or 'knowledge' components of creativity, and an operational analysis of creativity in terms of the opportunity costs and material conditions that pertain in any generic state. This distinction is suggested as the foundation of an evolutionary economics of creativity.

4.5   TOWARD AN EVOLUTIONARY ECONOMICS OF CREATIVITY

An evolutionary economics of creativity therefore distinguishes between generic and operant creativity. Generic creativity is analysis of the rules, knowledge and ideas (that is, the behavioural, social and economic 'technologies') associated with creativity. Operant analysis is of the operant conditions that relate to the particular context or material situation of the new idea. It is generic creativity that evolves, but it does so under operational selection pressure.

A generic theory of creativity would thus seek to extend the notion of bounded rationality to the concept of 'bounded creativity'. Boundedly rational economic agents use decision rules (heuristics) to make satisfactory choices (Earl 1986). Simon (1978) called this behaviour satisficing, reflecting the observation that economic agents rarely optimize, but seek to achieve outcomes that meet minimum sufficient criteria. The analytic significance of bounded rationality for creativity is that it shifts attention to the nature of the 'rules' over creative actions and how these rules are acquired and used. We may therefore extend the concept of bounded rationality, in terms of created and selected and operationalized decision heuristics (Earl and Potts 2004), to analysis of creativity along the same line – creativizing. This is consistent with the adaptive (natural selection) and strategic (sexual selection) theories of creativity in section 4.3 above.

Like bounded rationality and satisficing, bounded creativity and creativizing implies the use of rules for action behaviours associated with creativity. It is these generic rules for creativity and their interaction with the economic order that are the analytic focus of an evolutionary economics of creativity. The generic economics of creativity would thus be based on the existence of creative rules for action with evolutionary economic analysis focused on how they are originated, adopted and retained. This differs from endogenous growth theory, for example, where creativity is a monotonic function of resources invested, making it an operational not a generic theory. It also differs from search models by focusing on the coordination of the process of creativity rather than the outcome. The upshot is that creativity involves investment in the generic rules of knowledge creation at both the individual and social levels. The extent of such 'generic' investment is the extent of a creative economy and a creative society.

Consider several implications. First, the cost of the means of creative production will determine the extent of creative endeavour. Changes in these costs will affect the supply of creativity. As the real costs of ICT fall, for example, and as digital access and literacy rises, the operational cost of creativity also falls. As it does supply increases, and variety too. Technological change and global economic development increase the equilibrium supply of creativity.

Second, the cost of acquiring creative dominance involves differential costs. It is easier to be creative about haircuts, say, than neuroscience because the latter has higher costs of acquiring sufficient knowledge to be in a position to begin to be creative in the first place. The extent of creativity generation will be a function of the extent of such specialization (and thereby the implicit costs of entry) as limited by the extent of the market. Economic growth, which permits greater specialization, is thus in itself a driver of creativity precisely because of its development of such specialization and the growth of opportunities it affords to creativity. New technologies, economic growth and trade thus all increase the value of creativity.

Origins of creativity lie deep in human evolution. Yet the effects of 'the ability to see new things' are a driving force of modern economic growth and development; the more organized and complex our economic systems become, the more important creativity is as a primary resource. The recent rise of the creative industries has focused policy attention on the role of creativity – and in turn the creative industries – as a driver of economic growth and development. Still, creativity lacks a general economic analysis. An evolutionary foundation via both adaptation to environmental change and strategic social signalling has been suggested here (distinguishing between generic and operational analysis of creativity) to outline an evolutionary economics of creativity.

NOTES

1. Garnham (2005), Cunningham (2006), Potts and Cunningham (2008).
2. The work of Michael Hutter's group on 'cultural sources of newness' at WZB in Berlin is another candidate for a more general theory. Their work however falls more within the ambit of economic sociology. See also Stark (2009) on dissonance as a source of creative discovery.
3. There is a substantial literature on the process of creativity that begins with Wallas's (1926) four-stage model of the creative process: (1) preparation; (2) incubation; (3) illumination; (4) verification. Rossman (1931) then proposed a seven-stage model: observation of a need; analysis of the need; survey of information; formation of objective solutions; critical analysis; invention; and experimentation.
4. Simonton (1999), Woodman et al. (1993), Becker et al. (2006).
5. Curruthers (2002) argues that creativity is an indicator of intelligence and problem solving ability that would have been selected for through both natural and sexual selection. Dissanayake (1992) argues that the arts could have been co-opted by sexual selection to act as fitness indicators, but that their original function was to promote group survival. See also Dutton (2009) and Boyd (2009).

6. Magee (2005: 30) notes there is little work on the economics of invention: 'it is generally believed that invention is of no economic importance, the true economic value of an idea coming of age only with the successful completion of the process of innovation. . . . it is often contended that invention simply cannot be modelled.'
7. Shackle (1972) argued that this sort of imagination was inherent in all acts of choice, as all choice involves some aspect of speculation about future utility or value.

5. Creativity under competition and the overshooting problem

with Peter Earl

Prolegomena

This paper was written in 2009 when Earl audited one of Potts's lectures on Hyman Minsky's 'financial instability hypothesis' and realized that a similar argument could be made about the competitive organizational dynamics of creativity. This is a truncated version of a longer paper yet to be published.

5.1 INTRODUCTION

A widely observed phenomenon in the creative industries is the tendency for creative budgets to blow out and for creative concepts to escalate in complexity as suppliers chase ever-shifting norms of what is hip, cool, hot, or attention arresting. Infamous examples lie in the creative excesses of 'prog rock' bands of the 1970s, or in any turn toward debauchery, self-referential excess or kitsch in modern art. But this phenomenon is, we argue, to be found everywhere creativity and competition meet. It is not a uniquely modern form of decay but a logic of competition with predictable pathways and consequences.

Our hypothesis is that creative agents tend to compete by going deeper into their repertoire of ability and talent, which adds further depth, meaning, subtlety and complexity to their creative product, whether an album, a script, or a design concept. But as this happens, the norms of the genre become more complex through further layering of additional depth, meaning and detail. This creative competitive process can thus become an aesthetic 'arms race' that will systematically tend to overshoot consumer capabilities and demand (as with Minsky's (1975) Keynesian monetary dynamics model of debt overshooting).

Interestingly, this occurs much as Christensen (1997) argued that firms under competition would also tend to overshoot markets by adding ever more features to a product, thus moving up the product complexity gradient to overshoot markets. Christensen studied industrial high technologies and emphasized that the switch to new markets thus tended to involve new firms not caught in this escalation. But we think his main point of competitive overshooting applies just as much to the creative arts, in which the marginal addition of creativity to a given context also rarely follows a smooth path to an asymptote of stable perfection. More often it just turns expensively weird and self-indulgent before collapsing in a smouldering pile of artistic self-indulgence and infamy. This can make for great theatre, and there is no doubting that it's also probably fun. Admittedly it does also have broader economic spill-over effects in variety creation. But there is no escaping that it ultimately makes for bad creative business: someone ends up paying for it.

Overshooting is a common problem across many creative domains. Yet we have no economic theory to explain it. Standard theories of production assume diminishing returns. Applied to the generation of novelty this assumes that rational managers will only allow creative concepts to be pursued as far as optimal and not more. Of course, overshooting need not imply irrationality. Instead, it might simply reflect a basic problem in the endeavour to economize in the production of creative goods. Rational choice about how far to push a concept is difficult because such work tends not to be consumable at all until it has been developed to an advanced state. Even when a partly developed 'concept' version of a product can be shown to target customers, reactions may be a poor guide to actual behaviour when the product is eventually launched. Customers' tastes and tolerance may change in the interim depending on their experiences and on what other products reach the market, as similar to the 'competitive investment' problem raised by Richardson (1960). Yet inherent uncertainties associated with creative products – including uncertainties about how far rival producers plan to take a particular concept within a particular timeframe – open the door not just to occasional errors by individual suppliers, but to collective creative excess.

Our initial examination of the problem of competitive creative escalation and overshooting is modelled on Minsky's (1975, 1986) financial instability hypothesis – hence the 'creative instability hypothesis'. Our theory is that the direction of escalation under competition is invariably toward pursuing the development of a concept or idea in a way that sooner or later runs into a rising gradient of complexity, subtlety or difficulty. Depending on the initial impetus, the gradient can be to any extreme of the characteristics in terms of which the product is seen. This can involve increasingly minimalist or anarchic creations that make it harder and harder to justify claims that the output falls into a creative category such as 'art' or 'music' rather than 'rubbish' (epitomized in the music industry by impresarios such as John Cage's silent 'composition' 4'33", or by the calculatedly shocking behaviour of the Sex Pistols). Or it may involve pushing the creative envelope in elaboration and complexity, making greater demands on resource budgets, briefs, organizational tolerances, and suchlike. This escalation will tend to overshoot the mass-market by going beyond the audience's attention or absorptive capabilities. And this market overshooting will often have negative economic consequences for the creative organization, risking loss of audience and consumer demand.

There is an obvious Schumpeterian aspect to this model, seeing the world as a place in which creative overshooting is common because it is an expected strategic response to the competitive threat of other agents' creativity. This is competition not in price, but in entrepreneurial endeavours to advance ever more and new ideas (for the same price). This innovation process occurs over a flow of information (the music, the idea, the design) rather than over technologies that might be capitalized, making it perpetually contestable. Attention is the 'commodity' that must continually be produced and creativity is an input (Lanham 2006). This is also a process for which bounded rationality and differences between agents' information and knowledge matter. Central to this mechanism is that 'creative producers' (for example musicians, writers, artists) by definition have more experience and dimensions of appreciation of their 'creative product' than consumers (even fans). Competition will thus induce more of that knowledge and detail into the product, invariably adding complexity.

The creative vision of producers under competition will thus tend to overshoot the tolerance and absorptive capacity of the consumer. Eventually, inevitably, a line will be crossed where consumers can no longer keep up and stop paying attention. They move on to something else. The market has been overshot. This is a common phenomenon in all creative business.

5.2   THE CREATIVE ORGANIZATION

A creative organization has creativity as an input and some flow of information as an output. This implies two key ideas. The first is the notion of treating creativity, or creative labour, as an input into production (along with other factors, including capital) such that organizations compete by having more or better creative input – the latter being particularly important at the level of production teams such as bands or advertising agencies.

Creative labour is plainly not homogenous; indeed it is very difficult to assess quality *ex ante*. It is an experience good, in both consumption and production. But all creative organizations have this as a substantial input to production. There are of course other factors of production in creative output including labour management (producers), skilled contracted service (accountants, caterers, lawyers), coordination (elite roadies), manual labour (entry roadies) – as well as capital (gear, studios), and land (stadiums). Technological change is also a key driver of creativity, but we will not consider these factors here. Ours is a theory specifically of the marginal effect of one factor: namely creative input, *ceteris paribus*. The second point is that the creative output is an 'information good'. This may or may not be embodied in a physical form, but it will be something over which some manner of intellectual property could be claimed. The output of a creative organization is therefore a bundle, batch or more generally a flow of information.

Our model also refers to creative organizations that compete through creativity. These are often highly contestable domains due to relatively low entry barriers. There is of course a spectrum of contestability here: entry into a band or increasingly even film and videogames is relatively easy in consequence of digital technologies, whereas reputation effects, experience, licensing or regulations partially restrict entry into advertising and architecture, for example. But on the whole these are contestable industries, implying that creative organizations must continually push creative boundaries and seek at least to keep pace with ever-shifting industry norms. In such a contestable environment we expect to observe most firms reasonably tightly clustered about the aesthetic, stylistic or format norms that have been established by the industry 'leaders' or those who are at least perceived to be presently 'at the head of the pack'. Under such competitive conditions, we would expect that firms will be watching each other closely and strategically adapting their own actions based on the observed successes of others and of the creative directions in which they are moving.

Our model therefore assumes that creative organizations are rational, strategically oriented, and endeavouring to maximize both profits and the value of the assets they hold in a monopolistically competitive market. Creative organizations will tend to be small under these circumstances; the much larger organizations (such as big media companies) will tend to be network or holding companies. Our central assumption, then, is that these mostly smallish, strategically rational and often monopolistic creative organizations are continually engaged in competition for the consumer's attention and resources by ever figuring out new ways to apply or extend their creative capabilities.

5.3   BOUNDED RATIONALITY AND THE CREATIVE CONSUMER

Creative overshooting can be explained by connecting the model of the creative organization to a boundedly rational model of the consumer of creative output. The main implication of assuming bounded rationality is to suppose that agents will seek to make satisficing decisions, or 'good-enough' choices made by adapted choice heuristics rather than seeking optimal choices (Simon 1978). But there is a further implication, as explained in Earl (1986), namely that consumers will be expected often to employ non-compensatory decision rules when appraising complex products or facing a large range of consumption options. Such decision rules can be seen as templates that draw the line between what is acceptable and what is not within a genre. These templates can evolve through time and may be sourced from peers or experts, such as professional music, drama or art critics (Earl and Potts 2004). They will often relate to the dimensions of aesthetic and product differentiation in the producer discriminations, but commonly lack fine or 'critical' discrimination, and also allow other concerns.

Consumers have less expertise about the product than the creators, so there will be many opportunities for consumers to completely fail to understand what the point of the product was or to miss its subtleties (for example, just think of your last visit to a modern art gallery). The creatives themselves will also be somewhat distant from their audiences and how their potential customers see their products and related concerns. This distance is likely to increase as they become more successful and cease to mingle on an everyday basis with their customers. By implication, there will be points in creative development beyond which the consumer will no longer be able to keep up. In crossing these points, creative production overshoots and enters an unstable space.

Another way of looking at this was suggested by Hayek (1952) in his discussion of the 'sensory order' (Earl 2010). Hayek's point, later developed by Shackle (1972) and Loasby (2002), was this: the human brain is continually trying to find order. Learning is discovering and acquiring a new order. So, the consumer is always open to being challenged and, as Shackle (1979) emphasizes, attention is grabbed by events that are surprising because they depart from past patterns. When there is no challenge because there is no new pattern to be found, boredom arrives and attention wanders. Creatives who turn out products that present nothing new will therefore tend to lose their markets: the status quo is not an option for durable creative outputs since consumers can simply reuse earlier products to satisfy their artistic needs. However, attention also requires a sufficient prospect of success in discerning a worthwhile pattern. At the other extreme, therefore, there are strangeness thresholds that arise from too much change, or change beyond comprehension. When this happens, the brain can no longer find order; it will all seem to be noise and no further attention will be paid by consumers. They will become bored again, even though the competitive creatives may be earnestly and honestly following one creative advance with another. But each consumer will have a tolerance that is lower, and often considerably lower than the producer's. If a creative product goes beyond the consumers' threshold of tolerance in a particular direction, attention will be withdrawn regardless of how well it exceeds requirements in other dimensions.

5.4   THE THREE-PHASE CREATIVE INSTABILITY HYPOTHESIS

A model of creative overshooting is suggested by Minsky's (1975, 1986) financial instability hypothesis (FIH). Minsky's financial instability hypothesis proposed three distinct income–debt relations for economic units: (1) hedge – where income covers full debt amortization; (2) speculative – where income only maintains debt; and (3) Ponzi – where only income growth maintains debt. Minsky argued that economic units will move through these successive phases under the force of competitive pressure. This causes the financial system to become increasingly fragile, eventually leading to collapse. The collapse is thus inherent in the mounting fragility of the financial system. The core theorem of the FIH is that although an economy does have equilibrium states of income–debt relations (that is, hedge positions), over periods of prolonged prosperity these units will transition under competitive pressure to more unstable states, eventually leading to financial collapse.

The creative instability hypothesis makes the same claims for a creative organization. But instead of income–debt relations, the CIH is modelled in terms of creative producer–creative consumer relationships mediated by the dynamics of consumer attention relative to producer creativity. Similarly, the CIH argues that in the course of a creative opportunity playing out, the creative organization will transition through three distinct phases of escalating creative investment. We call these: (1) mainstream, in which creative production is well organized and managed, and successfully maps to consumer tastes; (2) edgy, in which creative agents push the boundaries of the art's style and medium, but still carry many consumers along; and (3) experimental, in which the creative producers are largely in the avant-garde realm of 'art for art's sake' and have substantially overshot most of their previous market. A fundamental characteristic of the creative economy, we argue, is that the creative organization swings between mainstream and experimental states and these swings are an integral part of the process that generates fashion and cultural cycles.[1]

From the critical perspective, this model of creative output might seem backwards. In arts theory, mainstream, like kitsch, is the final resting point of a creative program that begins on the experimental fringe (for example 'art school') before being picked up by a coterie of more sophisticated consumers (for example 'indie') before then transitioning into a comfortable but dull state of mass-market appreciation (that is, 'mainstream').

But this 'linear model' of creative production is flawed because it fails to recognize art and creative output as a competitive economic activity. It assumes there is only the artist and the consumer, and that the economic coordination problem is how to match them. Yet we want to de-emphasize how the artist goes to market, and instead to emphasize 'artist versus artist' competition. We suppose that this starts out in a 'mainstream' state, which is something that competitive forces should generate. Yet those same competitive forces will continue to push the organization beyond the mainstream state and into increasingly edgy and then experimental states, leading to overshooting. Our model thus predicts that 'mainstreams' should decay from within, as the competitive pressure to be ever edgier becomes pressure to be experimental, which may eventually lead to market collapse.

CIH 1: Mainstream

The initial phase of the creative instability hypothesis (CIH) begins with a well-managed creative organization that successfully produces the creative output its market audience demands. This is 'mainstream' because the creative organization creates and delivers creative product (a flow of information) to a stable population of consumers who appreciate and value it. They do so under competitive pressure, where other creative organizations are also competing for that same audience/market. So, in the CIH, mainstream is not actually in equilibrium but is modelled as evolutionarily unstable in a competitively contested space.

The sort of organizations that attain this state under competitive conditions will tend to be well managed, in the sense of being broadly conservative in creative budgets and briefs. Management (that is, the 'suits') will have a tight rein on creative content and execution and will occupy a space of proven business models for creative production and delivery. This sounds pedestrian and unadventurous, but a well-managed organization really is central to the successful delivery of a flow of creative content to expectant consumers, irrespective of whether these are B2B contractual relations, as an advertising agency, or whether B2C, as in music, film, or video games.

Consumers in this mainstream state are satisficing. They maintain consumption patterns that work and change them when they no longer work, which mostly means when boredom sets in. They will do so by experimenting with new rules and using meta-rules to select new rules that work (Earl and Potts 2004). Due to the 'experience good' nature of many creative products, consumers may be surprised by the results of choices made by applying trusted rules if the creative strategies of those whom these rules favour have themselves changed unexpectedly. Consumers' native tendencies to desire novelty in some degree (Scitovsky 1981) and to value the search for patterns in streams of incoming stimuli (Hayek 1952), accompanied by tendencies towards 'sunk cost bias' (Thaler 1980), will all ensure that consumers will expend some effort to get to grips with these surprising products rather than immediately writing them off as mistaken purchases. If they succeed in creating new patterns into which such products fit, they will have adjusted their templates of tolerance into line with their experience. This is a mechanism by which consumer preferences can evolve at the margin (see Metcalfe 2001, Nelson and Consoli 2010).

As a monopolistic market, there will of course be variation in the creative organizations within each market niche. Some will have more creative freedom than others and will go in different directions. However, given that all firms are competing for this same attention, these variations will matter from a market selection perspective, as those that did relatively less well in each previous round will tend to update their strategies by copying those who did better. Success will be partly observable to others, and where that success was observed to be due to increased creative freedoms, the learning organization will then rationally afford more creative freedom to its own creatives to better compete. Competition for consumer attention, combined with the tendency of such markets to have strong social network feedbacks (Potts et al. 2008), will make the relatively more successful creative economic units better resourced and able to 'unleash' their creatives. By this process, the competitive escalation begins.

CIH 2: Edgy – pushing the envelope

The second phase of the CIH we call 'edgy'. Edgy is the creative product supplied under this intense competitive pressure. Its production involves 'pushing the envelope' by taking a genre into a more extreme form than before, stretching the capabilities of the 'creatives', and the tolerance of those who manage them. There will now be increased risk of failure because, for example, the product is harder to replicate reliably in live performances, due to rising demands on talent, or harder to explain to potential customers. But taking such risks may offer potential for much higher returns. The organization at the creative edge is highly competitive and is, in effect, seeking to be the leader of the idea-space that others may then follow. Every creative organization wants to be this. But the only way to do that is by creating a new 'edge' by forming new kinds of connections: by pushing the envelope in exciting and risky new ways.

The lesson will come to pass, a lesson arriving simultaneously in many creative organizations, that 'creativity pays' (in the Minsky FIH model, the equivalent lesson was that 'leverage pays'). Proposals to increase creative budgets will be passed; previously rejected projects will be green-lighted; the creatives will be 'let off the leash'.

This is the start of the upswing where 'creatives' are in greater demand and afforded increased 'creative' freedom. Specifically, high failure rates will generally lead to temptation to back what is going well and to allow one's creatives to push the envelope of what has been succeeding, leading to recording artists spending forever in the studio, over-elaborate staging of live performances, and excess in music that takes it into sharply diminishing or negative marginal returns. But at the same time, we should expect that this increased creative freedom will eventually yield new creative directions.

Pushing the creative envelope is risky not only in terms of its technical challenges but also because of the difficulty of anticipating the extent to which potential customers with differing templates of tolerance and abilities to form new patterns and decision rules will be alienated rather than attracted. With norms on the move, there is no easy way to judge between prospective returns at the margin of exploration versus those at the margin of exploitation of what already exists. Overshooting has not necessarily happened yet, but all the conditions for it are now in place.

CIH 3: Experimental

The third phase of the creative instability hypothesis is 'experimental' (in the sense of 'experimental music' or 'experimental art'). Such avant-garde economic units will be characterized by 'art for art's sake' and with output heavily skewed to the inclinations of the creatives themselves, now largely unmoored from previous normal business constraints or concern with consumer demand. Common characteristics of this third state will often include indulgence of 'bad behaviour', tolerance of ideas purely on reputation, and rampant unaccountability and the normalization of pet projects. Creative producer sovereignty will have mostly displaced any lingering consumer sovereignty, or indeed managerial control. By this stage, the creative output of the organization may well be high, even spectacular, but it will also be highly variable too, with the ever recurrent risk of being variously spectacularly awful and/or massively unprofitable. The viability of an organization in this competitive state will come to depend upon continuously staying at the front of sufficient public or market attention.

This third phase of the CIH will come to an end with a collapse of some sort of the markets or models. One way this can occur is when the economic unit loses control over expenses, or adopts unsuitable business models or fails to adapt existing business models to the new context. Another way is when the creative outputs move beyond what audiences and consumers can keep pace with. The collapse may quickly happen – especially where creative products are consumed socially and buyers take their cues from reviewers or acknowledge fashion leaders in their social circles. A further pathway of failure is that the creative firm may not feel the failure, but rather the clients of such firms, for example, with the advertising that wins awards but not customers, or the architecture that is striking but uninhabitable, or the music that is technically brilliant but unbearable, or the film that is challenging but unwatchable. It is noteworthy that many such 'failures' in this third stage of the CIH are often not actually experienced by the creatives themselves, but rather by their commercial backers. This is just as in Minsky's model of the FIH where it is the investing shareholders, not the charismatic entrepreneurs, who are left holding the bill for failure.

The collapse occurs as the market was overshot; as creativity was overinvested. The extent of overinvestment may be worsened by a backlash from exhausted customers whose rejection of the latest products entails not simply failure to revise their templates of tolerance to accommodate them, but a re-evaluation of what they had previously found acceptable and the construction of new templates that favour alternative genres. When this happens a fan-base can shatter; the overshooting is irreversible. The creative agents cannot simply revert to putting out the kind of products they had created before they overshot the mark. Rather, they will need to now completely reinvent themselves, usually with entirely new consumers. This may necessitate forming many new connections and not just creative ones, but also with new creative team members and new contracts for the supply of creative input. They may now need to 'sell out'. This will be a chastening time for extant creative suppliers. But it will also afford new opportunities for the new generation of creatives.

And thus the cycle continues again as the now disgruntled consumers look again for something new and recognizably good. This becomes the new mainstream, from which the competitive process starts over again. Some geniuses can span the cycles (in contemporary music for example

Bob Dylan, David Bowie and Madonna have reinvented themselves through successive waves), but most cannot and do not, and moreover often have little incentive or energy to do so. For where do you go next, once having gone to the creative extreme?

Creativity is a brutally competitive business, where every incentive is to go further and deeper, but with every step you take, you move further away from the consumers that support you. There does not seem to be any stable equilibrium here. Such cyclical creative overshooting seems endemic to creative competition in a market order. Just as business cycles seem endemic to market capitalism, so too do creative cycles.

5.5 CONCLUSION

This chapter has offered a model of Schumpeterian competition (the CIH) where creative firms compete by continual creation of novelty, and with predictable Minsky–Christianson type results in terms of overshooting leading to endemic market turbulence and recurrent endogenous dynamics. This models an evolutionary process where the less successful copy the more successful, who took greater creative risks, thus advancing the creative space of the market. But it is also a market process in that this producer advance is not always able to be kept up with by consumers. Sometimes and invariably they fall behind and lose interest. Thus the market collapses, and with it the elaborately constructed creative edifice.

And that's the ultimate economics of this story, namely that the production of creative novelty is ultimately constrained by the consumption of such novelty at the margin. This margin, moreover, is rarely a monetary budget constraint but most commonly an attention and comprehension constraint. Yet this is just as hard, and when violated has significant consequences. When producer creativity exceeds consumer competence a constraint has been violated and a market will collapse just as predictably as if they had violated a price point.

With competitive escalation of the producer side, the consumer side of novelty production is commonly overshot. This is the essence of the creative instability hypothesis. The Schumpeterian economy is thus creatively unstable. It has a tendency, under competition, to overinvest in creative input, which is destabilizing at the level of the organization, although for the whole economy, this mechanism will also tend to accelerate the rate of economic evolution.

The CIH presented here is a theory of the dynamics of creative industries businesses under market competition. It explains why survival is hard and why renewal is inevitable. But what else might the CIH apply to? Beyond the creative industries there are numerous forms of organization that compete through creativity. An obvious example is academic departments. In the mainstream state there will be tight control over creative work and projects, with pressure for rapid results and no sabbatical without a business plan with promised publications of particular kinds. At the opposite end is the world of academics allowed years on projects with no budgets and sabbaticals with no accountability. Departments with 'superstars' would be likely to be more indulgent of phase 3 'experimental' behaviour, making them more unstable by this account than those with lesser creative investments. In relation to product development, a sense of the cycles that the creative instability hypothesis predicts can be observed in, for example, automotive design and manufacturing firms such as Ford and Mazda, with radical inspired efforts interspersed with dominance of 'bean counters' causing unoriginal designs that concentrate on cost cutting rather than pushing the boundaries. This suggests a further dimension to the analysis of the firm's organization, strategy and markets over a product life cycle in relation to the ebb and flow of creative investment. This offers a new angle on Schumpeterian creative destruction by highlighting the importance of creative investment and the state and mechanisms of control over that resource and imitation of those strategies (Earl et al. 2007). Minsky argued that the market-capitalism economic system is financially unstable, and according to us it is also creatively unstable.

Yet this is not necessarily a bad thing, because this creative instability may actually be part of the mechanism of economic evolution in which overshooting creativity, just like overshooting products (Christenson 1997) and overshooting finance (Potts 2004), is actually an evolutionarily viable outcome because of the variety generation and creative destruction it brings, which in turn refreshes the space of opportunities across the broader economy. That this means that creative businesses may be disequilibria phenomena may well be the price we pay for the creative impetus and consumption opportunities that we ultimately value as consumers. Some of the finest achievements of modern culture have occurred indeed precisely in phase three of the CIH (I have my own list, but perhaps you, dear reader, have a different list). But phase 3, the experimental phase, which is a natural market outcome of creativity under competition, makes for the competitive forces that push creatives to do better and more, and more importantly, induces new entrants who might creatively venture new and better ideas. We all ultimately benefit from that, even if individual creative businesses are brought to the abyss. This is a further (admittedly brutal) aspect of the evolutionary genius of market capitalism in respect of a creative economy.

NOTE

1. Cf. 'A fundamental characteristic of our economy', wrote Minsky (1974: 269), 'is that the financial system swings between robustness and fragility and these swings are an integral part of the process that generates business cycles.'

6. Creative labour markets and signalling

with John Banks

6.1 CREATIVE INDUSTRIES' LABOUR MARKETS, UNCERTAINTY AND SIGNALLING

Labour markets in all industries have their idiosyncratic features and structural characteristics and the creative industries are certainly no exception. We have already met one such feature in Chapter 4, namely the tendency toward extremes of wealth in winner-take-all markets (De Vany 2004, Potts 2006). Other features highlighted by Caves (2000) include the 'motley crew' aspect of *ad hoc* teams, the significance of the apprenticeship system, and the role of labour organizations such as guilds and unions. Furthermore, work in artistic labour markets (as a subset of creative industries' labour markets) has consistently highlighted the lower-than-average returns to creative endeavour in proportion to human capital (Throsby and Hollister 2003, Menger 1999, 2006). Indeed, the peculiarities and challenges of arts, cultural and creative labour markets and careers is a common motif of the economic and sociological analysis of arts, culture and creative industries.[1] Menger (1999) is worth quoting at length on this:

> Artistic labor markets are puzzling ones. Employment as well as unemployment are increasing simultaneously. Uncertainty acts as a substantive condition of innovation and self-achievement, but also as a lure. Learning by doing plays such a decisive role that in many artworlds initial training is an imperfect filtering device. The attractiveness of artistic occupations is high but has to be balanced against the risk of failure and of an unsuccessful professionalization. Earnings distributions are extremely skewed. Risk has to be managed, mainly through flexibility and . . . multiple-job holding at the individual level. Job rationing and an excess supply of artists seem to be structural traits associated with the emergence and the expansion of a free market organization of the arts. (p. 541)

> Artists as an occupational group are on average younger than the general work force, are better educated, tend to be more concentrated in a few metropolitan areas, show higher rates of self-employment, higher rates of unemployment and of several forms of constrained underemployment . . . . They earn less

than workers in their reference occupational category . . . whose members have comparable human capital characteristics and have larger income inequality and variability. (p. 545)

The training system may play an unintended role in the self-congesting spiral of oversupply, since teaching positions and kindred activities in nonprofit art organizations shelter artists from occupational risks. (p. 567)

The upshot is that creative or artistic labour markets do not work particularly well. This poses particular challenges for the viability of arts, cultural and creative careers, as for arts, cultural and creative industries. Yet the problems with arts, cultural and creative labour markets are not a simple litany of things wrong with the free market (cf. Ross 2009). It is certainly true that all of the standard criticisms – about excess supply, precariousness of labour contracts, strong insider–outsider distinctions, importance of informal networks and connections, and now the problem of the competition from the 'free labour' of consumer co-creation – all adversely impact on creative industries' labour markets. But we argue here that none of these issues are problems with markets *per se* or egregious instances of market failure. Rather, they all stem from one overriding concern that has hitherto received little attention in analysis of artistic, cultural and creative labour markets, just as it has also been much over-looked in analysis of the 'problem' of consumer co-creation. The issue concerns the relationship between demand-side uncertainty and supply-side signalling.

Neither (fundamental) uncertainty nor signalling (technically 'signalling games') receives much more than passing comment in most treatments of these subjects. (There are some partial exceptions: see, for example, Jones (2002) on signalling strategies in creative careers.) Yet we wish to associate both of these phenomena as two sides of the same problem associated with entry into creative industries' labour markets. In one case this shows up as over-education or overskilling associated with excess supply at the entry level of such labour markets (this problem is far less prevalent with established careers where reputations effects dominate, thus reducing fundamental uncertainty), but also and for much the same reason with consumer co-creation, which is routinely portrayed as a new 'post-market' gift economy (for example Quiggin and Potts 2008), but which as Banks and Potts (2010) show can be elucidated with reference to other labour markets and the emergence of new market institutions. The problem is not market failure but insufficient appreciation of the evolved institutional complexity that is necessary for markets to function under such endemic conditions of uncertainty. These institutions revolve about the demand for and supply of signalling.

Signalling matters in creative industries on both the demand and supply side of the labour market. We examine the signalling aspect of creative labour markets at the point of market entry in terms of signalling games (Spence 1973, Yachi 1995). The idea is this: in creative labour markets, new entrants are an unknown quantity (they are subject to uncertainty on the demand side). These agents therefore endeavour to signal their creative qualities to prospective employees by undertaking various actions that only a 'high-quality' creative could have. Yet the problem remains that false signals can invade a message-space: anyone could say that they are a creative. The coordination and incentive problem thus becomes how to send a *credible signal* not easily faked by an agent who was not a true 'creative type'. Thus the problem is how to separate true creatives from those who might merely aspire to be. In biology, this strategy is called the 'handicap model of sexual selection' (Grafen 1990). Here, the information of 'true type' (say, high creativity, or good genes) is encoded in a 'handicap' that only the true type could sustain, such as hypertrophied tails on peacocks. A non-true-type could not sustain that 'handicap', thus it serves as a credible signal of underlying true value. The problem is that it is not enough just to be a 'creative' but to persuade others, and specifically employing others, that you are indeed what you say you are.

This seems to be a generic problem in creative labour markets. We suggest that signalling games are rife in creative labour markets in at least two places: first, in consumer-co-creation, which is not 'working for free' under this interpretation (*a lá* Ross 2009), but is manifest as a visible 'handicap' that acts as a signal for future labour markets or even venture finance; and second, in overinvestment in creative education and training, which also works as a credible signal for entry into creative labour markets. This curious institutional feature defines (and necessarily so) creative labour markets.

Why does this happen? We seek to emphasize that these difficulties arise for a single overarching and deep reason: namely, uncertainty in the choice to contract or commit resources (by a firm) to a 'creative' (as an employee or contractor). It is uncertainty on the demand-side of the labour market, and particular at the entry level, that is at the core of the perennial problems experienced by those seeking to transition from arts, cultural and creative industries' training and education to the entry and early stage labour markets prior to the accumulation of significant experience and reputation, which is a manifestly effective and credible signal.

So, while it undoubtedly remains difficult to *be* a creative, and it is abundantly clear that pursuit of a creative career must be weighed carefully with self-knowledge of the drive required to succeed and difficulties required to be endured (Towse 1996, Throsby and Hollister 2003, Menger 2006), it is also difficult to *hire* a creative, especially a young one. This is owing to the uncertainty involved in commitment to an unknown quantity and the difficulties in structuring incentives to perform well. It is uncertainty on the demand side of the labour market that prompts most of the difficulties, peculiarities and problems that occur in this market. This applies to consumer co-creation as well as to creative education and training.

Our argument builds on two ideas. First, uncertainty on the demand side of the labour market is a situation of asymmetric information that induces those on the supply side (that is, aspiring creatives) to invest in signalling their true creative potential through what are not just typically but necessarily costly displays (Spence 1973). This is the 'signalling games' aspect. The second part follows that overinvestment in education and training (overskilling or overeducation)[2] is a likely form of signalling in creative industries' labour markets.[3] Many difficulties of arts, cultural and creative labour markets may be traced to signalling contexts where overskilling has evolved as an institutionally adapted mechanism.

The overskilling hypothesis in creative labour markets cuts against the grain of the standard theoretical explanation and policy response to persistent market failure here. In the standard 'cultural economy' model, labour market failures issue from insufficient demand by consumers (Baumol and Bowen 1966) or perhaps from under-appreciation by businesses of the value creative labour can add (Work Foundation 2007). Both diagnoses tend in the direction of seeking policy solutions to increase public funding to arts, cultural and humanities education, or to arts and cultural organizations in order to correct the perceived market failure of insufficient private demand. This has the effect of subsidizing the creative labour market (over-supply is thus interpreted as insufficient demand). Yet our argument follows a different line that still recognizes market problems but traces their causes to the problem of signalling quality of creative labour supply under uncertainty. The problem lies with insufficiently developed market institutions, not with insufficient demand.

6.2 SIGNALLING AND OVEREDUCATION

The overskilling hypothesis is notably absent from analysis of creative labour markets. Specifically, most economic analysis of education and training in arts, humanities, cultural and creative industries labour markets hews to a Pigovian welfare-theoretic model of market failure. This argues that the gross benefits of arts, humanities and creative industries education and training are poorly captured in competitive labour markets. The existence of such spillover benefits is widely analysed (Heilbrun and Gray

2001), verifying the common argument for institutional labour market failure on the supply side as a positive externality, usually with demand side subsidy as a solution. But this common assessment may well be wrong.

The standard theory argues that because benefits of arts and creative education and training are poorly captured in labour market wages, this causes under-investment (from an aggregate social welfare perspective) in creative education and training. But an alternate theory of demand-side failure and runaway signalling games makes the opposite argument, namely of a market failure of sorts, but not in the direction commonly supposed (of uncounted non-monetized benefits leading to under-investment), but rather due to systematic overinvestment in skills, credentials and training in order to enter into these labour markets in the first instance. Thus we focus here on the transition from education and training, to entry level creative labour markets because this seems where the core problem exists. Labour markets for experienced creatives mostly work well; indeed, often too well (Rosen 1981, De Vany 2004). Supply of training and education in the creative arts is, for the most part, just another monopolistically competitive industry. But the 'market failure' problems arise specifically in the transition from creative training or education to entry into creative labour markets. It is not the markets that are failing, but the efficacy of the institutions of entry.

The market failure is not due to uncompensated positive externalities or insufficient monetary incentive. Rather, oversupply (these are good jobs) and institutionalized wage agreements (these are fair jobs) lead inexorably to queues forming at the entry level of these markets due to demand side uncertainty. From the individual perspective, these queues are rightfully perceived as unfair allocation mechanisms that do not reflect or account for the true value of the individual's creative talents and potentials, that is, their 'true type'. But how can you signal that credibly? The rational response is to engage in costly signalling games that invariably result in overskilling via overinvestment in education, training and credentialing, as well as overinvestment in social networks, all in the endeavour to send appropriate signals to potential employers to alleviate their uncertainty.[4] At the same time competitors (other entry level creatives) are endeavouring to do likewise. The result is predictable systematic and mass overinvestment and runaway signalling.

This model of creative labour markets is based on the theory of strategic signalling that emerged in the 1970s with the application of game theoretic approaches to strategic interaction with asymmetric information. Still, it was the 1990s before economics and biology significantly advanced the sender–receiver model of communication to further account for strategic communication in signalling games (Grafen 1990, Godfray 1991,

Yachi 1995). In the sender–receiver model, a key concern is signal–noise ratios, or the efficiency of communication. But in signalling games the key concern is the signalling of 'true type' (a problem of asymmetric information), leading to effective coordination. This problem arises because of the possibility of false signals, which were never a part of the sender–receiver model.[5]

A credible signal must carry or encode a cost that can only be reliably carried by a 'true type'. Spence (1973) argued that an expensive and demanding graduate education may function in exactly this way as a labour market signal because the opportunity cost of such education is greater for agents of low innate ability; hence gruelling elite education (that is, overeducation) is a credible signal of innate high ability. Only a person with high innate ability is not wasting substantial time and money at an elite education institute, so an expensive education (the 'handicap') is a credible signal of high innate ability, even when no useful learning occurs.

This theoretical insight is consistent with a different line of research into graduate overeducation (Freeman 1976, Groot and Maassen van den Brink 2000) which is commonly found to be on the order of 30 per cent. Graduate overeducation is viewed as a serious problem at the individual level of overinvestment (or poor returns to investment) and at the social level as wasted resources (Hartog 2000). This in no way disputes the significant returns to education. Rather, it seeks to recognize that these returns are not uniform across or within groups and that overeducation is the predominant form of labour market mismatch. The form of this failure is wasted spending on education and training that bears little relation to the skills and capabilities actually required in a job. Labour economists call this the problem of overskilling in job matching (Mavromaras et al. 2007). They analyse it in several ways, including job quality, measures of job satisfaction, evidence of labour market queuing, and educational attainment (Kler 2007).

The same phenomenon seems equally applicable in creative labour markets, specifically in the importance of the 'right' arts schools, training programs or higher degrees as entry requirements into subsequent jobs. Observe that the essence of the signalling game response arises from the information problem of needing to signal 'true type', that the seller of creative labour is indeed a high quality creative. But due to asymmetric information the inherent and inescapable problem is making that claim credible. You may know that you are a high quality creative, but how do you prove it without first getting a break, as an entry point into the labour market? And you can't get that break until you can prove it. It's a common trap.

The solution is credible signalling: in effect doing things that only a 'true type' high quality creative could do. These are the hoops through which you must jump and the perpetual credentialing, networking and résumé building exercises that are the nature of the game in markets for such 'experience goods' where 'product uncertainty' is rife. It is entirely uncontentious to point out that this has been long recognized as a major feature of creative industries' outputs (Hutter, forthcoming), but it equally applies on the input side too in creative labour markets, occupations and careers.

The standard line on creative education and labour markets is that, under competitive market conditions, demand will be sub-optimally low due to unaccounted (and thus un-incentivized) positive externalities. We do not reject that argument but instead focus on a further and potentially more important class of 'market failure' due to signalling games and matching problems under conditions of fundamental demand-side uncertainty. It is this uncertainty and the emergent and designed institutional solutions to that uncertainty that should be the proper focus of policy responses with respect to problems in creative labour markets.

This does not argue for diminished public support for arts and creative industries, with the supposition that if the problem is overinvestment then the solution should be less investment. That argument has always failed to distinguish between social incentives (that is, positive externalities under a social welfare function) over individual incentives (that is, getting a well-matched job in an entry level labour market). Rather, we recognize that the problem in arts, cultural industries and creative industries' labour markets is more specifically associated with entry and the signalling game institutions that have evolved. Signalling games are not pathologies to be extinguished but (variably) effective institutional mechanisms that occur in the context of uncertainty; they seem particularly prevalent in creative labour markets. The point is to figure out how they might be done better and more efficiently. An analysis of signalling games' market failure will thus seek to develop better and more efficient signalling mechanisms that might lead to better matches that may be less wasteful and more effective from both the individual and social account.

6.3   CONSUMER CO-CREATION AND THE 'PROBLEM' OF FREE LABOUR

And then there is the problem of 'free labour' as it is known in the more left-leaning political economy literature (Ross 2009), or the problem of 'consumer co-creation' as it is known in creative industries' circles. Due to recent digital information, computation and communications technological revolutions (for example Leadbeater 2008, Shirky 2008), media consumers increasingly participate in the process of designing, producing and marketing media content and experiences. Recent years have seen the rise of user-generated content and user-led innovation as significant cultural and economic phenomena.[6] Media consumers are now increasingly media producers. Following Jenkins (2006b) on participatory culture and von Hippel (2006) on user-led innovation, co-creative media culture occurs when a non-trivial component of the design, development, production, marketing or distribution of media product proceeds through the direct and voluntary involvement of consumers or users. Consumer co-creation relations are of increasing economic and cultural significance in many industries (OECD 2007), including the videogames industry. As an assemblage of media technologies and consumer-participatory culture practices, videogames are at the generative edge of consumer co-creation (Green and Jenkins 2009). In this new model, players use editor tools embedded throughout the game to create and edit new levels and objects. They can then share these creations with other gamers.

Why do they do it? The standard line is that these actions are based on non-market or non-pecuniary motivations.[7] This portrays a 'gift-society' where people work on projects because their intrinsic motivations are well primed with communitarian spirit (Zeitlyn 2003). Benkler (2006: 17) and Bruns (2008: 29) in particular argue that this new modality of organizing production does not rely on market signals or systems but instead that the value and innovation potential of these co-creation relations indicates a limit to the market that is emerging from the market itself. Commercial endeavours to tap into these actions are then framed as an extraction of surplus value from the consumer co-creators, contributing to the precarious employment conditions of professional creatives (Ross 2009).

But is this what's really going on? Is this really a 'non-market revolution'? Our perspective is that there are actually more markets involved than simply those for labour and final products. Drawing on ethnographic research with an Australian-based games developer, we explored the front-line practises and motivations involved in online games development by these consumer co-creators. We proceed from this ethnographic material (see Banks and Potts 2010) to derive two theoretical explanations for consumer co-creation that avoid the either/or distinctions of market/non-market, cultural/economic and intrinsic/extrinsic motivations that have taken root about this issue. Our explanation of co-creative relations in co-evolving market and non-market contexts elucidates the complex interrelationships between multiple contexts, incentives and motivations, as well as the emergence of markets and dynamics of institutions. This involves a co-evolutionary dynamic of both economic and cultural change.

We frame this in terms of the theory of multiple games (Page and Bednar 2007) and the theory of social network markets (see Chapter 8 below). Both involve further aspects of the signalling hypothesis.

The most obvious question in consumer co-creation concerns motivations to participate in such relationships, for both consumer co-creators and businesses, and the specific nature of the costs and benefits accruing to each. Our study illustrated the difficulties involved in navigating these relationships in the context of extant behavioural and social norms, community practices, business models and institutions. Note that there are two distinct lines of analysis and explanation here: either (1) viewing consumer co-creation as an extension of market exchange, and thus a product of incentives associated with existing institutions; or (2) viewing consumer co-creation as the emergence of a new non-market model of production centred about socio-cultural explanations.

The first, broadly associated with economic explanations, recognizes that consumer co-creation is a voluntary (rational, incentivized and non-coercive) exchange. It is axiomatic that both sides benefit, else the exchange would not take place.[8] Labour signalling and learning-by-doing are presumed to be behind otherwise seemingly altruistic motivations.[9] This emphasizes consumer co-creation not as a production relation, but as a voluntary exchange relation with complex and subtle incentives associated with investment in labour market signals. These extend beyond labour and goods markets to include exchange of less tangible and fungible goods, such as reputation, opportunity, learning, recommendation and access. These involve future labour markets that create additional incentives that operate in markets for reputation, markets that may only be monetized indirectly if at all and are difficult to observe. This shadow or secondary market aspect is easily and often confused with non-market motivations and context.

Cultural and new media studies researchers, however, have not viewed consumer co-creation in terms of market-exchange, but have instead maintained emphasis on it as both a production relation on one hand and a non-market relation on the other. Within this frame, there are many claims of exploitation that derive from a Marxist theory of surplus value creation. Ross (2009: 15) for example argues that in amateur content production platforms 'the burden of productive waged labor is increasingly transferred to users or consumers'. The humanities-based literature thus seeks to find socio-cultural explanations for the observed phenomenon of voluntary work and social production.[10] In this model, the firm itself is transformed into an organization that 'works' for the public good by abandoning the propriety model and freely distributing its product, as for example with canonical examples Linux and Wikipedia. There has recently been much discussion of this model and its prospects for generalization (Leadbeater 2008, Shirky 2008). Consumer co-production is here an expression of a burgeoning new era of non-market production and innovation driven by democratization of the means of digital production and the surpluses it creates (Lakhani and von Hippel 2000). Benkler (2006: 56) argues that a combination of excess capacity and democratic distribution of computing power, coupled with the public good nature of information and the modularity of problem-space, is ushering a revolution in which peer production and 'nonmarket behavior is becoming central to producing our information and cultural environment'.

Although these two perspectives – broadly economics, and cultural and media studies – arrive at very different analytic frameworks and explanations of consumer co-creation, both hew to an exclusivist line of analysis: either consumer co-creation is a market-based exchange activity governed by extrinsic incentives, or it is a non-market cultural production governed by intrinsic incentives. Only one explanation can be correct. Yet that does not fit the facts of our case study. A central finding was that complex motivations were at work over multiple markets with ample evidence of once-free-providers able to monetize reputation effects in subsequent labour markets. This favours the market-based economic explanation. Yet there was also considerable conflict between norms, expectations and institutions, all of which implied that cultural factors and emergent institutions also mattered. We therefore proposed a 'third' explanatory model of consumer co-creation to integrate market exchange explanations and cultural production explanations. This seeks to reframe both into a more general co-evolutionary analytic model in which 'economic' and 'cultural' factors are conceptualized in a dynamic open relationship: each affects the other such that consumer co-creation emerges in respect of the practices, identities, social norms, business models and institutions of *both* market-based extrinsically motivated exchange relations, *and* culturally shaped intrinsically motivated production relations.

6.4 INSTITUTIONAL CO-EVOLUTION OF MARKETS AND CULTURE

A co-evolutionary model of consumer co-creation is neither an economic nor cultural analysis *per se*, but employs both modes of explanation to account for the dynamics of consumer co-creation. This has multiple dimensions, including market outcomes, practice and identity, institutions, and so on. In a co-evolutionary analysis cultural factors (identity conceptions, received practices, power relations) affect the space of economic outcomes, and economic factors (implicit contracts, incentives, markets and business models) affect the space of cultural outcomes. This sets up a dynamic co-evolutionary process where change in one affects the other, which then adapts, inducing a change that affects the other, and so on.

Our specific concern was consumer co-creation in videogames, but the broader point was that the new media context is replete with instances where either economic or cultural analysis approaches fail to gather the full set of concerns because economic analysis tends to ignore cultural factors, and vice versa. It is noteworthy that signalling is precisely such a phenomenon that is clearly visible only from this dynamic co-evolutionary context. Toward redress, we proposed two models of co-evolutionary analysis: multiple games and social network markets.

6.4.1 Multiple Games

Economic models of human action routinely allow complex motivations and incentives but not complex contexts. Analysis of consumer co-creation is framed as a market exchange context or a socio-cultural production context but not both. Yet most human action is rarely neatly decomposable and commonly consists of situations of simultaneous multiple contexts that do not permit multiple actions but require a single action that plays out across all contexts simultaneously: this is the context of a multiple game. Consumer co-creation, we suggested, is a paradigmatic instance of a multiple game.

Multiple games theory (Page and Bednar 2007) is a recent extension of game theory to analysis choice situations where an agent uses a single strategy to interact in multiple conceptual spaces or 'games' that are otherwise incommensurable. Standard game theory allows much complexity in the agents, strategies and rules of the game, but always supposes that only one game is being played. A multiple game differs in that a single strategy is played over multiple games, with each game representing a different set of rules, payoffs and even players.[11] Multiple games theory recognizes these multiple contexts of action in consumer co-creation – intellectual property production, future labour market signalling, learning and feedback, equity stakes, cultural identity and opportunity, cultural participation, community norms – but also that these dimensions are incommensurable. This is important, because were these dimensions commensurable it would be possible to sum the costs and benefits with each dimension appropriately weighted to reflect the agent's cultural and economic preferences, to arrive at a single rational choice or 'play'.

Yet this was not observed. Our subjects showed no evidence of neatly compartmentalizing different aspects of context and resolving these into actions reflecting the various inherent trade-offs. Rather, they behaved 'as if' these multiple contexts and distinct tensions were not there at all: that is, they resolved them into a seamless dynamic context over which a single action was 'played', with which they identified in all contexts. This is what multiple games theory predicts, whereas a standard economic or cultural analysis would predict the opposite – namely that the various motivations would be experienced as distinct and thus inherently conflicted trade-offs.

This frames consumer co-creation as a context of institutional evolution over the populations of agents that have resolved the 'multiple game' into a singular action, and thus institution, against those that have not. This is not about conflicted motivations of market self-interest versus cultural participation. Co-creative agents all operate in an institutional context where these objectives and motivations are commonly in conflict and require resolution. Yet our case study specifically highlighted, and perhaps typifies, a context that distinguishes those who have resolved these 'multiple games' acting in a way that, in effect, presumes this is already a new institution, from those who continue to act in ways that reflect past and extant institutions. This gave rise to internal signalling communities.[12]

The resolution of a multiple game into a single action also implies a new single identity that is not manifestly composed of the various parts of the resolution, but that reflects this wholeness and consistency of action.[13] We observe this in the evolution of occupations and professions where, as various skills and actions combine into new specializations, they also come to express a new identity (see Chapter 7). This matters for internal consistency and resolution, but also for social signalling and coordination, so that agents of the same 'type' may recognize each other in order to effectively cooperate, and agents of different types may understand their respective motivations and expectations. The consumer co-creators in our study were highly adept at developing such identity mechanisms and reinforcing community norms. In turn, problems consistently arose when there were failures to correctly identify agent types and relevant norms and expectations: that is, in distinguishing agents playing a 'multiple games' strategy from those who were not. Multiple games theory provides a new analytic window into how complex and conflicting motivations and incentives can self-resolve via institutional evolution. An exclusively economic or cultural analysis would inherently miss this co-evolutionary process of signalling, multiple games, identity dynamics, and institutional evolution.

6.4.2 Social Network Markets

Consider also the interaction between market and non-market contexts. This relates not only to how each furnishes conditions for the other, but also how they transform into each other. This can be analysed with the theory of social network markets (Potts et al. 2008a, and Chapter 8). A social network market emerges when consumer choice shifts attention away from price information and toward observations of other agents' choices as a rational reaction to uncertainties about product quality arising from novelty or complexity. In situations where price is a weak signal as to quality and expected utility (books, movies, and so on) agents thus economize on information search costs by using other agents' prior and signalled choices and investments. Whether this arrives spontaneously or by design, the result is a social network market. Coordination in a social network market is not through price signals, as in mature markets, but through the social information signals observed in the behaviours of other agents.

The role of consumer co-creation through social networks can thus play a significant role in shaping demand in situations involving substantial novelty or consumer uncertainty, a common situation in digital media and online gaming.[14] Social network markets help explain producer willingness to engage in this business model (as a marketing mechanism), and also indirect benefits of consumer co-producers (social network status). Consumer co-creation in social network markets presents an option beyond market (economic) or non-market (socio-cultural) actions. However, much social production literature (for example Benkler 2006, Quiggin and Potts 2008) argues that it is intrinsic motivations, centred on self-identity and engagement, that underpin the rise of consumer co-creation. Extrinsic motivation – via prices, money and markets – are assumed to operate against intrinsic motivations, inhibiting or crowding them out (Zeitlyn 2003). Yet conceiving consumer co-creation in terms of social network markets avoids the either/or assignment of intrinsic socially motivated or extrinsic economically motivated behaviour. Instead, it allows a complex interaction between the two motivations and domains (Johnson 2002) as in the multiple games approach above.

By seeing consumer co-creation through the lens of a social network market, we emphasize a demand-driven dynamic in which the agency and choices of creative citizen-consumers and their social networks are fundamental to the evolution of markets. For example, the purchase of a video-game and investment in its online social networks may be prompted by a group of fellow game enthusiasts (a local social network), or from positive reviews by other gamers on distant but still connected social networks. Yet these 'non-market' social networks interact and co-evolve with 'market' contexts: they may give rise to potential for-profit businesses in their own right, as well as instrumentally shaping the creation and development of markets themselves (Malaby 2006).

Consumer co-creator agents seek both economic opportunity *and* the social status signals and intrinsic rewards earned from participation in social networks. Creative citizen-consumers increasingly transact across these motivation and incentive domains and as they do so they give rise to new institutional forms about which other cultural and economic institutions then re-coordinate and evolve. This foregrounds consumers as entrepreneurial deal-makers, agreeing to exchanges and negotiating the terms of these relationships based on self-interest paid in money or attention to the provider in a two-way transaction of complex network choices.

6.5   CONCLUSION

This chapter has argued that many problems and difficulties of creative labour markets may not be due to classic market failure (resolved with income transfers), but may instead accrue from the persistent and overwhelming presence of 'signalling games'. In a signalling game, agents will do things that don't seem rational – giving labour away for free, or deliberately overskilling – in order to send a credible signal to creative labour markets. This, of course, is the outcome of a competitive process and, as in the previous chapter, indicates yet another wrinkle on the interaction of creativity and market competition. Yet neither is an argument against market competition in creative labour markets. By pointing to the signalling aspect as a prime motivation for otherwise inexplicable behaviours (such as voluntary consumer co-creation), this evolutionary 'signalling' framework offers a new economic approach to the co-evolution of cultural and economic incentives at the intersection of market and non-market behaviour.

Credible signalling builds reputation, and reputation is social capital; a capital that is then fungible over future market and non-market contexts. Creative production occurs in a social context that gives rise to arbitrage opportunities over market and non-market spaces. The currency through which these transactions occur is not always monetary; indeed as often it is reputational, in the sense of being an investment in the wealth of a credible signal. We suggest this insight, which arises out of the fundamental uncertainties involved in the experience-good nature of creative production – on both the input and the output side – is instrumental to the analysis of creative labour markets and a proper subject for further research.

NOTES

1. For example Throsby (1994), Towse (1996, 2006), Gill and Pratt (2008), Oakley (2009), Banks and Hesmondhalgh (2009), Ross (2009).

2. See Freeman (1976) and Hartog (2000).
3. Note that signalling contexts do not always lead to overskilling as other mechanisms might be harnessed; also, overskilling is not always caused by signalling (Lindsay 2005).
4. It is noteworthy that there is also an artistic and creative 'look', often well cultivated and reinforced at art schools and so on, that while associated with 'cool' is also unmistakably a form of signalling.
5. This extended to animal signalling in the 'handicap model' of mate attraction in sexual selection and predator deterrence in natural selection (Zahavi and Zahavi 1997).
6. For example, Jenkins (2006a, 2006b), Croteau (2006), Bruns (2008), Shirky (2008), Hartley (2009a), Burgess and Green (2008).
7. Lessig (2004), Benkler (2006), Quiggin (2006), Bruns (2008).
8. Lerner and Tirole (2002), Johnson (2002), Llanes (2007), Boldrin and Levine (2008).
9. Lee et al. (2003); Mustonen (2003).
10. Kücklich's (2005) concept of 'playbour', which articulates the blurring of the boundaries between the cultural and the economic domains, is a key example.
11. The idea of multiple games theory was first proposed by Long (1958) and then Bowles and Gintis (1986). In the Page and Bednar (2007) model of 'games theory', the rationale for a multiple game is an extension of bounded rationality (Conlisk 1996) to suppose that strategies are costly to construct (or compute) and so playing the same strategy in multiple games is a form of satisficing (see also Miller and Page 2007).
12. Note this can also be usefully seen through the lens of the emergence of communities with new norms and rules, largely self-organized and self-enforcing in the manner of the institutions of a common pool resource (Ostrom 1990).
13. See Akerlof and Kranton (2000), Kirman and Teschl (2004).
14. See Neff (2005), Williams (2006), Castronova (2005, 2006).

7. Identity dynamics and economic evolution

7.1 ECONOMIC EVOLUTION REQUIRES IDENTITY DYNAMICS

The concept of identity is central to cultural studies and much of the post-modern humanities where it connects a person's self-image to group affiliations, thus expressing the 'personal political' of identity politics. Examples include gender, racial, class, sexual, cultural and religious identity in the prime instance, but extend outward to encompass identity in terms of community, nation, and other social aggregates with respect to which an individual 'identifies'. Identity is also a prime concern of personal and social psychology (sense of self), philosophy (selfhood) and anthropology and ethnography (sense of place and group affiliation). But until very recently, almost the only part of the non-physical sciences (cf. Breger 1974, Greenfield 2008) that did not have serious interest in identity was economics.

The concept of identity has recently entered microeconomic theory through the work of Akerlof and Kranton (2000, 2005, 2010), Davis (1995, 2003, 2007), Kirman and Teschl (2004), Livet (2006), and Sen (1985, 1999b, 2004). Each makes a different argument, yet all broadly converge on identity as a useful additional concept in modelling choice in socially framed situations, focussing on particular identities as additional constraints over choice. Identity thus enters economics as an additional parameter that constrains individual choice as a function of each individual's particular identity endowment. In this way, identity is made a further argument in the agent's utility function. Let us call this choice-theoretic approach equilibrium identity statics (Akerlof and Kranton 2000, 2010). Unlike the cultural studies and other approaches that turn on the political and power implications of identity, this is clearly an economics of identity in that it seeks to examine the individual choice implications of particular identity endowments.

Yet the economics need not end there, for this endowment may not be exogenously given but may actually be endogenously and continuously transforming in an analogous manner to the growth of knowledge or technology in an evolving economy. Indeed, this is precisely what we should expect. If economic evolution requires agents to originate, adopt and retain new 'generic rules' or ideas, then it is entirely reasonable to allow that individual identities will also change through the process of economic evolution. Indeed, economic evolution may not be possible without such processes. Let us call this evolutionary identity dynamics.

Economic evolution implies that agents change not just the information they learn, but the knowledge (or generic rules) they carry and thus the capabilities and connections they can make. Economic evolution requires that some agents become generically different, with presumably a changed sense of self, or identity. Yet while neoclassical economists were laggard in noting the implications of identity statics (on choice constraints), evolutionary economists have been no more cognizant of identity dynamics (a notable exception is Herrmann-Pillath 2008, 2010, discussed below). For the most part, new knowledge is assumed to be easily 'updated' in the internal scheme of each agent, effectively supposing that identity dynamics are costless and instantaneous. Yet economic evolution may be subject to constraints caused by identity lags and driven by the emergence of new identity differentials associated with changes in a person's 'sense of self' due to the effects of the adoption of new ideas or positional shifts in social networks or in an institutional milieu. Identity dynamics may be hypothesized to occur differentially, irregularly but persistently to economic agents in an evolving economic order. The limits of economic evolution, in this view, are thus bound up with the limits of identity dynamics: if agents cannot change generically whilst maintaining coherence, differentiation and valued social connections, then the economic system will be evolutionarily constrained. In turn, the capability to undergo such identity changes will affect the rate of evolutionary economic dynamics. The argument advanced here is that an evolutionary function of the creative industries is in facilitating such identity dynamics (also Chapter 9).

My argument builds on the work of Carsten Herrmann-Pillath (2008, 2010), who also seeks to integrate the economics of status orders and agent identity into a unified framework of cultural and economic co-evolution. He writes (2008: 1):

> Status orders and agent identities appear to be major determinants of the nature of economic systems, resulting in contingent boundaries between systemic categorizations of production and consumption, or notions of productive processes versus non-productive ones. From that perspective, the major novelty in the emerging creative economy, viewed as a new kind of economic system, is the structural change of the social networks, which become less hierarchical and more integrated, resulting in the endogenization of identity formation. Changes in the agent identity trigger the further evolution of the economic system.

Herrmann-Pillath rejects the strong universality hypothesis of agent rationality, arguing that economic systems build on contingent agent identities that change through time. Economic orders are thus historically contingent culturally as well as technologically and institutionally. He argues that agent identities are not exogenously given, as in the Akerlof–Kranton model, but are endogenous through experimentation, interaction and selection. This process, he further argues, as Potts and Banks did in the previous chapter, unfolds at the dynamic intersection of market and non-market activity and context.

What has been missing in the economics of identity, and which underpins a theory of identity dynamics, is an evolutionary generic model where identity is neither a given (free) endowment nor an equilibrium outcome, but a 'generic asset' subject to investment, adaptation and maintenance (Dopfer 2004). This adaptive and evolutionary 'investment in identity' perspective in turn illuminates how creative industries outputs contribute to the process of individual adaptation to economic change. Economic evolution requires identity dynamics and creative industries outputs are the inputs into such identity dynamics. This offers a further reason to underscore the significance of the creative industries to the process of economic evolution.

7.2 IDENTITY IN EQUILIBRIUM AND EVOLUTION

7.2.1 The Akerlof and Kranton Model of Identity

George Akerlof and Rachel Kranton (2000, 2002, 2005, 2010) have sought to integrate several major findings from psychology and sociology on the behavioural and motivational aspects of identity into neoclassical economics. They have done so by augmenting the standard utility function with a loss function calibrated on the difference between the utility of actual behaviour and self-framed (not socially constructed) identity. They rightfully claim this makes for a more realistic and scientifically consistent basis to microeconomic analysis. From this theoretical extension, they elaborate a raft of applications of the economics of identity ranging over employment, education, organizations and macroeconomics. They argue that identity matters to economic analysis because it selectively but consistently constrains individual interactions and choices. Their point is that the inclusion of identity is effectively a forced scientific move in economics due to the manifest empirical importance of identity in observed human economic behaviour.

John Davis (2003, 2007) is critical of their model for failing to distinguish between personal identity and social identity. This matters in an evolutionary context where agents not only choose an identity[1] but also continuously update their identity as a function of their social networks (Kirman 2005). Davis points to Sen's (2004, 2007) conception of multiple identities, a point also recognized by evolutionary behavioural economists (Earl 1986, Earl and Potts 2004). Specifically, Akerlof and Kranton's (2000) utility maximization model introduces the identity I of agent j as an argument in the utility function U which is defined in relation to the actions a of the agent (a_j) and those of other agents (a_{-j}):

$$U_j = U_j (a_j, a_{-j}, I_j).$$

The identity function of agent j is:

$$I_j = I_j (a_j, a_{-j}; C_j, e_j, P).$$

Identity depends on j's actions and those of others; upon j's assignable social categories C_j (each social category C has an associated set of social prescriptions P of behaviour appropriate to that category); and upon the extent to which j's own given characteristics e_j match the social ideals of j's categories C, as indicated by P. For Davis (2007), the identity or 'self-image' function I_j is really a 'social image' function because it is constructed by the agent's characteristics e_j in terms of their distance from given social prescriptions P. This models identity in terms of the individual adapting to a given set of socio-behavioural categories and prescriptions: hence a general identity equilibrium occurs only when all agents' actual behaviour e_j maps uniquely to the social ideals of j's categories $C(P)$. The neoclassical model of identity is therefore an analysis of *equilibrium identity*, individually and socially. But this is misleading if the categories C and proscribed behaviours P are themselves changing due to the actions of other agents whose socially observable characteristics e_j shift the definitions of C and P (as for example in the 'multiple games' discussed in the previous chapter). The Akerlof–Kranton model thus presumes the invariance and stability of C and P to construct the equilibrium in I upon which their choice-theoretic inferences depend.

7.2.2 Evolutionary Critique

The evolutionary critique of the equilibrium model of economic identity focuses on how economic change affects the identity of the agent. In an evolving economic order, individual positions, opportunities and knowledge all change, pressuring identity to also change. This may occur, for example, when once entrepreneurs become large business holders or bankrupt, or when once general employees become highly paid specialists.

Or it may occur over generations, when a working-class mother provides resources for a professional-class daughter. Commonly, this occurs as people change jobs or careers, or experience changed income or acquire new skills or resources leading to different economic lifestyles and opportunities. Indeed, this process plays out both individually and demographically as agents move through the various stations of life in an open economy, or experience economic mobility. This process is most often treated sociologically, but it can be integrated via analysis of micro generic change in the identity of the economic agent.

Central to the evolutionary critique is the notion that identity is not a given and fixed state of an agent or even a stable distribution of identity parameters over a population of agents. Instead, in an open evolving economy identity will continuously adapt within each agent and evolve across a population of agents. The basis of the evolutionary economic model is that identity is bound up with the 'generic rules'[2] agents originate, adopt and retain, and is part of the process of economic evolution. The evolutionary critique of the neoclassical model of agent identity is thus analytically equivalent to the critique of the neoclassical model of technological change: it makes dynamics exogenous to the model. Instead, an evolutionary model of identity dispenses with the augmented utility function (U_j) and comparative static identity function (I_j) approach – a point also argued by Sen (2004) and Kirman and Teschl (2004) – and proceeds with a behavioural–evolutionary model based on agents and their origination, adoption and retention of generic rules. An evolutionary model of identity thus integrates the micro concept of identity with the analytic framework of generic rule evolution.

7.2.3 Generic Identity

The general theory of economic evolution is based on the distinction between generic and operational analysis (Dopfer and Potts 2008). An economic system is 'made of' generic rules carried by agents that form the populations and structures of knowledge that compose an economic order. Change in generic rules or knowledge – not in operations or resources – defines economic evolution. The same point applies to agent identity. An agent is composed of generic knowledge, operational actions and resource endowments. From the evolutionary perspective, it is the content and efficacy of generic knowledge that is 'what evolves'. Identity here does not relate to the agent's operational actions and cultural endowment (as in the Akerlof and Kranton model). Rather, it relates to the agent's underlying generic knowledge-base, structure and connections. Identity dynamics are thus affected by the process of origination, adoption and retention of new ideas and rules an agent carries. This evolutionary process of knowledge growth and change and subsequent re-coordination into a new 'personal order' (*á la* Hayek 1952) works to transform each agent into a different person through each such generic change. Economic evolution thus both drives and is constrained by identity dynamics.

From the evolutionary economic perspective, identity is generically constituted by the rules an agent carries and the sense and extent to which they work as a coherent system, and the interactions this system then makes with other agents or groups of agents. This model differs from standard psychological and sociological conceptions of identity that are based on a 'sense of self' or a self-image connected to given social categories. As Akerlof and Kranton (2000: 720) explain: 'Identity is bound to social categories; and individuals identify with people in the same categories and differentiate themselves from those in others'. However, rather than social categories, the evolutionary identity model is constructed in terms of generic rules that agents identify with, when effectively internalized. In the evolutionary model, agents 'identify' with other agents who have also internalized and externally signalled similar rules. Identity is constructed of generic similarity that is integrated to create coherence in the agents' inward and outward perceptions and actions.

Identity is defined in evolutionary economics as the generic set and operationalized function of the rules a carrier has originated, adopted and retained. This 'cognitive technology' then has 'competitive advantage' in the construction and maintenance of an identity with strategic costs and benefits that will be proportional to the particular rules adopted and under selection pressure in relation to the environment in which such rules operate. Identity dynamics are to the micro-agent what technology dynamics are to the macroeconomy, namely a change in underlying generic structure through an evolutionary process (an 'identity trajectory') of 'creative destruction' of the content and system of generic rules that shape an agent's economic identity. The model of evolutionary growth through technological trajectories (or meso trajectories, Dopfer and Potts 2008, chapter 4) can similarly be applied to the process of identity dynamics in an individual agent: just as a new technology enters a macroeconomy as a meso trajectory, a new idea may enter into an individual agent as a micro trajectory that changes the agent's identity.

7.3 IDENTITY DYNAMICS AS A MICRO TRAJECTORY

In evolutionary economics, a micro trajectory is the process by which an agent (*Homo sapiens oeconomicus*, Dopfer 2004) originates, adopts and retains a novel generic idea. Yet it is also a trajectory of identity dynamics as an agent goes from one generic state to another, becoming generically different. This should immediately be distinguished from learning dynamics in relation to new information, which are operational dynamics. Generic dynamics instead relate to the effect of a micro trajectory that changes the knowledge-base of what the agents know and how they behave and see themselves, that is, the identity of the agent. New information changes the inputs into the agent's generic identity; but new knowledge adopted and retained changes what and who the agent *is*: these are generic identity dynamics and they are consequence of a micro trajectory.

A micro trajectory has three phases: micro 1-2-3. Micro 1 is origination as the new idea is created or accessed. Micro 2 is adoption as the novel idea is adopted and integrated into the system of ideas composing the agent's identity. New ideas can fail at this point if they do not fit with the extant system or if it cannot integrate the new idea. Micro 3 is retention and normalization of the new idea, such that it becomes embedded into the ongoing and normal operations of the agent. This three-phase process of a micro trajectory (under a novel generic rule) is how the economic agent personally experiences economic evolution as a changed sense of self.

Modelling identity dynamics as a micro-trajectory has several implications. First, it provides a way of conceptualizing the multiple selves problem in cognitive and behavioural research on identity. This is conspicuously missing from the utility function approach. This disjunction has been highlighted by Sen (2004, 2007) who argues that economic agents have multiple roles they occupy in society (for example, father, employer, Hindu, cricket-fan, and so on) and thus are constituted by multiple identities that need not be continuous or even commensurable at any point in time. The concept of multiple selves is easily accommodated in a rule-based framework, as each 'self' corresponds to a subset of rules adopted within a system of micro trajectories. Further, there will be meta-rules specifying which rule set is applicable in any given context. Indeed, multiple identities are precisely what a generic micro trajectory model would predict.

Second, a generic model enables a consistent treatment of preference endogeneity in which agents' preferences are variable through time rather than given and fixed (Hodgson 1997). Earl and Potts (2004) modelled this in terms of a 'market for preferences' in which boundedly rational agents adopt the decision rules of other more experienced agents when making choices over infrequently purchased novel or complex goods and services. Identity dynamics are thus a 'market-like' behaviour of observation and adoption of the knowledge base of the choices made by other agents on a 'social network market' (see also Chapters 6 and 8).

Third, an identity dynamics model of micro trajectories connects individual and social identity via entrepreneurship in social networks. Indeed, it is conceivable to talk of 'identity entrepreneurs' who extract value from novel identity constructions that might be adopted by other agents. The social milieu in this view is not given, but continuously emerges from the interactions of differentially endowed and specialized agents, each proposing, configuring and projecting identity constructs creatively assembled from connections and refractions from other agents. (Note this is analogous to the Romer model of new technologies.) This evolving identity order is then modelled as an emergent outcome of individual identity dynamics in which rules are differentially originated, adopted and retained over social networks.[3]

7.4   CREATIVE INDUSTRIES' SUPPLY MECHANISMS OF IDENTITY DYNAMICS

Economic evolution is a meso trajectory that unfolds as micro-agents adopt and adapt a novel general rule. In doing so, they become (marginally, generically) different: these form micro identity trajectories (dynamics) from the evolutionary economic perspective. A meso trajectory stabilizes when a population of agents adopt and retain a rule, such that it becomes an element in the knowledge-base as an institution. A common context occurs in choice situations over novel goods where the agent lacks information or experience and thus takes the choices of other agents as a signal of the quality or expected utility to be derived: for example, choice over restaurants (Kirman 1993) or movies (De Vany 2004). This gives rise to social network markets, an important institutional form in an evolving economy.

Yet social network markets require an additional mechanism not requisite in a standard choice model, namely: identity matching. This occurs when agents map the observed characteristics of the agents who have already made a choice onto their own identity. Observed choices from a matching 'identity' are positively weighted and integrated. This process of identity matching, particularly with respect to peer references, is foundational to marketing techniques and fashion dynamics (Chai et al. 2007). The creative industries, in this view, produce social network markets that create value in the production of the identity categories C and in the representation of the sorts of proscribed behaviours P, where these categories and behaviours are subject to continual evolutionary variation and selection.

This suggests a new evolutionary mechanism by which the creative industries contribute to the operations and dynamics of a market economy. In a purely static economy with no new markets, products, technologies or business models, the definition and common knowledge of *C* and *P* may not actually be part of the economy but instead be acquired culturally or even socio-politically. This would occur if *C* and *P* were highly stable or only slowly changing, as has been true for most of human history. Yet in an evolving economic order continually buffeted by new technologies, commodities and work and lifestyle opportunities – an evolving and institutionally modern economy – identities may be required to be far more fluid and adaptable, giving rise to substantial scope for the continuous construction and reconstruction of identities. So while the static economic function of the 'creative industries' is the production and delivery of entertainment and culture, the evolutionary function turns on the ongoing reconstruction of identity and its spillover into identity matching, refinement of new lifestyle specializations and niches co-evolving with the origination, adoption and retention of novelty.

As economies become wealthier they are characterized not just by higher levels of production and consumption, but also by a greater variety of goods and services (Beinhocker 2006). Yet a widely overlooked hypothesis is that this greater variety may also then extend to identities. Economic evolution involves the multiplication of identities in the same sense that it involves the multiplication of specializations and knowledge (Cowen 2009). Furthermore, if the social network markets model of identity matching is correct, then we would also expect that a greater variety of identities would feed back to drive a greater variety of goods and services as niche identities and niche markets emerge and are institutionalized. At the meso level then, economic evolution drives identity evolution.

Even the most reticent consumer values an identity in creative consumption. At the aggregate level, this is observed in a widely estimated positive (>1) income elasticity of demand. As we become wealthier, both consumption and creative demand increase. The evolutionary theory of identity dynamics explains this consumer behaviour not as increased utility from consumption of previously income-constrained goods, but by the identity signalling effect such public consumption accrues (as Thorstein Veblen argued in 1899). Displays of creative consumption function as signalling mechanisms to socially networked or otherwise connected agents, not just of the particular value of the particular good or services in question (the restaurant, car, clothes, furnishings, and so on), but also of the identity of the agent who leads such endeavours. Economic evolution is a prime space for identity dynamics, and vice versa.

A further angle on identity dynamics can be considered in the macro domain. Macro identity dynamics do not concern the identity profile of a macroeconomy (say the 'branding' of Canada or France for example), but rather refer to the role of identity dynamics in the context of macro growth and development (the transitions occurring in China, Vietnam or Russia, say). Akerlof and Kranton (2005) argue that identity considerations explain why Keynesian macroeconomic analysis better explains changes in policy variables than New Classical macroeconomics, where strong rationality assumptions imply that policy changes should have no effect on identity. They argue that neutrality assumptions ignore identity in determining how people feel they should respond, which returns the standard Keynesian conclusions of the role of government in stabilizing macroeconomic fluctuations and expectations (Akerlof and Shiller 2009). Yet a different approach to macroeconomics and identity follows from an evolutionary view of the macroeconomy as the emergent product of individual actions subject to ongoing change in the content of that activity due to entrepreneurship and innovation. A Schumpeterian approach to identity thus emphasizes the role of agents investing in the construction of new identities derived from new technologies, businesses or lifestyle opportunities. Rather than the Akerlof and Kranton model of policy, which seeks government intervention into identity to stabilize the economy, an evolutionary identity perspective on macroeconomics focuses on generic not operational macro policy.

The macro process of creative destruction involves identity dynamics in at least two ways. As entrepreneurship and innovation it leads to the destruction of some markets and therefore jobs; some identities will be 'destroyed' and other identities will be 'created'. Consequently, identity dynamics may be an important explanation for relative growth rates in terms of resistance to change and differential adoption of new technologies and knowledge on economic growth. Identity constraints on economic evolution are not implicitly macroeconomic in nature but ultimately trace to microeconomic incentives in terms of the fungibility of identity and its dynamics. The growth of knowledge is ultimately constrained by micro identity possibilities and dynamics. Economic evolution is ultimately constrained as much by identity dynamics as by technology dynamics. Identity dynamics, in turn, carve the possibility space of economic evolution. Technological change commonly far outpaces identity change, yet economic evolution requires their eventual re-coordination. The short side of the market is thus not technological dynamics (which most evolutionary economists focus on) but rather identity dynamics, which few have.

7.5   CONCLUSION

Agent identity means a sense of self. This has been a major focus of intellectual inquiry in philosophy, neuroscience, cognitive, behavioural and social psychology, anthropology, sociology, political and cultural studies and history. But until very recently, identity has not been of concern to economics. Akerlof and Kranton (2000, 2010) changed that by integrating identity into the neoclassical utility function to explain systematic biases in the framing of choice. Identity thus matters, in their view, in economics because of its effect in biasing and framing choice.

This chapter has sought to challenge this idea and instead to develop an evolutionary economic interpretation using not identity-based choice biases but rather adaptive identity dynamics. Rather than conceptualizing identity as departures from rationality, identity instead enters evolutionary economic analysis in terms of entrepreneurial adaptation and market selection. The evolutionary economics of identity are thus focused on identity dynamics and the problem of maintaining and developing identity in an open and changing economic order. This is an analogous problem to that of a firm seeking to maintain competitive advantage in a world of changing technologies, preferences and markets. Identity dynamics are thus viewed as a special case of evolutionary adaptation.

A focus on identity dynamics, as a corresponding micro-agent trajectory, exposes a significant lacuna in the theory of economic evolution. Identity dynamics are, in this view, a necessary condition for economic evolution to occur at the level of the micro agent. This point is routinely overlooked in evolutionary economic analysis where such dynamics 'just happen'. Yet there are many instances where they do not, or in which identity dynamics are arrested or deviated to frustrate the adoption and retention of new ideas due to cultural, socio-political or social network effects, or deficient material or cognitive resources. Economic evolution requires agents to become different, and the limits to economic evolution are thus also the limits of the possibilities of agents becoming different as the limits of identity dynamics. Without identity dynamics, economic evolution does not and cannot occur.

I have only suggested that the creative industries may play a significant role in this process (this theme is taken up more fully in Chapters 8 and 9), but it should be immediately apparent why they are likely producers of inputs into this process. Identity dynamics involve social interaction, social adaptation and many forms of media and creative input and feedback. When we unthinkingly model the outputs of these industries as art, culture, leisure or even experiences we miss the fundamental reason why these 'goods' are of value to people in the first place, or the problem that they solve for consumers. We value these goods and services because they help us become different people, whether the people we want to become or need to become. In an open evolving economy we should not be surprised to observe increasing demand for the output of such industries.

NOTES

1. Akerlof and Kranton model this in game-theoretic terms, thus fixing identity in terms of a parametric pay-off function.
2. See Chapter 1 (section 1.5), or Dopfer and Potts (2008).
3. Potts (2000), Davis (2003), Kirman (2005), Potts et al. (2008a).

8. Social network markets

with John Hartley, Stuart Cunningham and Paul Ormerod[1]

8.1 INTRODUCTION

The concept of creative industries has been a feature of academic and policy literature for over a decade. During this time, the standard definition has not changed much from its initial DCMS (1998) conception – namely, as an extension of the cultural industries definition to incorporate the copyright industries. The creative industries are defined in terms of an industrial classification of what they do, or what they produce and how they do it. And although there have been many grumbles and even dismissive critique of the details of the classifications – too narrow, too broad, too inconsistent with extant classification, too arbitrary and opportunistic – the broad notion that an industrial classification should proceed on industrial lines is seemingly on firm foundation. The creative industries are thus implicitly defined and classified according to industrial sectors.

The standard industrial classification system was developed over half a century ago when the economy had a simpler structure that could be categorized more readily than now by the type of industrial activity in which a firm was engaged and the nature of its material inputs and outputs. Since then, the economic system has become considerably more complex and service-oriented. Yet there is a general problem with this standard industrial classification (SIC). Specifically, industries do not actually exist in microeconomic theory: they are not natural categories in themselves. What exists, of course, are agents, prices, commodities, firms, transactions, markets, organizations, technologies and institutions. These are what is economically real at the level of the individual agent's transformations or transactions. An industry is a derived concept. The concept of creative industries is therefore loose and can benefit from a further attempt at analytic moorings.

The cultural and creative industries fit uneasily into the industrial era framework for two main reasons: first, because they share many generic

characteristics of the service economy; and second, because they are to
a large extent an outgrowth of the previously non-market economy of
cultural public goods and private imagination seeking new views and
representations of the world. Both are instances of the emergence of new
markets. Yet the creative industries have come to prominence as these
once marginal activities have grown in significance, market value and
contribution to individual wealth and GDP.[2] So, we propose that a better
analytical foundation for the creative industries can be provided by taking
the perspective of an emergent market economy rather than an industrial
one.

Economic evolution occurs as new ways of being are originated,
adopted and retained. The economics of the creative industries, then, is
not the same as the economics of the agricultural or industrial economy,
as implicitly represented in neoclassical economics.[3] The central economic
concern is not with the nature of inputs or outputs in production or consumption *per se*, or even with competitive structures, but with the nature
of the markets that coordinate this industry.[4] We think they are both
complex and social, and that this offers a useful analytic foundation.

In creative industries' markets, complex social networks play at least
as significant a coordination role as price signals. For evolutionary and
complexity economists, this is unsurprising. What is new is the suggestion
that it might apply not only to science and technology, as is conventional
in evolutionary economics, but also to the arts and culture. Markets for
novelty as social networks are thus moved closer to the centre of the
economic analysis of innovation and growth.

Consumer choice in creative industries is governed not just by the set of
incentives described by conventional consumer demand theory, but also
by the choices of others. For example, see Arthur (1989), de Vany and
Walls (1996), Ormerod (1998, 2005, 2006), Kretschmer et al. (1999), and
Beck (2007). Schelling (1973) described this entire set of issues as being
'binary decisions with externalities'. There is overwhelming evidence that
this choice dynamic applies generally to the creative industries (De Vany
2004, Potts 2006, Beck 2007). So our new definition of the creative industries therefore proceeds not in terms of individual 'artistic' or creative
novelty in a social context, but rather in terms of individual choice in the
context of a complex social system of other individual choice. The creative
industries are in this view then properly defined as a class of economic
choice theory in which the predominant fact is that, because of inherent novelty and uncertainty, decisions to both produce and consume are
largely determined by the choice of others in a social network.

These social networks function as 'markets' (Earl and Potts 2004) in
which the creative industries are defined in market-based choice-theoretic

terms that are, we believe, best analysed in a complex systems theory framework. So recognized, it becomes apparent that the creative industries are also a crucible of new or emergent markets that, typically, arise from non-market dynamics (for example internet affordances) and that often then stay at the complex borderland between emergent and ongoing social networks and emerging and established markets.

The upshot is that the analytic distinctiveness of the creative industries rests not upon their cultural value or sublime nature (that is, their non-market value), but upon the overarching fact that the environment of both their production and consumption is essentially constituted by complex social networks. The creative industries rely, to a greater extent than other socio-economic activity, on 'word of mouth', taste, cultures, and 'popularity' such that individual choices are dominated by information feedback over social networks rather than innate preferences and price signals.

This manner of 'industry definition' overlaps significantly with the extant definition of the creative industries. It offers an analytic foundation that sharpens economic analysis by isolating the central features that matter: namely, (i) agent cognition and learning, (ii) social networks, (iii) market-based enterprise, organizations and coordinating institutions. These three terms are strongly homologous with the triad that forms the 'unit of analysis' in media and communication studies, namely audience (reader, viewer, consumer), content or distribution (for example TV network or press with their associated content or text), and producer (especially large-scale state or private corporations). Reconfiguring this standard formula of a 'textual system of modernity' (Hartley 1996: 32) as agent–network–enterprise has the advantage of removing the assumption held in most political-economy accounts of media that there is a one-way flow of causation along this 'value chain', from (active) producer via text-distribution to (passive) audience. In our formulation, the interrelationship among agents, networks and enterprise is dynamic and productive; all are engaged in the mutual enterprise of creating values, both symbolic and economic. Our definition thus both builds upon and improves a longstanding model of communication flows from media and communication studies. This is particularly important in light of the increasing significance of consumer-generated content and user-led innovation in new media (Hartley 2008).

When triangulated, these components (agent–network–enterprise) point to a definition of the creative industries in terms of the system of activities organized and coordinated about flows of value through the enterprise of novelty generation and consumption as a social process. This perspective entirely transcends the arts/culture basis as well as the neoclassical welfare theoretic basis to arrive at a 'type of market' classification in an open system. The creative industries, in this view, are defined as the set of industries in which the choices about both production and consumption are predominantly shaped by generic and operational feedback from social networks.[5]

8.2 THE SOCIAL NETWORK MARKET DEFINITION OF CREATIVE INDUSTRIES

A new social network-based definition of the creative industries refers to: *The set of agents and agencies in a market characterized by adoption of novel ideas within social networks for production and consumption.*

The creative industries are the subset of commodities and services over which consumers do not have well established decision rules for choice (and so must learn them) or where the 'use value' is novelty itself (Caves 2000); and where also, significantly, producers do not have deep knowledge or power regarding what products will be of value. The creative industries are thus the domain of new generic rules that are ostensibly socially both produced and consumed. Creative industries, in this new evolutionary view, are central to the growth of knowledge process of economic evolution. All new technologies have some aspect of this, yet the creative industries are ostensibly characterized by the dominance of both social production and consumption through the flow of novel rules.

Before considering what industries are included and excluded from this definition, let us first review the analytic foundation. A social network is defined as a connected group of individual agents who make production and consumption decisions based on the actions (signals) of other agents on the social network. This definition gives primacy to communicative actions rather than to connectivity alone (cf. much new social network physics). *Social* here means the ability of one agent to connect to and interpret information generated by other agents, and to communicate in turn. *Network* means that these are specific connections (often technologically enabled), and not an abstract aggregate group such as a nation, a people, or the like. The literature and models of social networks will be briefly reviewed below, but for now we consider four salient properties.

First, a social network is not necessarily just the group of people an agent knows (for example, family, friends, colleagues). These are plainly social networks and often important social networks, but there are many others too. Social network feedback provides social network information that agents use in making choices, and are reticulated throughout the economic system.[6]

Second, a social network is not necessarily regular, but may contain hubs, weak and strong connections, close and distant connections. Social networks commonly exhibit a complex topology in economic space. Yet the inherent complexity of social connections incident from the individual does not necessarily imply that social networks themselves are highly complex. Indeed, a main finding of network and complexity theory is how similar many seemingly different networks are in terms of their emergent structural and dynamic properties.[7]

Third, a social network implies social origination, adoption and retention processes as a social process of micro trajectories. This renders social networks generally more complex than physical networks, in that the switching mechanisms (that is, human agents) are orders of magnitude more complex than neurons or genes in cognitive or genetic regulatory networks. Yet because human social and communicative action is more directly knowable than physical networks we may yet seek more realistic and parsimonious models of the higher-order complexity of socio-economic processes by integrating the behavioural, economic and social sciences with studies of anthropology, culture, media, and so on, in the context of creative industries.

Fourth, social networks are not separate and distinct from familiar categories of social and economic system coordination, such as mature markets, firms, coalitions or institutions. Rather, the creative industries are a particularly dynamic part of the structure of a social and economic system. In some aspects of the economic system, social networks play a more significant role than in others. This is what suggests social networks as a basis for identifying and classifying the creative industries as predominantly characterized by economic actions in the context of social networks, a definition over both production and consumption.

By defining the creative industries in terms of social network significance, the logical implication is that other industries and markets have less social network significance. Yet we think this is a defensible proposition. First, it rules out industries such as agriculture, mining, extraction and the primary industries in general, because they are constituted by physical resources and known technologies in production and as inputs into stable and generally mature technologies and markets. This does not deny the role of technological change and new markets in these industries, but emphasizes that social networks have a lesser role in explaining the dynamics of consumption or innovation in production (cf. Griliches 1957).

Second, it also excludes manufacturing industries that are successful according to a matrix of stable prices and technologies within which to combine, through efficient and scaled organization, resources and technologies to create commodities for supply (Porter 1990). Again, there is little role for social networks in this process, which is largely driven by efficiency through competition on the supply side, and income and wealth effects on the demand side. This is largely what both Keynesian economics and industrial organization theory have shown. Again, this does not exclude the role of social networks in, for example, the diffusion of innovation in manufacturing (Williams et al. 2004). Instead, it emphasizes that these are not the prime analytic consideration in defining these industries. The creative industries are not about mature technologies; they are about the evolution of new technologies (particularly those relating to human communication, knowledge sharing and cultural exploration).

Third, this definition also naturally excludes skilled professions that are largely about learning and applying complex knowledge (excepting components of these industries that do involve social networks). This is often mediated by advertising and marketing services, which are then properly classified as social network services, along with media and publishing. The software component of the extant creative industries classification is also naturally included in this definition of social network services, as the domain of information technologies at the human interface. The creative industries are services; specifically, services to the growth of knowledge and economic evolution in a socio-cultural context.

Social network services then are a subcomponent of the creative industries, the other component being content as new ideas. This distinction allows a logical systems view of the 'standard' creative industries definition, but also a clear point of departure for critical review toward further inclusions and specific exclusions. At base is the structure and process of the creation and use of the creative industries as part of an evolutionary system or mechanism. This is in no way a distinction between organizations and markets, or public and private, or commercial and humanistic; these aspects are everywhere in this distinction. Rather, it signals that there is an important distinction between services that build and maintain social networks (that is, infrastructure and connectivity) and services that use these to create value (that is, content and creativity). This relation is symbiotic: each depends on the other, and the whole is symbiotic with other sectors – the creative industries are a further mechanism in the complex emergent system of economic and cultural co-evolution.

Creative industries, in this view, are part of the innovation system of the economic order, and not just of industry space. They are themselves composed of systems that build and maintain social networks (for example advertising, architecture, media and ICT software) and systems that create value on these social networks through content (for example film, TV, music, fashion and design). This distinction is far from clean; for example, media companies often both create networks and supply content. Yet the basic principle is we think generally and usefully applicable:

- *The creative industries are the set of economic activities that involve the creation and maintenance of social networks and the generation of value through production and consumption of network-valorized choices in these networks.*

Several notable exclusions and differential inclusions are prompted by this new definition. First, and perhaps controversially, it potentially factures the definition of cultural industries along the lines of 'old' and 'new' culture – where old means heritage, antiques, museums, classic arts and performances, and 'new culture' means anything experimental about which quality is unclear. This does not diminish the role of 'old culture', but reassigns it to the social education system as knowledge becomes embedded as self-evident or infrastructural, needing only maintenance and continuity. The new cultural industries, historically and contextually conditional, are rightfully included in the definition because their production and consumption is heavily influenced by social networks for the simple reason that their value is uncertain (a point recognized in labour market signalling in Chapter 6). New cultural technologies are part of the creative industries, old cultural technologies are not necessarily so. What is in and out of the creative industries classification will thus evolve and shift as industries emerge and mature: there is no permanent or ultimately true definition of the creative industries in the industrial sense.

Second, it extends the set of creative industries into often low-brow cultural and highly commercial domains such as tourism, sports and entertainment. This has always been a contentious point in the standard definition, as it includes factors rightly regarded as not within the ambit of 'public good' policy attention. Yet because we can never know where new value will come from (because of uncertainty and the growth of knowledge), artificial exclusions of some socially produced and consumed services on the grounds of low-brow consumption is not a viable analytic proposition.

A third re-evaluation relates to design being much elevated as compared to the standard definition, in which it is just another creative industry. In essence, design is the new engineering, but between physical and social technologies (Nelson and Sampat 2001, Arthur 2009). Both architecture and software are therein frontloaded into this definition as the design of physical and information spaces for social interaction. In the standard classification, the performing and visual arts were implicitly regarded as central to the cultural industries, which were in turn tendered as the foundation of an extended conception of the creative industries (Throsby 1994, 2001). Yet in the social network definition, design and media are elemental not because they are transcendental, but because they are manifestly functional in the creation of new spaces and opportunities, and therefore of new choices and markets. As such, the core business of the creative industries is the representation and coordination of new ideas.

So, what do we gain and lose by this new definition? The main loss is of a political/ material definition of the creative industries; yet this is not necessarily a bad thing. What we gain is a non-political definition that registers the properties of the structure and process of a market order, not the concerns of aggrieved or self-interested parties in a democratic order. In the early 20th century, for example, automobiles, social clubs and romantic tourism were significant creative industries. By the late 20th century, these industries had mostly matured and creative industries had become deeply embedded in these sectors (as for example automotive designers, software designers and package holiday designers). Yet the creative industries did not just quietly embed along the industrial way, but moved on to new domains (digital content, games, new media, and so on). What we gain is a definition of industries as charged by their generic novelty, in the sense of being the industries of new ideas with products of uncertain social value. This contrasts with a definition based about the set of industries which produce known cultural goods subject to operational failure in a competitive environment. This sheds much ill-fitting and unnecessary baggage in the standard creative industries definition.

This model also links directly into analysis of the entrepreneurial process and the formation of new markets and organizations; and in general with the process of innovation as an experimental endeavour of what Schumpeter called 'creative destruction'. This then connects directly to analytic models of social process of the adoption and diffusion of new ideas on social networks. In consequence, this new view reconnects cultural studies back into modern science in a fundamental way through recognition of its basis as the study of emergent complex socio-cultural systems and their interaction with economic systems (Lee 2007).[8]

8.3 MODELS OF SOCIAL NETWORKS

The standard definition of the creative industries had the advantage of immediate relevance to extant policy platforms. Yet a social network definition of the creative industries offers license to import wholesale analytic models from late 20th century mathematics and science, in particular from network and complexity theory.[9] Social network theory is the application of network and complexity theory to the dynamics of social processes, and there has been considerable analytic interest and development in the theory and tools for analysis of complex social networks. Furthermore, this connects to the complex network framework of markets and other economic systems.[10]

Analysis of the creative industries fits easily into the framework of social network models of production and consumption. Social network theory provides an analytic modeling language that parsimoniously represents the essential features of the sorts of organizations and institutions that characterize both the production of creative industries output (see Caves 2000) and the processes by which consumers make choices over new products (which are often experience goods) of uncertain quality. The analytic implications of adopting a social network market definition are at least interesting, and possibly considerable.

First, this offers a first-principles rationale for developing the so-called 'trident' methodology for statistically tracking the extent of 'creative embedding' in the general economy (Higgs et al. 2008) in terms of network structure based on social network classification. This advances the early creative industries' mapping documents, which could only ever seek to infinitely elaborate maps of the existing classification, which is perpetually out of date.

Second, it makes possible the classification and mapping of the types of social networks in the creative industries according to theory network types and metrics. Network theory provides a framework to classify and map the connective structure of the creative industries. This further allows us to refine the idea of 'emergent socio-markets' by recognizing that many industries (and arguably all industries) start as hobbies by enthusiastic amateurs or shunned obsessives, or through unpredicted breakthroughs – in other words, outside established market norms. It is this liminal zone between the social and the market – not just in start-up conditions, but when it is normal in established sectoral activity – that defines the space we are trying to delimit.

Third, a new economic model of the creative industries developed from social network theory opens paths to further unification of analytic frameworks in behavioural economics, institutional economics, media and cultural studies, and other domains that study agent behaviour and changing environments in terms of the generic rule basis of the creative industries. A better understanding of the micro rules of creative industries' activities may then be developed into new simulation models or used to calibrate existing models of socio-economic processes. The network foundation further suggests a basis for macroeconomic analysis of how the process of growth in the creative industries connects to other sectors and to macro-economic growth when the creative industries are re-interpreted in terms of the innovation system, not the welfare system (Potts and Cunningham 2008).

A fourth point connects the network perspective to evolutionary and complexity theory as tightly interconnected concepts. The upshot is that evolutionary and complexity theory can be developed consistently in the economics of creative industries when defined in terms of social networks. Social systems are naturally complex systems; a point that once recognized offers an analytic basis for further integration with other behavioural and social sciences and cultural, political and media studies, which are also studies of complex systems. The particular complexity of the creative industries lies in the social network markets that form about the production and consumption of novelty. As such, analysis of the creative industries is properly based on the economics of complex social networks.

8.4 POLICY IMPLICATIONS

Although a speculative new classification is hardly the place for explicit policy conclusions, what this new definition highlights is the extent to which the policy landscape is changed by a social network definition of the creative industries. In the prime instance, the standard social welfare theoretic basis is replaced by an innovation system definition in which the creative industries are repositioned from a lagging to a leading sector, and from which their policy needs are appropriately re-assessed (Cunningham 2006, Cunningham and Potts 2010). As a welfare sector, their prime concern is public resource transfer to maintain existing activities. But as a leading sector, their prime concern is to apportion risk and uncertainty to the appropriate social domain best able to carry it, and to develop institutions that facilitate experimental behaviour and accommodate the dynamic costs of change.

The standard (DCMS) definition of the creative industries is based on an extension of the cultural industries, and so inherits a propensity to view creative industries' policy in terms of market failure in the provision of public goods.[11] The social network definition, on the other hand, is much closer to the sorts of policy prescriptions that derive from evolutionary or Schumpeterian economics, and in particular the apportioning of the risks and rewards of innovation, the development of capabilities for innovation, and the compensation of the losers from innovation. This approach focuses attention on institutions in relation to education, finance and insurance, taxation, property law and other such aspects of an enterprise economy. This also adds further concern with social technologies and social infrastructure and the adoption patterns and coordination properties that result. Yet unlike standard models, there is no implicit presumption of a market failure argument, but rather what is presumed is an ongoing process of adapting existing institutions and developing new institutions, offering a potentially important role for institutional or Schumpeterian entrepreneurs. The domain of policy is thus shifted from a top-down re-compensatory model to a bottom-up model of experimental facilitation and innovation.

The social network market definition also allows us to model how technological change may impact on the creative industries by evaluating the hypothesized effect on social networks, or of the differential effect of different structures of network. This offers a theoretical basis for evaluating the effects of public sponsorship of not just how new technologies affect the creative industries, but how the creative industries may affect the adoption and retention of new technologies.

8.5 CONCLUSION

Evolutionary economists argue that economic growth is ultimately caused by the growth of knowledge. Cultural economists argue that the creative arts, broadly conceived, produce knowledge. The concept of creative industries puts these two observations together. What we have added here is the further observation that this takes place in markets that are predominantly coordinated as social networks: these are social network markets.

In this view, the creative industries are not well defined as a set of industries, as in the standard DCMS definition, but are better defined as a class of markets – namely markets characterized in both supply and demand as social networks. This new conception offers in the prime instance an analytically coherent way to connect the economics of evolutionary growth with the social science and humanities studies of how people socially adopt novelty for retention as knowledge.

The creative industries are thus the set of economic activities in which production and consumption outcomes are predominantly determined by market-like processes on social networks. This is significant because the origination, adoption and retention of novel ideas is the primary cause of economic growth and development. Creative industries products are not defined as such because they are creative *per se*, but because they are novel and of uncertain value in the creation of new opportunities. That is a subtle but important distinction in which value is the outcome of complex networks of individual interactions. This is true of all commodities to some degree, or at some point in space and time.

The creative industries, in turn, represent the domains of economic activity in which social networks are the predominant factor in determining value. The creative industries are thus re-conceptualized as not just another public goods sector but as essential to the process and structure of economic and socio-cultural evolution, the leading edge of which occurs in social networks that result in emergent structures of coordination. The social network market perspective thus offers a basis for analysis of how socio-cultural and economic systems co-evolve. Such a framework should be central not peripheral to analysis of economic growth, development and policy.

NOTES

1. This paper was published as J. Potts, S. Cunningham, J. Hartley and P. Ormerod (2008) 'Social network markets: A new definition of creative industries' *Journal of Cultural Economics*, 32: 167–85. This edited version is reprinted here with kind permission.
2. See Howkins (2001), Cunningham (2006), Potts (2006).
3. For example Baumol and Bowen (1966), Throsby (1994), Heilbrun and Gray (2001).
4. This position is also advanced by Caves (2000), but in terms of information and transaction cost economics, as opposed to a conception of the market process.
5. This explains why contemporary emergent producer–consumer integration (as in the neologisms prosumer or produser) and the so-called pro-am revolution (Leadbeater and Miller 2004) is a feature of this process, along with the emergence of new organizations and markets.
6. For example Schelling (1973), Kirman (1993), Ormerod (1998), Ormerod and Roach (2004), Beck (2007).
7. For example Watts (1999), Strogatz (2001), Barabasi (2002), Christakis and Fowler (2009).
8. Cf. Garnham (2005).
9. See Watts (1999), Strogatz (2001), Newman (2003), Ormerod (2006), Vega-Redondo (2007).
10. See Kirman (1993), Potts (2000), Foster (2006), Ormerod (1998, 2005), and Dopfer and Potts (2008).
11. Hesmondhalgh and Pratt (2005).

9. Creative industries over an innovation trajectory

Prolegomena

This chapter is an edited version of a 2009 paper in *Economics of Innovation and New Technology* (18(7): 663–73) that examines the role of creative industries services over the three phases of an innovation trajectory – origination, adoption and retention. It suggests an evolutionary model with creative industries as not just another growing sector *per se*, but as demand-side elements of an economy's innovation system.

9.1 INTRODUCTION

Economic evolution is a dynamic market process in which new ideas, technologies, business models or elements of knowledge enter the economic system, displacing and disrupting the extant structure of such 'generic rules' (Dopfer and Potts 2008). Schumpeter (1939, 1942) called this process of sequential and parallel waves of entrepreneur-driven innovation 'creative destruction'. 'Creative' refers to the new ideas. 'Destruction' refers to their effect on existing ideas. The process of economic growth and development is not simply a process of expansion and accumulation, but crucially also involves re-coordination and re-configuration of existing activities and structures. This makes economic growth an evolutionary process.

Since Schumpeter, analysis of economic evolution has mostly focused on the 'supply-side' of the origination and diffusion of new technologies. This tends toward an industrial analysis that for the most part has been predominantly concerned with epochal physical technologies and associated manufacturing sectors (steel, chemicals, microelectronics, biotechnology, and so on), as well as service sector components relating to finance, transport and communication.[1] But something fundamental has long been missing from this account, namely analysis of the demand side of innovation.

The demand side is mostly assumed to be passive or neutral in the Schumpeterian model of economic evolution (as too in the neoclassical model of economic growth). The economic problem associated with new goods and services – the *raison d'être* of evolutionary economics – is assumed to lie mostly on the supply side in respect of problems of industrial and market coordination. Yet the question then arises as to whether there may be equivalent problems on the demand side, specifically in terms of how consumers learn to want new goods and how they integrate the consequences of these into their 'consumer lifestyles' (Earl 1986). A moment's reflection reveals that the same creative destructive forces obviously also operate here – for example creative destruction of an agent's sense of identity (Chapter 7), and of social networks (Chapter 8) – although these have traditionally been regarded as problems for psychology or sociology (*á la* Veblen, and the rest), not for economics. But these are manifestly economic problems to the extent that many businesses and indeed industries exist that (while not necessarily explicitly focused on this at first sight, perhaps seeing themselves most obviously as in the media or fashion or design business, say) are nevertheless deeply involved in adding economic value through their contribution to facilitating adaptation to such creative destruction on the demand side. This, I propose, is the evolutionary economic role of the creative industries.

Economic evolution means that people come to do new things, to interact with new ideas, to live in new ways; and the creative industries can add value by facilitating this process of economic evolution. This is less apparent in mature technologies or industries, for which structures of coordination and integration have already stabilized, and in which habits and routines and institutions of thinking and actions are already embedded. But it is of manifest significance when the economy is deeply and rapidly evolving through the effect of new technologies and discovery of new opportunities. The rapid growth of the creative industries of recent times (Potts and Cunningham 2008) may not just be due to wealth effects, or the benefits of ICT and globalization, but may reflect the deeper order of market-based economic evolution in which all new ideas are born into a social context and must develop in that space.[2] The creative industries, in this view, are thus a further element of the innovation system and correspondingly an essential part of any general evolutionary theory of economic growth and development.

The logical next step is to unpack the mechanisms of this process, which requires distinguishing between two evolutionary effects:

1. *Creative industries driving economic growth* The evolution of the creative industries with respect to the whole economy, in the form of structural change in which creative industries activities increase relative to the set of all economic activities.

2. *Creative industries facilitating economic evolution* The evolution of all economic activities in terms of creative industries activities, where the creative industries generate and facilitate the process of economic evolution through innovation.

This distinguishes between a supply side view (1) of creative industries as a growth-driving sector (see also Chapter 12, model 3), and a demand side view (2) of the creative industries in facilitating the processes of adaptation and retention in economic agents. This chapter focuses on this second model, seeking to present the case for how creative industries businesses are best understood as a mechanism in the process of economic evolution by their operations on the demand side in the context of an innovation trajectory.

In significant part, science and technology (mostly new technology) drive economic evolution. But creative industries further induce and enable the diffusion potential of a new technology or idea through their role in adapting and embedding these new ideas and opportunities into the minds and actions of economic agents. This is 'micro' creative destruction: the creative industries are the economic mechanism through which this most commonly occurs. That is why they are best understood (from both the analytic and policy perspective) not as just another industrial sector, but as part of the innovation system.

The standard theory of economic growth and evolution is based on factor accumulation, technological change, institutional efficacy and innovation, all driving productivity growth. For the most part, there has been little sense that the arts and culture play a positive or driving role in this process; indeed, quite the opposite (cf. Heilbrun 1991). The arts and cultural sectors are widely classified as high consumption in the form of culture, leisure, entertainment, and so on. These are antonyms of work and productivity and thus of no industrial strategic importance. This implies that as an economic system grows and becomes wealthy, it can afford more such cultural consumer goods through subsidized production. Economic growth thus enables the protection of the cultural/creative industries behind a wall of special treatment financed by the power and growth of the industrial economy (Netzer 1978, Grammp 1989). This model underpins the cultural economics canon of market failure, productivity deficits, non-market value and justified special treatment. How, indeed, could leisure activities ever be productively useful? It made no sense.

A failing of the modern theory of economic growth and evolution is that it does not account for economic evolution as a process in which a new idea is introduced into a social and cultural system (that co-evolves with the economic system, as in Chapter 6). Cultural economics has thus systematically under-represented the dynamic value of the arts and creativity to the economic order due to an implicit focus on cultural, socio-economic and technological equilibria. The neoclassical framework of cultural economics commonly overlooks the observation (readily available to introspection) that at an individual level change is often costly and difficult before it is beneficial and rewarding. Change is not a free good; it requires resources and benefits from the supply of services that contribute to the 'creative destructive' process of adaptation and change in micro agents in a socio-cultural context. Novelty is uncertainty before it is opportunity.

There are few incentives to evolutionary behaviour in a closed equilibrium world. Consequently, the efficacy of social structure in an open society (in Karl Popper's sense) will be a determinant of the scope for economic evolution. The cultural economics perspective focuses on the welfare of the cultural industries and the cultural goods and services they provide, but pays only passing attention to the dynamic evolutionary services they provide to the rest of the economy. The evolutionary economics of creative industries, in turn, focuses not only on the industrial dynamics of the creative industries (the growth model, as above) but also on its role in facilitating innovation and economic evolution through its services on the demand side.

9.2   HOW CREATIVE INDUSTRIES FACILITATE ECONOMIC EVOLUTION

Two related hypotheses connect the creative industries with economic evolution. The first is the growth model in which the structure of the economic system is evolving, with the creative industries becoming a more significant component of the economic order. The second is the innovation system model in which the creative industries are themselves part of the process of economic evolution across the economic order. These need to be distinguished, as they involve different mechanisms and have different analytic and policy implications. These are overviewed in Table 9.1 below.

9.2.1   The Growth Model of Creative Industries

In the first model of creative industries dynamics, evidence from creative industries mapping documents since the late 1990s clearly indicates that the creative industries' sector is growing at about twice the all industries average in value-added and employment (Potts and Cunningham 2008). By definition, all industries do experience this at some point, just as all

Table 9.1   Two models of creative industries dynamics

Model	Phenomenon	Example	Caused by	Analytics	Policy
Growth model of CIs	Relative growth of the CIs	Fashion and design industry grows faster than all-industry average	Factor increases, ICT, microeconomic reform, globalization, wealth and demand effects	CI as a meso trajectory, Uniform growth	Competition policy
Evolutionary model of CIs	Role of CIs in innovation	Fashion and design increasingly incorporated in all new products and services	Adapting new technology to human/social context, adoption and retention services	CI over meso trajectories Complex growth	Innovation policy

eventually grow at a less than average rate. Such is the restless nature of industrial evolution (Metcalfe 1998, Hanusch and Pyka 2007).

The creative industries are increasing in significance, and this has seemingly been occurring since the late 1980s/early 1990s. Why? The 'drivers' of this process are difficult to isolate and test, and there has been little analysis of this recent phenomenon. But a raft of explanations may be offered that include:

1. *Increased investment in, and supply of, input factors* The simplest explanation for relative growth in creative industries is increased investment in input factors (as modelled in a neoclassical production function). Increased capital investment may follow from increased sectoral profitability (which is widely reported), or opportunities to replace labour with capital, especially ICT. There is substantial evidence (DCMS 2001) that the sector has above average employment growth. A further source of labour growth arises from opportunities to access labour off-shore, although statistics here are patchy. So increased investment and increased supply of inputs (labour and capital) may explain the relative growth of this sector.

2. *Qualitative improvement in input factors* A related explanation for relative sectoral growth is qualitative improvement in input factors through increases in human capital, or through improvements in technology embodied capital. There is evidence for both. Average education levels in the creative industries are high (as are wages, although less so)

and have been rising since the early 1990s. But the largest effect has been in the ICT revolution associated with telecommunications, digitization, personal computing and the internet. The creative industries are heavy users of these technologies and their wide-scale adoption has revolutionized many aspects of production, delivery and even consumption of their output (Leadbeater 2000, 2008). So qualitative improvement of input factors may explain the relative rise of the creative industries.

3. *Growth of demand*   The growth of the creative industries may also be due to income effects associated with the substantial rise in global wealth since the early 1990s and the opening of global markets. This benefits all industries, yet it may have disproportionately benefited the creative industries due to their supply of income-elastic (>1) goods and services. So the rise of creative industries may be explained in terms of Engel curves and income elasticity, or more broadly as a shift in demand curves.

4. *Institutional change and efficiency*   A further explanation is institutional change in the direction of capitalist institutions penetrating this sector (see Chapter 12 below). Many parts of the creative industries escaped the regulatory reform in the 1980s that shook up other industries. They also harbour many not-for-profit organizations, whether legally or as vehicles for lifestyles. Furthermore, cultural and creative industries have historically been a well-protected sector with many institutions that pre-date capitalism (for example patronage, national esteem). However, there is mounting evidence that this has begun to change, in part due to the ICT revolution and the opportunities created, but also to the effects of globalization (Cowen 2002). This institutional change has affected organizational forms, business models and market strategies and thus may be a further explanation for the recent relative growth of the creative industries.

In each of the above, the relative growth of the creative industries is attributed to favourable forces from the rest of the economy, variously as increases in inputs, improved technologies, increased demand in consequence of wider economic growth, or institutional changes that create new opportunities. No analysis that I am aware of has sought to account for what proportion of growth can be explained by each; unfortunately I shall not offer one here. Still, it is likely that each has some explanatory power and that together they may explain some and perhaps much of the growth differential of the creative industries. Or, like Solow's classic work on production function estimation, a substantial residual may well remain. Let's assume for now that it does, and thus that these four factors explain only part of the economic significance and relative growth of the creative industries. This is of course a speculative position, but I want to proceed with this because I think it is important to think through the implications of such a residual, even if its contribution is only to help frame analysis of the growth model. So, if this residual does exist and is significant, as I suspect, how might it then be explained?

My hypothesis is that the multi-factor productivity (or technological change) analogue is that the creative industries themselves may be a kind of 'innovation technology' in the sense of furnishing 'evolutionary services' or 'coordination spillovers' as part of the innovation system, and specifically in the process of adoption and retention of new technologies. This, I suggest, is the evolutionary model of the creative industries.

9.2.2 Evolutionary Model of the Creative Industries

The evolutionary model of creative industries dynamics offers a very different interpretation of the value created by this sector. Instead of thinking of the creative industries as industries that produce a particular set of goods – entertainment, say – they might be better modelled as producing a coordination service – namely the generation and facilitation of change at both the individual agent and socio-cultural level.

The analytic framework proposed by Dopfer and Potts (2008) offers a way to unpack the role of the creative industries in the process of economic evolution in terms of the analytic unit of economic evolution: a meso trajectory – a three-phase process of the (meso 1) origination, (meso 2) adoption and (meso 3) retention of a generic rule into a population of carriers (see Table 9.2 below). The creative industries are involved in all three phases. As such, their economic significance derives not just from their operational economic value as cultural and creative industries products, exports, employment and so on, but also from their contribution to the process of generic change. The creative industries, in this model, will have greatest significance in an evolving economy and least significance in a static economy. So let us now consider these three phases in turn, and the role of the creative industries in each.

Meso 1: origination
The first phase of economic evolution is the origination of a novel idea. Dopfer and Potts (2008) call this 'meso 1', as the process of imagination and entrepreneurship in creating something new and developing it to the point that it may be adopted by others. This is the onset of innovation.

The creative industries contribute to this broadly in the provision of new ideas that then get developed, and often in deep collaboration with other industries. Music and video games are good examples of this, but

Table 9.2   Creative industries over phases of a meso trajectory

	Meso 1 Origination	Meso 2 Adoption	Meso 3 Retention
Process	Entrepreneurship and novelty	Innovation, creative destruction	Embedding and normalization
CI example	Art, music, publishing, fashion	Advertising, media	Design, film and TV
Function	Generating creative response, tools for imagination and exploration, models of change, experimental space	Social network creation and control, connection of new technologies to new lifestyles, (often non-linear) selection mechanism	Rendering of new rules into embedded functionality in the mind and as social rules

so too are fashion and design. Furthermore, the creative industries also provide services to generate and develop new ideas (what Dodgson et al. 2005 call 'innovation technologies'). This is especially true of publishing, TV, film and radio, which provide the space for the creation and analysis of ideas prior to them entering into economic space. A media rich society (supposing of course a free media society), for example, is not just good for democratic politics, but also for the origination of innovation through the opportunities it furnishes for discussion of and experimentation with new ideas. It should not surprise us that thriving media industries, in both populist and specialized media, offer a rich and fertile ground for the new ideas that are the basis of economic evolution.

This implies that the creative industries may in fact be a precondition for economic evolution – along with open markets, property rights, good governance, science and technology, and so on – by their production of the socio-technical space for generic origination. New digital media may well be particularly rich sources of and conduits for such origination (Jenkins 2006a). This hypothesis implies that societies with underdeveloped or restrictive media (along with other creative industries) should not experience economic evolution, which seems plausible when we think of Communist Russia or North Korea, or the differential performance of East and West Germany. Any default setting that attributes the creative industries to the entertainment or leisure industries should further acknowledge that a significant point of entertainment and leisure in humans comes from engagement with new ideas. This is why a rich fashion industry may also be a catalytic precondition for economic evolution (Hartley and Montgomery 2009). An externality of this preference for discussing ideas, even as entertainment, may well be a facilitating social technology for innovation and economic evolution.

Meso 2: adoption

The second phase of economic evolution – meso 2 – is the adoption of the novel generic rule into a population of carriers. This is the innovation process of creative destruction in action – often modelled as a partially stochastic adoption–diffusion process – through which a new rule-population emerges and the knowledge base of the economy changes. The creative industries are important to this process simply because it is an inherently social process involving many social and cultural technologies and mechanisms. When dealing with uncertainty, we look to others, sometimes directly to their individual advice or choice; at other times indirectly to the effect of their choice on price or sales, or even more indirectly, through others' representations of these effects (that is, social network markets; see Chapter 8, also Earl and Potts 2004).

The creative industries play a significant role in this process. This is most obvious in the commercial fields of advertising and marketing, which seek to inform and influence choice through construction and projection of various messages and rules for choice. This aims to affect the patterns of generic adoption through the production of rules for choice regarding the novel idea. This function extends through film, TV, radio, and other creative industries activities that create and process social information and focus attention (Lanham 2006). Alternative energies and genetically modified organisms, for example, are both physical technologies that have had their adoption process significantly influenced by the creative industries, as is currently the case for Web 2.0 and climate change. Indeed, I would offer the simple challenge of proposing innovation that has affected economic evolution that has not been facilitated and/or shaped by the creative industries.

The adoption and diffusion of new technologies is affected by the creative industries through their role in handling and processing social information about these new ideas, new things, new possibilities and consequences. The creative industries facilitate, accelerate and stabilize the adoption of novel generic rules into the economic order. They thus function as a selection mechanism, selecting against particular ideas and amplifying others. Again, without the creative industries, according to this hypothesis, an economic system would experience less evolution (and growth) because the adoption process would be either inhibited by uncertainty or constrained to the speed of personal knowledge. The vast acceleration in generic evolution from Gutenberg onwards (Eisenstein 1980), and again with telephony, radio, TV and the internet, all suggest that the creative industries provide the evolutionary service of adoption facilitation. Hartley (2009a) emphasizes this as the spread of new literacies, which then marks the transition to socio-cultural retention.

Meso 3: retention

The third phase – meso 3 – is the retention of the new idea into the economic order, along with its ongoing replication. This is often described as a process of normalization, habituation and embedding that refers to a world of stable parameters and low uncertainty, as the world the neoclassical model describes best.

But from the evolutionary perspective the creative industries play a further important evolutionary role in facilitating this process through the design of ways of being and their normalization. The example is the new representation, through whichever media, that transforms the new into the normal (a new signifier with culturally stable meaning), thus 'institutionalizing' novelty. Almost all creative industries feature in this function. There is interactive software that seeks to embed technologies into interfaces that accord with what actual human beings find comfortable and intuitive. There are books, films or TV that normalize a previously radical perspective. And there is the contribution of design and architecture to embed these ideas in plastic or stone. Of course, fashion, design and architecture, as with all other arts, also perform this same function (with variation) in proposing novel ideas in meso 1.

My further speculation is that this meso 3 process may well be the major contribution of the creative industries to the process of economic evolution through the normalization and embedding of adopted novel generic rules. This is obviously a difficult aspect to isolate, as it is a 'level effect' that will show up only in residuals, when it works well, or in balkanization processes of isolation and regression when it does not. The upshot here is a somewhat counter-intuitive perspective: namely that the value of the creative industries to economic dynamics is not that they are disruptive and 'creative' in the Romantic sense, but that they are effective forces of consolidation and normalization in respect of new ideas. They are a processing technology operating mostly on the demand side of economic evolution, and particularly with respect to the embedding and conservation of recent evolutionary advances.

The retention of new technologies into a socio-cultural system of interacting individuals is assumed in standard models of economic growth, and evolution is assumed to just happen, and for free. But that is a mistaken view. Embedding, normalization, habituation, routinization, institutionalization: these are all competitive domains with significant resources afforded to them across all sectors of any economy. And this, I propose, is also the domain where the creative industries are of greatest economic effect and value.

These three phases of an innovation trajectory do not neatly decompose the creative industries, with architecture only in meso 3, for example, or design only in meso 2. Rather, each creative industry tends to have different functions at different phases, and rising at different points with varying significance and intensity. In this view, the creative industries facilitate economic evolution through their role in providing the capabilities that incline agents toward generic novelty, adoption and retention. At any point in time, these will invariably seem indulgent or wasteful, or otherwise analytically and politically insignificant. But through time, these processes do have deep structural significance and act as significant shaping forces on the pathways of economic evolution.

9.3 TOWARD A CREATIVE INDUSTRIES MODEL OF ECONOMIC EVOLUTION

The analytic unit of economic evolution is the meso trajectory, each phase of which induces a process of creative destruction that results in a newly evolved and emergent order of agents, markets, firms and laws. The end result is an industry. Yet in the framework I have outlined here, the creative industries are not actually best understood as industries in this operational sense, but rather may be more clearly understood as mechanisms to connect new technologies and new economic opportunities to the dynamics of socio-cultural space. If so, this makes them an essential component of the innovation system of any economic order.

The extent and efficacy of the creative industries thus, I suggest, offers a partial measure of the evolutionary capabilities of an economic system. This implies a revision of the standard Schumpeterian model of economic evolution – which is ostensibly supply side and focussed on industry and technology – to integrate the role of the creative industries on the demand side of economic evolution.

This is simply to recognize that when technologies change, people must change too, along with cultural practices and social institutions. Following this line, when seeking to explain the causes of economic growth, we would thus extend the same analytical treatment that is routinely afforded to science, technology, engineering, manufacturing and distribution to the arts, practise, design and social coordination. We would recognize that the creative industries are part of the innovation system, and not just another bunch of growing industries.

The evolutionary growth and development of an economic system depends upon several ultimate causes (property rights, open markets, rule of law, and so on) but it also involves several proximate causes that include the new ideas brought by both science and art. Yet whatever the relative balance of significance, these are ultimately complements. Economic growth and development is, in part, caused by the creative industries through the new possibilities they create through their role in shaping and conditioning individual adaptation to and demand for novelty (Witt 2001). This is codetermined with their 'macro' role in the ongoing process of modernization. It is no accident that creative industries' firms are among the worlds' largest, or that individual fortunes are disproportionately due to creative industries' entrepreneurship (as in Chapter 3 above). Just as business and financial services, along with science and engineering services, have become an increasingly important aspect of the modern economy, so too have creative industry services, and for the same evolutionary dynamic reason: namely, the creation of the future through coordination of personal experiments and the adoption and retention of the resultant novelty. The creative industries are thus a crucial part of the mechanism of economic evolution through renewed imagination of individual lifestyles and socio-cultural possibilities (Earl 1986).

Yet Schumpeterian economists have widely overlooked the role of creative industries in the process of economic evolution. This has come at the cost of: an underdeveloped theory of the dynamics of demand and novelty; insufficient recognition of the role of consumers in the process of innovation; a poorly conceptualized analysis of technological re-use and adaptation; a misleading survey of the extent of organizational, regional and national innovation systems; and also a poor integration of the connection between culture, institutions and economic dynamics.

These are the opportunities before us to develop evolutionary and Schumpeterian analysis to better integrate an important and growing component of both the economy and the innovation system, namely the role of the creative industries in the origination, adoption and retention of new ideas and technologies. The creative industries are misunderstood as industries *per se*; they are better understood as emergent elements of the innovation system.

NOTES

1. See for example von Hippel (1988), Nelson (1993), or the classic text by Freeman and Soete (1997).
2. See Leadbeater (2000, 2008) and Benkler (2006) on this theme; also Howkins (2001, 2009).

10. Fashion and economic evolution

Prolegomena

This paper was first published in *Policy* in 2007, and was based on Chai, Earl and Potts (2007). It seeks to elucidate the positive role of fashion (and fashion cycles and the fashion industries) to the process of economic evolution.

10.1 FASHION: BAD OR WORSE?

Fashion is fun and frivolous. As such, the set of behaviours, commodities and industries associated with it are usually not regarded as part of the economic growth process, and certainly not as something that economic policy might consider relevant. Indeed, quite the opposite: fashion is widely conceived as a bit like astrology or barrels of whiskey, namely perhaps fun, but expensive in an opportunity cost way and something we really are generally better off without. Yet, I argue that this view is mistaken, and that fashion is in essence entrepreneurhip on the consumer side of the economy.

Analytically considered, fashion is the tendency of consumer preferences to move together, although in a seemingly random way. This has interesting implications for social and cultural analysis, as it signals a degree of social conditioning of individual tastes, a mechanism of which involves the publishing, advertising and media industries. Economists, however, have tended to be suspicious of fashion, which they define as the tendency of a group of consumers to adopt some personal mode of expression – as embodied in consumer durables such as clothes, furnishings, music, cars, leisure pursuits, and so on – only to adopt a different mode soon after, and certainly well before the physical assets embodying the fashion are fully worn out.

Immediately we see the economic problem: namely waste, as otherwise serviceable assets are unnecessarily depreciated. This waste occurs as actual utility fails to match expected utility, resulting in a misallocation of resources and significant write-offs of consumer assets. Worse, there is a widely held suspicion that the whole concept of fashion is the aggregate product of irrational (perhaps teenage) minds. At best, fashion is some species of coordination failure that systematically afflicts the shopping classes. As Oscar Wilde said, 'fashion is a form of ugliness so intolerable that we have to alter it every six months'. It certainly, in any case, has nothing to do with the inherent logic of new technologies and economic growth.

Conservative commentators have long argued that the existence of fashion remains an unseemly blight on an otherwise rational society. Sometimes this expresses as grumpy-old-man syndrome, where nothing new is as good as things that were, and at other times as the moral questioning of consumer priorities. Interestingly, there is a full political spectrum of darkness here, as fashion is also seen by many leftist commentators as embodying the worst aspects of a hyper-capitalist society, with its throwaway values of conspicuous consumption. Fashion, here, is a bourgeois indulgence that is certainly not to be encouraged. Indeed, this was made policy in Mao's China. So, although some people might enjoy fashion (a guilty pleasure, always) – and also recognizing that Australia does have a vibrant and growing fashion industry, making for many jobs and exports – the prevailing consensus remains that fashion is, at base, a species of gambling or 'social discourse', neither of which has a legitimate place in the rational economic order.

Yet is it possible that we have this all wrong? Could a rational society not just accommodate fashion, but actively require it as a mechanism of competitive advantage and productivity growth? In this view, fashion would instead be recognized as a valuable mechanism in an economy that is continually buffeted by new technologies (that is, a Schumpeterian economy), and therefore continually faced with new opportunities for consumers to reorganize their systems of consumption.

Fashion would thus be good for the same reason that Friedrich Hayek first argued that recessions are good for the economy: namely, that by periodically liquidating capital asset positions, they provide periods of 'structural cleansing' that enable the re-coordination of asset positions and the uptake of new technologies (Hayek 1931, Caballero and Hammour 1994). This is, of course, a significant cause of the productivity growth that ultimately results in economic growth. In turn, we suggest that fashion fulfils a similar role in the consumer economy by providing a mechanism to periodically liquidate certain elements of a consumer lifestyle, thus triggering the incentive to learn about new things and to demand new goods. Fashion cycles are thus rightfully bad in a static economy, as they simply cause a loss of consumer surplus, yet they might well be essential for evolving ones.

10.2   MODELLING FASHION

When economists model fashion, they tend to frame it as a problem of information cascades – that is, feedback on social networks – resulting in destabilizing dynamics (Simmel 1904, Pesendorfer 1995).[1] Fashion is thus a kind of amplified noise that is, from a welfare perspective, best minimized. The economics of fashion is thus analysis of an instability that is to be corrected. When sociologists and humanities scholars analyse fashion, the question is similarly framed; they also tend to see a degenerative process inherent in social networks. They too view fashion as something to be better understood in order to mitigate its harmful effects or at least to manage them (Veblen 1899).

The consensus on fashion modelling seems to be that fashion is: (a) an inherent but unfortunate part of the cultural and economic condition of man, due to negative externalities from social learning and status signalling; (b) bad, because it is wasteful, irrational and destabilizing; and (c) not to be encouraged. Yet the argument for a positive valuation of fashion derives not from comparison of an economy variously with and without fashion, as is the standard practice, but by reconsidering the value of these destabilizing dynamics in the first place, and in particular their value in a world of plenty, and therefore uncertainty.

There are many reasons why people engage in fashion: first, for attention, as a form of social communication through commodity signalling and demand for novelty (Bianchi 2002); second, from rational laziness, as a form of cognitive economizing on choices that are difficult or expensive to reverse (Earl 1986, Loasby 1999); and third, for fun, as being fashionable has its rewards when you get it right. These micro-motivations are well understood and, indeed, much celebrated when individually successful. However, the process can still be expensive and messy, as it results in the consumption abandonment of clothes, music, furnishings, appliances, cars and so forth long before they are physically worn out or fully depreciated in consequence of rising social costs of continued consumption.

Yet, considered at both the level of the agent's lifestyle and the whole economy, this accelerated depreciation, which seems *prima facie* costly for the individual, may in fact be socially beneficial. In a world with a continual flow of new goods and technologies, and in which there is the ever-presence of consumer mistakes in physical or social capital investments, then fashion functions as a periodic mechanism to speculatively liquidate some elements of a consumer's lifestyle, thus making room for the adoption of new ideas and the mitigation of past mistakes. Life can be cruel within a fashion cycle, but these are 'repeated games' in which failure is more a variety of experience than a terminal blow. Fashion is a game played through multiple rounds, with, at each round, the opportunity to re-shuffle your own cards in light of those held by others. It is, we suggest, best understood as the consumer side of entrepreneurship: a willingness to engage in risk culture as a means of exploring new ways of consumer lifestyles.

In this evolutionary theory of fashion, the introduction of a novel fashion trend into the agents' environment acts as a potential trigger to re-evaluate their consumption strategies in the face of this novel stimulus. The consumption strategies they adopt in response to this novel stimulus then turn into new habits and routines. As the fashion trend becomes normalized, novelty dissipates to the point where a newer stimulus may now induce consumers to re-orientate their strategies yet again. Each fashion cycle thus begins with the origination of a novel attention-arresting idea adopted by a network of others, inducing internal re-organization of consumption systems in each. As the stimulus decays, inevitably with subsequent adoption, the value of resources associated with the fashion is depreciated. This creates new opportunities for producers and consumers to re-enter that market.

This perhaps seems like a lot of work, but it has important benefits, not just for those who succeed in producing and consuming a fashion, but also for those who got it wrong last time and made bad investments in assets, whether for fashion reasons or not. When a fashion cycle comes to an end, those who placed unfortunate bets are put back on a more nearly equal footing with those who succeeded in avoiding being seen, that time around, as fashion victims. To be fashionable now, both fashion victor and fashion victim must incur the costs of tooling up for the novel fashion mode. Fashion cycles therefore also play a major redistributing role in society that mitigates their seemingly wasteful 'throw away' aspect. Furthermore, the accelerated depreciation of fashion goods enables them to be enjoyed second-hand by consumer subcultures whose members could not hope to purchase if their early rates of monetary depreciation accurately reflected their physical depreciation.

10.3 FASHION AND GROWTH

The demand-triggering role of changes in fashion potentially mitigates a problem for affluent economies in the clash between progress and security when rising incomes open up new consumption possibilities and, with them, new risks. Consumption becomes much more like business investment when unfamiliar new or previously unaffordable products are involved, as it does when consumption has a social dimension and reactions of onlookers cannot be taken for granted. A key problem for sustaining economic growth in affluent economies, then, is that income available for discretionary spending does not have to be spent. Affluent consumers may have the ability to spend, but demand may dry up if they lack the will to spend. With Keynesianism, government was proposed as a means out of these traps; however, consumer fashion might be a better, and certainly more fun, mechanism.

In an economic downturn, concerns about the security of income streams may make consumers unwilling to spend, but so too may seemingly the overwhelming tasks of choosing the right product in a functional or social sense. If one does not have to buy something, one can simply leave the problem of choosing what to buy in the 'too hard basket' for a while. But in doing so, one is taking away someone else's income flow and inducement to invest. Government need not step in at this point – it is better that fashion does, via the pressure of social competition, to overcome such weakness of will and help keep the economy closer to its potential growth trajectory.

At the micro level of firms, fashion cycles are inherently disruptive. Attempts to insure against them by diversification, for example, carry costs in terms of foregone economies of scope. However, there are lessons to be learnt from research on the effects of investment spikes at the macroeconomic level, such as those associated with tendencies of firms to invest in lumps and bumps, rather than in small adjustments of capital stock, as standard economic theory suggests. The theme of lumpy replacement cycles has become increasingly popular with macroeconomists who face the task of explaining volatile investment patterns amongst firms (Cooley et al. 1997). A number of conjectures have been made about a link between macroeconomic fluctuations and investment spikes, as based on recognition that times of economic downturn are the best times to replace capital stock (Cooper and Haltiwanger 1993). In particular, Caballero and Hammour (1994) observed that job destruction is much more responsive than job creation to business cycles. This led them to argue that recessions are a time of 'structural cleansing' when outdated or unprofitable techniques and products are pruned out of the system. The consequence of this is productivity growth.

Fashion, in turn, may be conceived as the same mechanism operating on the consumer side. Fashion is thus irrational only in the sense that recessions are irrational, namely statically. But recessions are dynamically valuable in the same sense that fashion is, that is, in facilitating the adoption of new ideas and in triggering the re-coordination this requires. Without such mechanisms an economy or a lifestyle can become locked in to bad choices due to the cumulative consequences of past mistakes. Fashion, like recessions, is thus a 'refreshing' mechanism that partly forgives and annuls past mistakes.

Uncertainty about what will become the dominant standard in a market is good for productivity growth, as it promotes experimentation. This tends to slow once a standard has emerged and production becomes concentrated in the hands of the firms who have worked out the least-cost way of making such products. The driving force of innovation is the rich pickings that await those who place their bets on the winning standard, and who work out how to make it win by solving technological problems. In the context of fashion cycles, this argument must be cast more in terms of uncertainty about aesthetic issues than technological ones. But as such, it now properly involves both producers and consumers. When a product goes out of fashion, its producers and past consumers are forced into problem-solving mode. And although the liquidation of some of their assets is costly, the process of dealing with this setback is likely to result in them emerging with enhanced knowledge. Furthermore, since the end of one fashion cycle is not the beginning of a clearly defined new fashion, but a time for experimentation within a new genre, there is everything to play for. It pays to be bold and creative whether as a consumer or as a producer, given the possibility of becoming a leader and the fashion mechanism write-off to being wrong. Fashion incentives, in other words, may function as growth incentives.

Fashion cycles and the consumer's taste for novelty thus appear to play a potentially important – not wasteful – role in encouraging flexibility and experimentation in consumer strategies by promoting the development of consumer knowledge and experience. Competition for social standing is always deeper than displays of how much money one can afford to burn on a particular kind of consumption. It also involves the display of skill in placing the right kinds of fashion bets in order not to end up a 'fashion victim' (by failing to select a fashion rule also selected by the vast majority around the same time), but instead to select a minority strategy that gives a 'hip' sign of expertise and insight ahead of the field (Holbrook 1995: 319–62). And that sounds like entrepreneurial behaviour in an open consumer society.

The impact of television series such as *Sex in the City* on women's fashion demonstrates this principle, in which rules may embrace both the set of products to purchase and rules for the combinations in which products are consumed. The fashion-leading consumer has many of the capabilities of an entrepreneur, as an agent alert to gaps in markets and to new opportunities for constructing connections (Earl 2003). The extent of entrepreneurship in consumption is widely overlooked in modern economic (and sociological) analysis, yet if consumers were not occasionally moved by the 'animal spirits' of such risk culture, economic growth would be more limited, as would consumer surplus.

Societies that focus on the comfort of everyman rather than on the sublime pleasures of risk-taking should therefore be expected to have relatively lower growth rates, due to low levels of entrepreneurial creativity, in both production and consumption. In turn, societies that systematically encourage and facilitate such seeming pointlessness as fashion might turn out to be the most progressive.

10.4 IN PRAISE OF FASHIONABLE YOUNG THINGS: COMPLEXITY AND POLICY

A further issue here is the relation between fashion and lifestyle complexity and the extent that consumers are willing to adopt complex and challenging consumer lifestyles. Lifestyle complexity relates not just to the number of consumer dimensions, but also to the rate at which a consumer lifestyle is updated. Consumers who choose complex lifestyles which present a relatively large number of problems will in turn have less attention to dedicate to novel solutions to any particular problem than consumers who choose simpler lifestyles. We would thus expect more herd-like behaviour to be displayed by consumers with complex lifestyles, and thus greater effects of fashion. Similarly, we would expect that more fashion influenced consumers will more effectively adopt new ideas.

Such consumers may have only small areas in which they can develop expertise to choose for themselves. They may serve in those areas as trendsetters for their peers, whilst following the latter in other respects (Earl and Potts 2004). Yet the problem remains coordination of the fashionable fit of different elements of the evolving lifestyle. Busy consumers might even delegate to an outside authority with professional expertise the task of ruling on what fitted together. So, although complex, busy lifestyles seem incompatible with short fashion cycles, the rapid convergence of behaviour via externally supplied decision rules suggests that the greater the lifestyle complexity, the faster fashion cycles should run. Indeed, such consumers may become exasperated by it. In contrast, 'classic' styles of consumption, as those that evolve slowly, would seem to be the prerogative of those whose wealth has given them a longstanding ability to consume at leisure. Such 'old money' consumers are rich enough to keep many problems at bay – often by following long established social rules – and, having not just 'arrived' (unlike the *nouveaux riches*), they have built up the experience to know how to choose in novel domains. Their lack of experience outside their narrow range of deep expertise imparts a profoundly conservative bias to their choices, and their connoisseurship is such that relatively small changes in the products composing their lifestyles will be sufficient to attract their attention. Fashion will not affect them as much, indeed: they will be generally appalled by it. And yet, in both cases, fashion effectively functions as a mechanism to induce and accelerate learning in complex lifestyles, enabling these lifestyles to become more complex still, thus improving their productivity in generating valuable consumption services.

This raises an interesting policy point. For there are many (especially the 'affluenza' type) who argue that our lives are already too complex, and that we would all be better off with less consumption and simpler times. This line of thinking invariably concludes that government should seek to constrain, if not all consumption, then at least frivolous consumption, which is presumed to be mostly what rich people (or irresponsible teenagers) do. Fashion, in this view, is unsustainable consumption and ought not to be encouraged, as it gets in the way of rational economic progress.

Yet this is surely wrong, as it fails to appreciate the dynamic benefits of fashion (Postrel 2005, Lanham 2006). Fashion is good for the economy because it is a mechanism to promote experimentation, learning and re-coordination. Fashion accelerates the adoption of good new ideas and mitigates the costs of the past adoption of bad ones. It's expensive, of course, but it works in an emergent self-organizing sort of way. 'Fashion policy', then, should be like competition policy, in seeking to promote all forms of it, and acting only to free it up when artificial restrictions occur.

In modern economics and consumer theory, the standard view is that fashion is irrational and inefficient. From the Schumpeterian/Hayekian perspective, however, it seems to play a more positive role in stirring consumers to actions that result in the growth of experience and knowledge. Just as an increase in the strength of competition may prompt decision-makers to explore ways of increasing productivity, so a change in relative competitive strength between status-conscious consumers may force them to rethink their choices. Just as firms in featherbedded markets may fail to develop new knowledge, so consumers who opt out of social competition and take the 'quiet life' may fail to develop their ranges of experience and capabilities.

The absence of fashion, then, may well be worse than its presence. Such a lifestyle may appeal to older consumers who have already established where they are in the social order and with fewer years of life remaining have less incentive to take risks to acquire new capabilities as consumers. Yet, not so the young, for whom there are significant pay-offs to being fashionable. And that is good, for the experimental adoption of new ideas by the young is, ultimately, what drives long-run economic growth. Fashion not only enforces flexibility in consumer lifestyles, but also has a positive distributional effect on consumer welfare by erasing past consumer mistakes and minimizing the opportunity cost of adopting novelty.

Ongoing economic growth requires not just entrepreneurship and risk-taking from producers, but also from consumers, who must find the will to buy, learn and risk. Risk-taking behaviour inevitably causes mistakes. Yet fashion is not just a way of making mistakes, but also a mechanism for correcting them. Fashion thus facilitates economic growth by providing consumers the twin incentives to abandon old fashion rules and adopt new rules through: (a) periodically liquidating dated fashion goods and their related mistakes, and (b) providing alternative goods that, thanks to standardization, cater for the varying risk preferences of consumers. This process looks wasteful from a static account, but it is, we suggest, dynamically efficient in the promotion of the change and re-coordination that eventually registers as economic growth.

Fashion trends might be better understood not as bourgeois leisure, but as a process of creative destruction working through social pressure to provide a fresh and self-regulated impetus for consumer learning (see Chapter 8). Fashion cycles work to periodically loosen accumulated constraints on the demand side, facilitating both economic growth and personal development. Fashion, then, is part of how economies evolve, not of how they decay. Conservatives, who like growth but hate change, and liberals, who like the opposite, have both traditionally been down on fashion. Yet both may be mistaken. Fashion is perhaps better understood as another name for consumer entrepreneurship, and the more of that, the better.

NOTE

1. In critique of Pesendorfer, see Coelho et al. (2004).

11. Capitalism, socialism and culture

Prolegomena

This chapter is based on a working paper that argues that the rise of the modern cultural economy is in part due to institutional change toward a global market economy, giving rise to the emergence of recognition of creative industries and the creative economy. The title is a riff on Joseph Schumpeter's famous book *Capitalism, Socialism and Democracy* in which he sought to connect an evolving economy to an evolving political order. I suggest here that his arguments also extend to an evolving cultural order.

11.1 INSTITUTIONS OF THE *ANCIEN REGIME* AND THE CULTURAL MARKET ECONOMY

This chapter offers a Schumpeterian – cf. a Marxian or political economy – analysis of the institutions of the creative industries in relation to both the institutions of the pre-capitalist order (the *ancien régime*) and the institutions of the market capitalist order. We begin by recognizing that the institutions of the cultural and creative economy, as elucidated in Chapter 2, are conventionally (but wrongly, as is the theme of this book) analysed in opposition to the institutions of market capitalism.

Cultural studies, along with much of the arts, humanities and political economy, broadly proceed from an analytic foundation derived from or significantly influenced by Marxist formulations of the institutional structure of the economic system.[1] It was of course Karl Marx who coined the term capitalism as the antonym of socialism, as an economic order defined by the pecuniary motive and the rationalization of all aspects of economic life toward the drive to accumulate capital. This reflex view of capitalism as rapacious, unforgiving and anti-humanistic has since held significant sway in the humanities and socio-cultural sciences. It has thus underpinned modern analysis of the cultural economy and its institutions. Yet economists have mostly rejected this view for two broad reasons.

The first is recognition of the market order and price system as a mechanism that coordinates economic activity far more effectively than any planning system. This is due to its ability to deal with distributed local information via the price mechanism (Hayek 1945). This view is widely held by economists, although with varying degrees depending on the extent of information imperfections supposed. Still, most economists understand price competition in free markets to be a superior mechanism for the coordination of economic activity than any other possible system, and irrespective of how humanistic, expert-based or well-meaning that system may be. This is the modern mainstream accommodation between economics and the humanities-based analysis of arts and culture.[2] What is striking is the extent to which discussion of institutional dynamics remains so difficult. There is the market or price mechanism on one side and the institutions of culture on the other with little common analytic ground between. Instead, accommodation is practically worked out with operational politics via a negotiated regime of transfer payments, or special exemptions and regulations, or often personal political preferences that sum to the economic basis of modern arts and cultural policy (Cunningham and Potts 2010).

The second reason economists reject the Marxian view of capitalism is associated with the work of Joseph Schumpeter (1942). This goes beyond concern with the market or price mechanism to instead focus on the broader nature of capitalism as a set of evolved institutions to facilitate the process of economic change. The Schumpeterian model of capitalism centers on the key role of the entrepreneur and the process of innovation and the socio-cultural institutions that generate this evolutionary mechanism. (This is also of course associated with the Austrian economists: Menger, Mises, Hayek, Kirzner, and so on.) The market system is thus a set of institutions to promote the growth of knowledge by affording credence to the entrepreneurs who introduce new ideas and organize the means by which they may be socially adopted.

The motive for entrepreneurship is presumed to be profit. Yet entrepreneurs create for the same reason artists do, namely because they see opportunities to create value in the world (of whatever form) and seek to realize this (see McCraw 2007: Chapter 21). Creativity and its expression in action is a natural human drive that under the right institutional circumstances results in social good through the incessant flow of innovations that creates both individual wealth and aggregate welfare. For Schumpeter, capitalism is an evolved system of institutions through which economic coordination is achieved through market prices and the actions of entrepreneurs in the promotion of innovation. Economic theory and the history of the 20th century plainly reveal the efficacy of capitalism and its associated institutions of personal freedom as the main engine of material economic progress (Mokyr 2004, Baumol 2002, Beinhocker 2006, Ridley 2010).

The Schumpeterian perspective on cultural institutions is therefore in relation to their efficacy in the coordination of change. Yet there remains a significant rump of opposition to the notion that the virtues of capitalism and its institutions extend fully to the realms of humanism and culture. Indeed, it remains a widely held article of faith among the 'academic left' that capitalism is spiritually bankrupt, or at best amoral. Several stylized points are often axiomatically cited in defense of the proposition that capitalism:

1. draws upon base human emotions such as greed and self-interest, and is against social feelings such as empathy and altruism;
2. fosters a calculating rationalistic mentality and the pecuniary motive, and abjures the spiritual or imaginative cast of mind;
3. privileges the material and measurable over the psychic and imma- nent, promoting 'commodity fetishism' and 'false consciousness';
4. is non-inclusive, producing and accentuating inequality.

There are other points of critique, but these sufficiently capture the theme of alleged ethical and cultural corruption that burdens the institutions of market capitalism. I shall not attempt to refute these arguments here.[3] My purpose is simply to acknowledge the conventional lines by which capitalist institutions may be admitted to be good for material progress but flawed in the production and consumption of arts and culture. Indeed, the usurpation of capitalist values in the cultural sphere was famously critiqued by Adorno and Horkheimer's (1979) analysis of the cultural economy, implicit in which was rejection of the very notion of treating arts and culture as economic goods valued by market capitalist institutions, because they possess intrinsic value beyond the market and its institutions.

A line of reconciliation was subsequently opened as cultural economists sought to estimate the non-market value of cultural products.[4] This was coupled with analysis of the nature and extent of market failure in cultural products. Cultural markets were said to fail due to their high fixed cost and low marginal cost; their significant public good aspects; their extreme uncertainty in demand; and their special context of creative labour input.[5] Economic analysis of cultural industries and institutions routinely turns on an implicit premise that they are special due to their public good aspects (positive externalities) and widely subject to market failure. This is commonly argued to be a permanent condition, implying a continual institutional tension between the market and cultural system requiring political solutions to constrain market institutions in the arts and cultural domains, and to replace them with a designed bureaucratic mechanism. This accommodation occurs in most developed nations and enjoys broad public and political support.[6] The underlying premise is this: market capitalist institutions seem to work for some things, but not arts and culture, for which they are allegedly institutionally inappropriate.

And yet, is it possible that this thesis of perpetual institutional conflict might be wrong? I propose an alternate hypothesis here, not based on a new theoretic interpretation of cultural or capitalist institutions, but based on the observation that the institutions of the cultural economy themselves seem to have evolved over the capitalist epoch. This change has occurred almost imperceptibly, allowing the assumption to persist that these respective institutions are given, fixed and in perpetual conflict. Yet this change has, I hypothesize, begun to accelerate. Specifically, I associate this change with the rise of the creative industries and their accelerated growth since the 1980s. My central observation is that the timing of this rise coincides with the resurgence of global capitalism based on the epochal changes in the international trading and financial order in the late 1970s, the market-based reforms of the 1980s, the collapse of the communist bloc and the nascent rise of the newly industrialized economies, and so on. It may just be coincidence that the rise of creative industries and the resurgence of global capitalism seem co-integrated. Or it may be the case that the timing of the emergence of the creative industries, as a locus of post-industrial growth in the 1990s, may be an evolutionary consequence of the resurgence of the capitalist order on a global scale – namely. globalization. If so, then a plausible hypothesis to explain the rise of the creative industries is a shift in the institutions underlying the cultural economy in the direction of the institutions of the capitalist order.

11.2 INSTITUTIONS OF CAPITALISM AND PRE-CAPITALISM

What follows here is a potted history that will surely offend any passing economic historian. My purpose is not to give a detailed institutional history, but only to outline the types of institutional change that have manifestly occurred, and to connect these to changes in arts and cultural institutions that underpin the 'creative industries' or 'creative economy'.

Capitalism emerged in the late 1700s in certain parts of Western Europe. Economic historians do little but study and debate when, how and why capitalism emerged, and I shall not enter that fray here.[7] My point is simply that capitalism emerged into a largely static institutional and cultural world. For previous millennia, the economic order was that of the feudal system: the *ancien régime* characterized by a landed aristocracy where serfs, vassals and peasants toiled for their masters. The institutional characteristics of the *ancien régime* are many and subtle and with much regional variation. Yet their overarching character was that of adaptations to a world without change, a world in which change was almost imperceptible and certainly not normal. In the *ancien régime* material standards of living hardly changed for generations. The concept of economic growth or progress was without meaning or reference. This is almost unimaginable today; even the most vociferous Club-of-Rome type environmentalist at least knows that economic and institutional change can happen. Power in this world was tied to land ownership which conferred economic ownership of those who lived on that land, namely peasants and serfs. This really was a world governed by class in the Marxian sense. Yet this notion of class and institutions was not a political concept then, but something closer to a social ontology, an inborn fact of being carried by the institutional milieu. The overarching institutional milieu was of a fixed social and economic order in which technology and institutions were not variables.

Schumpeter sought to describe the institutional nature of the capitalist economy. This required first defining the institutional changes that ushered in the new era. McCraw (2007: 146–8) summarizes Schumpeter on the economic institutions of the *ancien régime* prior to the emergence of capitalism thus:

1. Spiritual life suffered grievous damage if people became immersed in materialism
2. Absence of belief in upward social and economic mobility
3. No widespread sense of personal freedom and individual autonomy
4. The governance of most occupations and crafts by cartels and guilds
5. Entailed estates marked by primogeniture
6. A primitive financial system lacking credit mechanisms
7. The absence of private property and a framework for the rule of law

These collectively construct an institutional complex that effectively prohibits economic change. All are of course general propositions without direct bearing on the institutions of the cultural economy. Yet each is worth examining, for the extent to which each institution has been maintained is indicative of the current changes in the institutions of the cultural economic order. My argument here is that it is the collapse of these atavistic institutions under pressure of globalization that explains the timing of the recent rise of the creative industries.

Schumpeter, like other economic historians, argued that capitalism did not arrive by revolution but rather absorbed and adapted most extant institutions. What shifted, however, was the temporal focus (toward the future, not the past), along with the individual and social attitude to novelty (potentially good, not bad). According to Ebner (2006: 500–501):

Capitalism evolved from the socio-cultural substance of preceding forms of economic organization, based on institutional elements that were cumulatively growing in economic and social influence. Thus Schumpeter accentuated the notion of institutional variety as a basic feature in the dynamism of economic development. . . . Schumpeter claimed that pre-capitalist institutions would contribute decisively to economic evolution in modern capitalism by providing institutional incentives as well as by shaping modes of economic behavior that could be conducive to the carrying out of innovation.

Schumpeter was clear about the institutional hybridization and variety inherent in the emergent capitalist order (see also Hodgson 1988, 2004). Schumpeter (1942: 114) argued that 'every society contains, at any given time, elements that are the product of different social systems' and that:

social structures, types and attitudes are coins that do not readily melt. Once formed they persist, possibly for centuries, and since different structures and types display different degrees of ability to survive, we almost always find that actual group and national behavior more or less departs from what we should expect it to be if we tried to infer it from the dominant domains of the productive process. (Schumpeter, 1942: 12)

Capitalism was not a radical break from the past but brought with it many of the old institutional orders, and necessarily so. In consequence, the Marxist line of cultural economy analysis that sets the institutions of capitalism in direct opposition to the institutions of culture is misleading from the start. It is thus possible that some of these pre-capitalist institutions have survived into modern times. Obvious candidates are the institutions of the arts and cultural economy.

It is thus useful to revisit pre-capitalist institutions and examine their atavistic status. It also becomes a live possibility that these institutions, many of which have remained invariant for aeons, may only now be undergoing evolutionary change due to recent institutional and techno-logical evolution in cultural production and consumption as driven by the re-emergence of global capitalism and the diffusion of its underlying institutions. The globalization of market capitalism (broadly in the late 20th century) has underpinned the greatest period of economic growth and development the world has ever known. While normally composed in terms of rising living standards, growth of trade and the large-scale alleviation of poverty, this has also had a significant effect on the cultural economy (Cowen 2002). My argument here is that this institutional evolu-tion has turned the cultural economy into the creative industries (Garnham 2005). This change is not due to government policy, academic insight, or any such planned or rationalized endeavour, but rather is an outcome of institutional evolution, as the institutions of the cultural economy, most of which date back to the *ancien régime*, have rapidly adapted and evolved toward capitalist institutions. The creative industries are one of the latest fruits to ripen on the tree of globalization.

11.3 INSTITUTIONAL EVOLUTION AND THE CREATIVE INDUSTRIES

Thus the rise of the creative industries may not only be due to the growth of wealth and technological change, but also due to institutional evolution in the market capitalist system. If so, this implies that specific institutions affecting the arts, cultural sectors and creative industries sectors have also changed. So let us consider this in terms of the pre-capitalist institutions that Schumpeter (as summarized by McCraw 2007) identified toward the modern era.

'That spiritual life suffers grievous damage if immersed in materialism'
That materialism is the opposite of humanism is axiomatic in the humanities. By implication, arts and cultural considerations are higher in the moral order than the economics of material reality. This pre-capitalist institution is widely operational in the cultural economy, particularly at its elite end (that is, 'art for art's sake', the spiritual honour of the 'starving artist' who strives for deep truth without contamination). Yet this monastic institution may be eroding. The young rich are now highly creative (Chapter 3) and the connection between artists, designers, musicians and celebrity is strengthening. In consequence, cultural expectations are shifting toward a normalization of excellence in art and high income, along with the large-scale emergence of the celebrity artist. There has also been a notable shift in the perception and incomes of embedded or commercial artists, such as industrial designers and their role in connecting fashion with new commodities. This is a marked change from the relatively recent past, when such materialistic alliances were considered impure or suspect.

If this pre-capitalist institution is eroding, the question is why now and not earlier? I suspect that much of this is due to the effects of the resurgence of global capitalism that has profoundly increased the reach of individual artists into global markets, transforming income possibilities that would have been limited if confined to their home region or even nation. In turn, this has increased both the supply of and demand for such output.

'Absence of belief in upward social and economic mobility'
The pre-capitalist era offered little social or economic mobility. People were born into a station in life and 'knew their place'. The institution of

class or caste is a natural concomitant of this belief. The institutions of capitalism required the destruction of this notion with the possibility of social and economic mobility. All economic systems involve specialization of occupation and thus involve some concept of class. Capitalist institutions, however, require mobility, both upward and downward, between these classes due to the choices and actions of each individual. The concept of class and the constraining of mobility has been a most difficult pre-capitalist institution to unseat. The various fascist and communist revolutions sought to do so by seeking class solidarity and then revolutionary change by subverting the order of classes. Yet the result was simply a new class structure, still without individual mobility. The arts and cultural sectors were drawn into this process, identifying in many ways with the causes of revolutionary class struggle. In practice, this centered on the value of the arts and cultural production toward the goal of social criticism and the detrimental personal, spiritual and environmental effects of the capitalist order.

Yet again, this may be changing. The new generations of Xs and Ys did not grow up with revolutionary class struggle – that was something their parents did – but instead have emerged into a media-saturated globalized world in which individual social, cultural and economic mobility is utterly normal. The creative industries, in turn, have been a significant driver of this institutional renormalization, particularly in film, TV and publishing. This effect has accelerated with the development and widespread adoption of new media digital technologies for self-publishing and user-generated content, transforming a passive class of media consumers into an emerging entrepreneurial class of media producers and consumer co-creators. You don't need to overthrow the system; you just need to get yourself out there.

'No widespread sense of personal freedom and individual autonomy'

Before capitalism, few people were free in the modern sense. Freedom was a privileged position held by the elite of lords, masters or tribal chiefs, and so on. Most people were slaves, serfs, or indentured servants. The incentives of the vast majority of the human population to work and create value were supplied through threat of violence or expulsion. Productivity was correspondingly extremely low, as with economic output. The institutions of capitalism are based about the freedom to trade in markets and to decide what to supply and what to consume. By shifting the locus of decision-making to the individual and away from the governing elite, the incentive effects of market-capitalist institutions began to unleash an enormous surge in productivity. Markets are not so much a precondition for economic freedom, as its basic embodiment.

The cultural and creative industries play a significant role in this process aspect of freedom. While freedom is enshrined in constitutional principles, such as freedom of speech, it is the application of this freedom through the arts and media that renders this freedom real and effective by continually testing and probing the limits, thus ever expanding the domain of freedom (Coyne and Leeson 2009). In consequence, this expands the scope of the market (*á la* Adam Smith). In turn, the suppression or control of the cultural economy acts to maintain the pre-capitalist institutions limiting personal freedom. The collapse of communism was a big step forward for cultural freedom, along with deregulation of media and communications industries. The creative industries have also been at the vanguard of individual freedom of expression in their uptake of digital technology and the internet. This vastly increased power to create information based on new digital literacy and access is presently having a profound effect on the production of value through the new freedoms it creates and enhances (Hartley 2009a).

'The governance of most occupations and crafts by cartels and guilds'
In pre-capitalism there was little labour mobility. Skilled occupations were preceded by long apprenticeships and controlled by guilds. They were a pre-capitalist institution adapted to a period of economic stasis. Because wages were set by operations of the cartels and guilds, they served to regulate labour supply by restricting entry and exit. Labour markets in the modern sense only existed at the very lowest end of the skill spectrum. These feudal institutions of labour supply have proven remarkably resilient institutions that have changed relatively little through the capitalist era. Indeed, they remain strongest in the modern licensed professions such as medicine, law and academia, although they extend through many occupations (Potts 2009e). Capitalist institutions have adapted to these pre-capitalist institutions mostly through accommodation in these restrictions of trade and enterprise.

This relates to human psychology as much as institutional politics. A job is something that for many has the status of personal property; it should not be appropriated by someone else. The result is wide support for continuity of these feudal institutions through the modern capitalist era, despite the significant opportunity costs, rents, and reduced supply these guild institutions impose. Yet because we each see only the immediate cost to ourselves in competitive threat and not the benefits such as lower cost of other services and increased demand for one's own services, occupational deregulation remains entrenched. Although far from optimal, it remains a highly stable equilibrium. Yet within parts of the creative industries, this institution is breaking down. The guild system collapses when the

distinction between professional and amateur collapses, something burgeoning in the open-source movement. There is much uncertainty about
the nature of this change, yet it is clear that new institutions are presently
emerging and that these institutions are adapted to a much more flexible
and distributed production model (as explored in Chapter 6). This is a
very recent phenomenon that seems intimately linked to the resurgent
capitalist institutions of individual freedoms and mobility coupled with
globalization.

'Entailed estates marked by primogeniture'

Entailment specifies a sequence of heirs and primogeniture is sole inheritance by the eldest son. The effect of this transfer of wealth was extremely
conservative; it discouraged risk-taking and the sale of land and other
wealth, preventing its widespread dispersion and ownership. This institution began to unravel in the 17th century and was mostly abolished by
the early 20th century. The abolition of this institution underpins modern
capitalism.

The institutions of the cultural economy may seem unconnected, but
there is one notable domain where the pre-capitalist institution of entailed
estates still dominates, namely public arts collections in which once works
pass into them, they are entailed in perpetuity by an elite class of custodi-
ans, thus preventing the dispersal of ownership. The dramatic fall in costs
and rise in quality of reproductive technologies has blunted the demand
for the abolition of art entailment, yet the technology to, for example, rent
such works already exists and would be a likely business model if public
galleries and museums were privatized. A more immediate change in the
institutions of entailment and primogeniture can be seen in the demand
for change in intellectual property associated with new institutions such as
'creative commons' (Benkler 2006). At first sight, this weakening of intellectual property and drive to place more works in the 'commons' might
seem the very opposite of a move toward capitalist institutions, but to
the extent that it emphasizes the value of dispersion and re-use of productive resources (that is, idea content) to find their best use, it is a logical
extension of the abolishment of that pre-capitalist institution.

'A primitive financial system lacking credit mechanisms'

Capitalism did not get underway until millennia-old institutions preventing lending of money at interest, and thus the creation of credit, were
overturned. In the pre-capitalist era, the only sources of finance were from
royal, aristocratic and religious patronage. Finance was required not just
for capital works, but also for voyages of trade, and for commissions for
art and architecture. Inventors and businesspeople had no way to raise

finance, which obviously stifled technology, business development and entrepreneurial activity. The capitalist engine, as Schumpeter explained, is powered by the creation of credit. The development of industry went hand-in-hand with the development of specialized banking and financial institutions.

The financial system and its institutions are the most complex and essential part of the capitalist system. Yet they are also the least visible because they do not actually produce anything material other than credit (and liquidity) through contracts into the future that connect the parts of the economy together. These are inherently built from the bottom up through extremely complex specialized networks. The financial system, like the legal system, is built up over a long period of time and is highly distributed and deep. This is why it cannot be created *ab nihilo* nor easily transplanted, as witnessed by the weak state of financial organizations and institutions in developing and transition economies. It is interesting then to reflect on the notable absence of arts and cultural financial institutions. Even media and publishing banks do not really exist to the extent that such specialized financial services exist in other sectors. Indeed, one reason media firms have grown so large is to effectively internalize finance within the organization in the studio or producer model, an inefficient method. The financing of large projects such as movies is in consequence extremely complex and poses significant costs due to unbundled risks (Caves 2000). The absence of well-developed financial institutions means that the key aspect of capitalist development – namely that the financier not the entrepreneur carries the risk – does not generally hold in the arts and cultural industries where risk for new ventures is typically still carried by those undertaking the venture (for example the artist, designer or producer). Capitalism didn't get started until precisely this institutional form was replaced with a credit system. The cultural economy is, in this sense, still significantly pre-capitalist. Notably, the pre-capitalist system of patronage has developed much further with government funding to the arts and culture, further crowding out opportunities for the creation of a viable specialized financial system.

'The absence of private property and a framework for the rule of law'

Private property is an institutional pillar of the capitalist order, meaning the right to own and dispose of property at the owner's discretion. The other pillar is the rule of law prohibiting arbitrary changes in that ownership and consistent treatment independent of persons subject to that law. The rule of law has a powerful incentive effect on entrepreneurship and enterprise because it does not then require investment in social and political connections to acquire special treatment or protection against the effect of others acquiring special treatment (Hayek 1973/1976). In the absence of the rule of law, corruption and rent-seeking flourish and the business enterprise becomes a largely political affair. Yet a capitalist system constantly experiences change from innovation in new forms of property via financial and technological innovation. It thus requires continual adaptations of law to account for these new circumstances. The most profound changes in new forms of property of recent times have been in intellectual property, and the creative industries have been central to these changes; indeed, part of their very definition. The adaptation and development of new laws relating to private property are currently being significantly shaped by the concerns and opportunities of the creative industries. Further, it is precisely a rule of law framework that enables the consistent application to other parts of the economy. The creative industries are very much allied with the institutions of the market capitalist system: indeed, they are significantly shaping its current evolution.

11.4 CAN INSTITUTIONAL EVOLUTION EXPLAIN THE RISE OF THE CREATIVE INDUSTRIES?

Although the institutions of capitalism involved a radical break from the pre-capitalist feudal era, they have nevertheless carried with them many of those pre-capitalist institutions (Hodgson 1988). Furthermore, these have been freighted and maintained by the cultural economy. This explains the traditional tension between the 'cultural economy' and the institutions of market capitalism. My hypothesis, however, is that something has changed in the past few decades concomitant with the rise of the creative industries as a somewhat lagged process on the resurgence of global capitalism. I have argued that the rise of global capitalism and the rise of the creative industries are connected. Specifically, we may be presently observing a deep institutional shift in the cultural economy as institutions associated with the pre-capitalist era are eroding. In the context of this institutional creative destruction, new arts and cultural institutions are emerging that are allied with and adapted to the institutions of capitalism. It is this process that I suggest is a major factor behind the specific timing and nature of the recent rise of the creative industries.

The creative industries then are not just a random cluster of industries currently experiencing a revival of economic fortunes, other things equal. There is evidence that these sectors are growing and are indeed 'drivers of growth'. But it remains unclear why this is occurring, and why now. My hypothesis is that this rise is a natural outcome of ramifying institutional changes and not merely the vicissitudes of shifting consumer demand or the fortunate arrival of new information technologies. Among scholars of the creative industries in cultural and media studies, urban geography, cultural policy and the like, a consistently inward analytic focus predominates that has largely ignored the broader sweep of history and the effects of institutional change in market capitalism. Yet these forces may not only be significant and decisive, but also counter-intuitive.

Capitalism, Socialism and Democracy, Schumpeter's (1942) most mature and popular work, devoted the first three chapters to a review of Marx's analysis of capitalism. For Schumpeterian economists to follow, this was a curious foundation. But his point was that Marx had got many things right in his characterization of capitalism but had completely misunderstood its dynamic implications. For Schumpeter, this was the essential point about capitalism: namely that it was a dynamic evolutionary system. Its *raison d'être* was not equity or efficiency, but the coordination of emergent change.

The rise of the creative industries is thus perhaps a further chapter in the Schumpeterian conception of the evolution of market capitalist institutions. As discussed in Chapter 2, this is obviously a very different conception of the role of arts, culture and creativity in economic life. But it is entirely consistent with a co-evolutionary conception of the relation between art and commerce or culture and economy as intermediated by market institutions.

NOTES

1. See, for example, Heilbrun and Gray (2001), Hesmondhalgh (2002), Du Gay and Pryke (2002).
2. Blaug ed. (1976), Heilbrun and Gray (2001), Throsby (2001), Towse ed. (1997, 2003).
3. I refer the reader, instead, to Cowen (1998), Friedman (2005), or McCloskey (2006).
4. Baumol and Bowen (1966), Blaug ed. (1976), Throsby and Withers (1979), Throsby (2001).
5. See Caves (2000), De Vany (2004), Garnham (2005: 19–20), Hartley ed. (2005). In contradistinction, see Jones (1995), Cowen (2002) and Cowen and Kaplan (2004).
6. Throsby (1994), Frey (2000).
7. The various works of Donald (and Deirdre) McCloskey, Douglass North or Avner Greif are good starting points.

12. Four models of the creative industries

with Stuart Cunningham

Prolegomena

This chapter is an edited version of Potts and Cunningham (2008) 'Four models of the creative industries' *International Journal of Cultural Policy* 14(3): 233–47. It argues for an empirically based view of the dynamic interaction between the creative industries and the rest of the economy.

12.1 INTRODUCTION

'Creative industries' offers a definition of the industrial components of the economy that have come to be newly represented as a significant and rapidly growing set of industries; an important sector, in other words, for policy attention. The ostensible purpose of the various creative industries mapping documents (starting with DCMS 1998) has been to estimate the 'significance' of the creative industries to the modern economy in order to reorient economic policy support in accordance with that significance. In doing so, however, these studies highlight an important point: namely that the economic value of the creative industries may extend beyond just the manifest production of cultural goods or the employment of creative people, and have a more general role in driving and facilitating the process of change across the entire economy, as evidenced by its dynamic parameters and degree of embedding in the broader economy. If so, this has immediate implications for the type of policy intervention appropriate to creative industries. This chapter seeks to address the issue by posing the question: what actually is the dynamic relation between the creative industries and the rest of the economy?

Rather than asking about the absolute size or static economic significance of a sector, it seems better to inquire into its relative performance with respect to economic dynamics. The four models of this chapter are the four possible answers to this question: namely (1) negative, (2) neutral,

(3) positive and (4) emergent. Each of these possibilities parlays into a very different policy model: in (1) a welfare subsidy is required; in (2), standard industry policy; in (3), investment and growth policy; and in (4), innovation policy is best. Very different policy frameworks thus follow from each of the four basic dynamical models relating the creative industries to the rest of the economy.

We outline the four possible primary relations between the creative industries and the rest of the economy. We then explain the relation of each model to different theoretical foundations, what we should expect to observe if the model were true, and the appropriate policy framework in each case. What we provide here is only a theory of the classes of models involved and an illustration of how different sorts of data might be applied to them. This seems to us a necessary first step in developing the economics of the creative industries. Yet, in doing so, we find evidence supporting models (3) and (4). And while clearly signalling the need for further theoretical and empirical work, this also points out the potential value of an innovation-based approach to creative industries and cultural policy. These four models are thus proposed as a starting point for further discussion of the intersection between economic analysis of the arts and culture on the one hand and modern analysis of economic growth (and growth policy) on the other.

12.2   FOUR MODELS OF THE CREATIVE INDUSTRIES

Let the economic value of the whole economy be defined as Y, and the economic value of the creative industries as CI, affording us the master equation:

$$CI = A \cdot Y$$

This says that the creative industries comprise some given fraction (A) of all economic activity. In a static model, this estimate is treated as the 'significance' of the sector. In Australia, A is estimated at 0.045. The estimate of A has been a central output of the creative industries mapping documents.[1] These estimates all find that the creative industries are indeed 'economically significant'. They are thus deemed comparable to other high profile sectors in their contribution to income, employment and trade – agriculture, for example, typically has an A value of 0.03. By implication, the creative industries are argued to deserve policy attention and support in proportion to that significance.

The problem with this line of reasoning is that it has no basis in economic theory. It is a matter of political expediency to afford an industrial sector policy attention in proportion to the share of income (or jobs, or exports) it generates, not a matter of economic logic. This is always true in any equilibrium-based (static) argument. Indeed, it is only when considering the failure of an industry that political and economic significance align in this static manner. But the creative industries' interaction with the aggregate economy is presumed to be positive, not negative. Yet, if so, then the basic economic-political significance may no longer hold.

Instead, economic significance needs to be reconstructed, which is what the four models approach does by shifting to a dynamic approach to significance. In this, the economic analysis of the relation between an industry sector and the rest of the economy is constructed in terms of the dynamic interrelationship, which we may specify by examining the dynamics of our master equation: specifically, how a change in CI activity (ΔCI) affects aggregate economic activity (ΔY).

We suppose that change in *CI* affects *Y* in some way ($\Delta CI \leftrightarrow \Delta Y$). The four models are the set of possible dynamic interrelations in which a change in CI activity has either: a negative (model 1), neutral (model 2) or positive (models 3 and 4) effect on the economy. This is plainly simplistic. Yet it offers a useful starting point to orient both empirical analysis and policy discussion in order to be clear and explicit about this hypothesized relation and its evidential support.

For analytic convenience, we assume $dCI/dY = 0$, meaning that economic growth affects the CIs no differently to the average of other industries, or technically that income elasticity is unitary. We strongly suspect that growth in income does disproportionately affect demand for the output of the CIs; but we set that aside here. Policy is analysed in terms of whether change in the creative industries changes aggregate utility welfare (or utility, *U*). Again, we presume $dU/dCI \in R$, such that a change in CI can increase, decrease or leave utility unaffected.

Model 1: The welfare model
In this model, the creative industries are hypothesized to have a net negative impact on the economy, consuming more resources or economic value than they produce. This model is specifically aimed at those who see little analytical benefit in discriminating between creative and cultural industries (Pratt 2005). A dynamically equivalent statement is that the rate of total factor productivity (TFP_{CI}) growth is less in the CIs than in other sectors (TFP_Y), as assumed in Baumol and Bowen (1966). In this model, the CIs are essentially a 'merit good' sector that produces cultural commodities that are welfare enhancing ($dU/dCI > 0$), but that are only economically viable with a transfer of resources from the rest of the economy

$(dY/dCI < 0)$. Furthermore, positive knowledge spillovers associated with production that would augment TFP_Y are excluded.

Hypothesis 1: $\dfrac{dY}{dCI} < 0, \dfrac{dU}{dCI} > 0$

In model 1, the creative industries are a net drain on the economy, although a net drain worth having as the net result is welfare positive. This is due to the production of commodities of high cultural value $(dU/dCI > 0)$ but low market value $(dY/dCI < 0)$, as production is inherently unprofitable because demand curves mostly lie below cost curves. The economic justification for such restitution must ultimately then rest on a market failure argument, with policy appropriately calibrated to estimates of this non-market value. Yet the question of whether market failure is an appropriate justification for intervention need not concern us, for it is sufficient to recognize that if $dY/dCI < 0$ then policy intervention can be justified if it is also true that $dU/dCI > 0$. If model 1 is true, then policy prescriptions should centre on income and resource reallocation or price maintenance in order to protect an inherently valuable asset (cultural production) that is naturally and continually under threat in a market economy (Galloway and Dunlop 2007).

It is broadly accepted by scholars of cultural economics (Throsby and Withers 1979, Throsby 1994) and supported by a raft of non-market valuation studies (Towse ed. 1997, 2003) that dU/dCI is positive. This is an unsurprising result that accords with intuition. It is, furthermore, not inconsistent with economic conceptions of rational economic man (Frey 2000). So, let us take that positive sign as evidential and focus instead on the sign of dY/dCI and what it means to say that dY/dCI is negative. Specifically, it means that growth in the CIs comes at the cost of aggregate economic growth, as their growth is not what 'the market' wants, but must be compelled to support through transfers.

Evidence for model 1 may accrue in several ways. These include: high levels and rates of negative profit among creative industries firms; low total factor productivity $(TFP_{CI} < TFP_Y)$; persistently lower income to factors of production in creative industries compared to other industries; and other indications that the economic viability of activities organizations within the creative industries is critically dependent upon resource transfers from the rest of the economy to maintain prices, demand or supply. If model 1 is true, we should observe not just an economically stagnant or low-growth sector, but also one with lower performance levels (return on investment, incomes, and so on). Such decomposition allows multiple opportunities for empirical assessment. This is, we think, an interesting empirical question to re-ask, for the implicit truth of 'model 1' is almost axiomatic in the field of cultural economics where few dispute the implicit assumption of below-average income or productivity growth.

Model 2: The normal model

Model 2 differs from model 1 in allowing that the creative industries are not economic laggards, nor providers of special goods of higher moral significance, but effectively 'just another industry': in effect, the entertainment or leisure industry. In this model, which is the default setting wherever economic analysis assumes competition, a change in the size or value of the creative industries has a proportionate (but structurally neutral) effect on the whole economy. This model presumes that the growth impact is also neutral, such that the creative industries would in aggregate contribute no more or less to technological change, innovation or productivity growth than the average of other sectors.

This model does not argue that the creative industries have no effect on income, productivity or welfare as that is trivially false, but that their effect is on par with all other sectors: such that $TFP_{CI} = TFP_Y$. Indeed, this is what standard economic analysis would predict as based on the competitive substitution of resources in a market-based economy to achieve equivalent returns at the margin. If so, this implies that the marginal welfare benefit of policy-based redirection of resources into this sector is zero in aggregate. There will be no economic welfare gains to special policy treatment. This supposes that cultural/creative goods are 'normal goods', in that as they vary in relative price, rational consumers would substitute between them and those from other sectors to equalize their marginal utility. An expansion of the creative industries would have no aggregate welfare benefit distinct from expansion of any other sector.

Hypothesis 2: $\dfrac{dY}{dCI} = 0, \dfrac{dU}{dCI} = 0$

Model 2 does not exclude the possibility that the economics of the creative industries are 'special' in terms of extreme levels of demand uncertainty, power-law revenue models, tendencies toward monopoly, complex labour markets and property rights, endemic hold-up problems, information asymmetries, highly strategic factor markets, and so on (Caves 2000). Rather, it emphasizes that these coordination problems are eventually solved under competitive conditions, just as the special circumstances of other industries lead them to discover specific institutional arrangements and coordination structures.

Model 2 emphasizes these as problems for management as well as opportunities for entrepreneurs, but ultimately insists that they are no different to the 'special' problems of all other industries, such as energy or tourism, which also have 'interesting' features associated with scale, coordination, uncertainty, networks, and so forth. The 'normal model' thus finds that the creative industries have comparable industry statistics to other sectors (Scott 2002, 2006). It then follows that they should properly require the same policy treatment as other industries.

The creative industries, in this view, are just another member of the industrial community, and they should rightfully then demand neither more nor less 'assistance' than that due to others. If so, the creative industries then require no special policy treatment, just the consistent application of policy mechanisms extended to other industries. In this view, the CI policy focus should not be on resource reallocation, but rather on consistent industrial policy treatment.

Model 3: The growth model

Model 3 explicitly proposes a positive economic relation between growth in the creative industries and growth in the aggregate economy, such that $dY/dCI > 0$. Here, the creative industries are a growth 'driver' in the same way as agriculture was in the early 20th century, manufacturing in the 1950s–60s, and ICT through the 1980s–90s. The key difference from models 1 and 2 is that model 3 actively involves the creative industries in the growth of the economy. This occurs in two ways: supply side and demand side. The supply side interpretation emphasizes the export of new ideas from CI to Y. The demand side interpretation emphasizes how growth in Y causes a proportionate increase in demand for CI services. In practice, it is difficult to separate these two forces without recourse to advanced microeconometric techniques, which are not attempted here. Model 3 may therefore be true, but with different policy implications depending upon whether causality runs predominantly from CI to Y – the supply-side growth driver model – or from Y to CI – the demand side induction model.

Hypothesis 3: $\dfrac{dY}{dCI} > 0, \dfrac{dU}{dCI} \geq 0$

In both cases, policy should then properly treat the creative industries as a special sector. This is not because it is economically significant in itself, but because it powers the growth of other sectors. This may plausibly lead to politically justifiable intervention, but unlike model 1, the ostensible purpose of this is to invest in economic growth, or to invest in the development of capacity to meet growth in demand. If model 3 is true, then there is a clear economic case for redirecting resources, not just for the benefit of the creative industries *per se*, but for the benefit of all.

Evidence for this model would come from association of the creative industries with growth. This would accrue not just in jobs and commodities (as in model 2), but in new types of jobs and new sorts of commodities and services. Model 3 proposes the creative industries as growth drivers not because of operational expenditure multipliers, but due to their role in the adoption, retention and absorption of new ideas and technologies. The creative industries would be thus assumed to create new industries and market niches and to stabilize and develop extant industries. Without such continued investment, aggregate economic growth would suffer. This is the opposite of model 1, in which economic growth suffers when there is such continued investment. Model 3 thus argues that the creative industries are good for the economy because they introduce and process the new ideas that drive economic growth.

Model 4: The creative economy model
These three models might seem exhaustive of analytic possibilities: yet a fourth model is also possible as an emergent dimension. Rather than thinking of the creative industries as an economic subset 'driving' growth in the whole economy, as in model 3, the CIs may be well characterized not as an industry *per se*, but rather as an element of the innovation system of the whole economy. This perspective has been argued throughout this book, particularly in Chapter 9.

Model 4 thus rejects the initial statics-to-dynamics master equation $CI = A \cdot Y$ and $\Delta Y_t / \Delta CI_t$. Instead, it re-conceptualizes the creative industries as a higher-order system that operates *on* the economic system. The economic value of the creative industries here is not in terms of their relative contribution to economic value (models 1–3), but due to their contribution to the coordination of new ideas or technologies, and thus of the process of change. In this view, the creative industries are mis-specified as an industry *per se*, and better modelled as a complex evolving system that derives its 'economic value' from the facilitation of economic evolution.

Model 4 is similar to model 1, in that it ventures an element of special pleading. Specifically, this is the same model as proposed for the effect of science, education and technology in the national systems of innovation approach.[2] The creative industries play a key role in originating and coordinating change in the knowledge base of the economy. In consequence they have crucial, not marginal, policy significance. In model 4, the creative industries have essentially dynamic rather than static significance and value. Culture and creative action is not then an industry *per se*, but rather an evolutionary dynamic mechanism across sectors. In model 4, the creative industries do not drive economic growth directly, as might a boom in the primary resource sector or the housing market for example, but rather facilitate the conditions of change in the economic order. If model 4 is true, then, the creative industries are part of the innovation system driving and coordinating the growth of knowledge process that underpins economic evolution.

Hypothesis 4: $\dfrac{dY}{dCI}$ *undefined,* $\dfrac{dU}{dCI}$ *open*

Culture is still a public good, but here it is recognized as such for dynamic not static reasons. Unlike the value of museums or classical arts, which seek cultural value through the maintenance of past knowledge, creative industries' value lies in the development and adoption of new knowledge. Evidence for model 4 accrues from ongoing regeneration of existing industries and the emergence of new industries in consequence of creative industries' activity. Model 4 thus requires observation of ongoing structural change and re-consolidation across the entire economy and with catalytic attribution of this to creative industries' operations. This is difficult to test. Yet this dynamic distinction between growth processes (model 3) and evolutionary processes (model 4) is important, for it carries the most radical policy implication: namely the possibility of a shift of policy from an economic engagement with respect to welfare as opposed to an economic engagement with respect to innovation.

12.3   EVIDENCE

What evidence do we have? Our preliminary sample of data on differential growth in creative industries' value added predominantly favours the *prima facie* conclusion that models 3 and 4 fit better than models 1 or 2. Yet the substantial variation in performance measures within the CIs caution that what is statistically true of the aggregate is not necessarily true of sub-sectors. For example: heritage and performance arts seem to fit model 1; publishing model 2; digital content model 3; and design and software model 4. So, this is a first pass with a new methodology, not a final conclusion. Yet we also emphasize that these findings all tend to point in the same direction: namely toward growth dynamics (models 3 and 4) rather than welfare dynamics (model 1) or equivalent dynamics (model 2). The current evidence mostly points toward the creative industries' growth model.

12.3.1   Comparative Growth Evidence

The basic finding for Australia, US, Britain, and the EU for 1999–2006 is that the creative industries, under various definitions, are growing at a

Table 12.1   Creative industries' relative growth

Country	CI value added (% GDP)	CI value added growth	GDP growth	CI growth ratio	CI employ- ment growth	National employ- ment growth	CI employ- ment growth ratio
Australia 2000–2005	6.0	10.4	4.0	2.6	3.8 1996–2001	1.9 1996–2001	2.0 1996–2001
New Zealand 1996–2001	3.1	8	3.7	2.2	5	3	1.6
Europe 1999–2003	2.6	5.4	2.9	1.9	na	na	–
UK 1997–2005	7.3	5.0	3.0	1.7	2.0	1.0	2

faster rate than the aggregate economy. This is primary evidence of structural transformation as driven by the creative industries, thus supporting model 3. Between 2000 and 2005 the Australian creative industries grew at twice the rate of the aggregate economy. The European Commission found that the growth of the cultural and creative sector proceeded in Europe at 12 per cent. In New Zealand, it was found that creative industries' value added has been recently growing at 8 per cent per year. In the UK, where the most comprehensive data exists, the creative industries have been recorded as growing at 5 per cent as compared to real aggregate GDP growth of 3 per cent. CI growth ratios are everywhere greater than 1.0. We may therefore infer from this sample that the creative industries are now, and have been for the past decade, growing at about twice the rate of the aggregate economy. In the absence of evidence of increasing transfer payments to the creative industries, this seems to reject models 1 and 2 and favour model 3.

12.3.2   Firms

At the micro level, we can compare data on the growth in creative industries' firms with aggregate growth in all firms. We may also compare the profitability of creative industries' firms and aggregate profitability. According to economic theory, these statistics should be related, as higher than average profitability would encourage a shift of resources into creative industries, increasing the number (or size) of firms. A broad finding is that the creative industries sector has a higher rate of enterprise creation than the economy as a whole, consistent with the observed growth rate of value added (Work Foundation 2007).

Profit data is not widely reported by creative industries. It can also be ambiguous, appearing low in both a declining industry due to low margins, and in a growing industry due to reinvestment. European estimates of average profitability of the cultural and creative industries for 1999–2003 was 9 per cent, similar to Australian estimates. This is good for the service sector, which in Europe ranges between 5 and 10 per cent. This is an unsurprising result, signalling the creative industries as comparably competitive, as model 2 hypothesizes. Similar profitability supports model 2, and enterprise growth supports models 3 and 4. Yet acknowledging the considerable variation within the creative industries, firm data only consistently rejects model 1.

12.3.3   Income

Income in the creative industries provides a good opportunity to discriminate between the negative, neutral and positive models. Australian census data indicates average income by six sectors for 2001. The all-industries mean was 31 per cent higher for creative industries, although with significant variation within.

Several explanations can be offered for the higher creative industries' income. One, the creative industries have higher human capital than the aggregate economy. Second, it may be that mean and median statistics do not accurately reflect the distribution of income, which is instead heavily skewed to a winner-takes-all situation. Indeed, there is substantial evidence for a power law rather than Gaussian income distribution here (De Vany 2004). A third possibility is that incomes are higher in the creative industries due to transfer payments from other sectors. This is dominated by heritage funding and public broadcasting, yet is broadly comparable with the EU and the US. Yet, to the extent these all constitute investment in social technologies, the net transfer may even be from the creative industries to the rest of the economy, which would be evidence against model 1 and for model 4.

12.4   IMPLICATIONS

There are good reasons we should expect this manner of growth in the creative industries, as discussed in Chapters 9, 10 and 11. The relative growth of the creative industries is not an anomaly, but what open-system economic theory predicts as based on the effects of technological change and a changed consumption set consistent with increased income. The evidence surveyed broadly (although only loosely) supports the model that creative industries' growth is driving economic evolution.

But if this is correct (and I emphasize that we only have plausibly suggestive evidence at this stage), what would it then imply for public policy? One perspective is to view the creative industries as the 21st century analogue of the creative destruction 'wrecking ball' that was 19th century engineering. The 19th and 20th century transformations that wrought epoch-making changes in the economy and culture occurred through physical, chemical, civil and electrical engineering, along with economic engineering. The same argument now applies to creative industries' 'engineering' of open systems (or more broadly of social technologies), rather than closed systems. If this metaphorical translation holds, policy implications follow directly from model 4 and with a substantial and significant role for public support based on innovation policy. However, an equally consistent perspective may be read from model 3, in which creative industries are growth mechanisms for the 'generic' adjustment and adaptation of the knowledge base of the economy.

Models 3 and 4 thus harbour a substantially differential commitment to public intervention. In particular, it is apparent that investment behaviour in the creative industries is crucial to understand as the services industry analogue of R&D. We find, for example, that growth is the primary way that success is spent in the creative industries. Indeed, as DEMOS (2007) find, the CIs 'grow by staying small', such that growth occurs as spin-off entrepreneurial growth. The creative industries, in this view, have dynamic economic value that contributes to the process of economic growth and development over and above their contribution to culture and society. This distinction is important, as cultural policy, which is traditionally based on model 1, may require some critical retooling to adapt to what appears to be a model 4 world.

NOTES

1. For example, DCMS (1998, 2001), Higgs et al. (2007).
2. For example, Lundvall (1992), Nelson (ed. 1993, 2002), Freeman (1995), Edquist (1997), and Dodgson et al. (2005).

13. Creative clusters and innovation

with Michael Keane

Prolegomena

This chapter is based on unpublished work with Michael Keane on the role of cultural and creative clusters in China. It picks up on the theme of creative clusters, a core plank in creative industries policy. We argue that creative clusters play a significant role in the innovation process, a point we think has received insufficient attention thus far.

13.1 ECONOMICS OF CLUSTERS

The economics of clusters – or what Alfred Marshall called 'external economies' and Paul Krugman calls 'increasing returns operating spatially' – is a simple concept that connects agglomeration to innovation (Porter 1996, 1998, 2000, Hall 1998). It is widely observed that creative industries seem to thrive in clusters. This chapter discusses the evolutionary economic explanations of this observation and the implications for creative industries and innovation. We begin with the economics of clusters.

Businesses in similar markets gain from spatial co-location (that is, a cluster) due to external economies. These accrue in several ways. First, because there are both greater and more diverse opportunities for specialized work: clusters attract a pool of skilled workers. This lowers the cost to firms of finding and employing specialized skilled workers, an effect that extends to other input resources that may be directed to the cluster in greater quantity and via scale economies at lower price. So clusters offer good input markets.

Second, the presence of many similar firms creates incentives for other businesses to establish specialist services to these firms that would not be viable if there fewer of them. These services become viable in a cluster. This enables firms to concentrate on their core capabilities, thus improving the average productivity and refining the competitive advantage of all firms within the cluster. So clusters enable greater specialization and productivity. A related point is that infrastructure, utilities, transport and other business requirements and institutions can be more efficiently supplied to a cluster, again lowering average costs and reinforcing the global competitiveness of firms within the cluster.

Third, a cluster provides a physical focus for consumers of the cluster output. By lowering the costs of search, the existence of the cluster as a market benefits consumers (Earl and Potts 2001, Potts 2010). Consumers also gain by the greater range of choice, including over quality, which enables them to move to higher utility functions on the same budget. The presence of a large number of shoppers creates a demand for other services such as food, accommodation or cultural amenities. While this increases competition for scarce inputs such as land or some labour markets, the presence of these services also benefits the producers in the cluster too, improving its attractiveness to mobile creatives (Florida 2002).

These demand and supply side factors interact to generate the increasing returns that drive spatial agglomeration and results in cluster formation (Jacobs 1969, Krugman 1991, Belleflamme et al., 2000, Blien and Maier 2008). With the exception of primary industries, industries with large transport costs or restrictions on mobility of inputs or outputs, or industries that have achieved regulatory capture, it can be generalized that most industries cluster in some degree for all the above reasons. The implication is that clusters form naturally (or emerge spontaneously) under conditions of competition and mobility. They are a natural form of emergent order in an evolving economy.

Clusters therefore do not need to be created artificially (although they can be artificially accelerated through mechanisms to make the proposed locus of the cluster more attractive, usually focused on side-payments to producers). This cluster policy often travels under the heading of regional development policy, a complex of regulatory and fiscal policy that typically targets some set of industries or part of one industry. This creates competition between regions that in equilibrium should escalate to the point where the marginal cost of the cluster policy equals the marginal benefit of the cluster to the region's economy and society. Such clustering is readily observed in most creative industries, and operates by all of the above mentioned mechanisms (Turok 2003, Pratt 2004, Cooke and Lazzeretti 2007) although in some cases these are being driven heavily and with differential success by government policy (Jayne 2005, Gwee 2009).

13.2 CREATIVE CLUSTERS AND EXTERNAL ECONOMIES OF INNOVATION

So, clusters form naturally in an open economy because of these standard economic forces. Yet there is also a dynamic logic to clusters in terms of creativity, learning, knowledge networks and innovation between firms that is not yet accounted for. Part of this is contained in the skilled labour markets within a cluster, where the movement of people between firms acts as a conduit for new ideas and knowledge. More generally, clusters drive innovation through the heightened competition within a cluster and the ability of firms to learn from each other, or to be spurred and challenged by others' developments, experiments and ideas. In clusters with mature technology or stable markets, this effect may be less important.[1] But in industries characterized by incessant and driving novelty and experimentation – for example fashion, art, film, television, music and other creative industries – this dynamic innovation dimension is likely to be the economic rationale of the cluster. The specialist services, labour markets and consumer markets will of course continue to be important, but the dominant economic force driving creative clusters will be competitive innovation between co-located firms. Clusters thus matter not because of external economies in production, nor external economies in demand – although both clearly remain important – but because of external economies in innovation.

External economies of innovation provide the central rationale for why creative industries need to cluster. This is particularly so for new, small and start-up creative industries businesses that derive much of their 'R&D' not from in-house production and investment but from learning from other firms through invited or tacit observation, as well as by tapping into and exploiting the social networks of learning that grow and develop within a cluster context. This extends to learning associated with new ideas and innovation that is often highly tacit and requires face-to-face interaction, feedback and observation. These external economies of creativity, research, learning, experimentation and innovation operate over social networks. 'Social network markets' (Chapter 8) and 'situated creativity' (Potts et al. 2008b) in clusters enable small and start-up businesses to be far more innovative and competitive than they could be outside of a cluster. While such clusters do form organically, there is from the regional perspective a strong strategic competitive rationale for public intervention to create the initial conditions for such clusters (Martin and Sunley 2002).

It is crucial to distinguish between cultural clusters and creative industries clusters because the foregoing arguments about external economies of innovation only apply to the latter; yet these two cluster concepts are often run together. Creative industries clusters are frequently constructed about extant cultural clusters, but there are important differences between these two states, and a successful transition from a cultural to a creative cluster requires more than simply relabelling.

A cultural cluster is typically organized about, and extracts value from, its demand side market dimensions. These are often purely 'transactional' benefits related to labour supply, institutional infrastructure (often via a single large production company, studio, gallery, or the like) and concentrated consumer markets. A cultural cluster is thus not necessarily a particularly competitive or innovative cluster. Normally, it will involve a well-defined niche (ceramics or painting, for example) and mature or largely non-experimental technologies. There may be many firms involved, and much product diversity, but it will be mostly routine operations, possibly highly regulated – either by implicit collusion or explicitly by law – and not necessarily marked by significant innovation or outward focus. This is often typical of 'cultural quarters' or arts districts (Roodhouse 2006).

A creative cluster may involve similar aspects to a cultural cluster, but it differs in one crucial respect: namely the significance of novelty and innovation and thus in the form and extent of both competition and cooperation between firms in the cluster. In creative industries clusters, firms are engaged in developing and exploiting competitive advantages that arise through new ideas, new technologies, new business models, new competencies and new markets, or new ways of exploiting any extant ideas, technologies, business models, and so on. This will involve simultaneous and overlapping competition and cooperation. It will involve significant strategic challenges and adaptive abilities, much of which will be tacitly known only to those within the cluster. A creative industries cluster may thus seem more chaotic or messy and less corporeal that a cultural cluster, and may not even stand out as such to those who are not part of it (unlike a cultural cluster, which is usually obvious to most passers-by). None of these knowledge-sharing and competitive learning aspects are particularly important in cultural clusters, which tend to be more settled; yet these knowledge dynamics are the *raison d'être* of creative clusters.

This distinction matters because cultural clusters are not always easily then converted into creative clusters (Wang 2004).[2] While cultural clusters do have important cultural and economic spillovers into the local or regional economy (Florida 2002, Mommaas 2004), it is only creative clusters that function as drivers of growth and innovation into the broader economy through their role in developing new ideas, products, businesses, business models, markets and industries. Cultural clusters can extract efficiency gains from extant economic activities through more efficient (spatial) market organization, but it is creative clusters that can supply dynamic benefits through the creation of new markets, new industry niches and new businesses. It is creative clusters therefore and not cultural clusters that have most to offer regional economic development.

It is perhaps therefore useful to distinguish between two classes of 'space' that clusters may represent: namely static spaces and dynamic spaces. Static spaces are the creation of markets and organizations that benefit from lowered transaction costs and organizational costs associated with close physical proximity. The cluster thus increases efficiency and productivity for a given knowledge base. This applies to manufacturing and assembly clusters that gain through the concentration of input resources, organization and coordination of conjoint activities as well as by concentrated markets. However, this same static space benefit also applies to 'cultural spaces' in that the same input and output logic applies, but with respect to cultural goods. Clusters occur in static spaces because of efficiency gains in organization of resources and markets.

'Dynamic spaces' also cluster, but instead of forming about transactions and organizational economies, they reflect the benefits of 'creative spaces' for experimentation, incubation and learning that leads to or facilitates innovation processes and the growth of knowledge. These 'dynamic spaces' or creative clusters may of course also share the same benefits as accrue to the 'static spaces' in terms of efficiency and productivity gains, but even if they do not, there remains an economic rationale for the cluster in its external economies of innovation. An important difference is that static spaces are often 'zero-sum', in that the gains from agglomeration of some activities or industries come at the cost of displacing them from elsewhere. However, dynamic or creative spaces are often 'positive-sum' because they may produce new activities and sources of value that did not exist in their absence. Rather than just efficient re-organizations of existing production, they are a model for developing new production and sources of value. These innovation and knowledge spillovers may then lead to sustained competitive advantage for the regional economy.

13.3   THE SIGNIFICANCE OF CREATIVE CLUSTERS

What may we conclude from this brief review of the evolutionary economic logic of creative industries clusters? The key point is that the creative clusters approach offers a new form of industrial growth and development policy that focuses on industries that have not traditionally been considered part of the commanding heights of industrial development. Indeed, under cultural industries rubric they are most directly associated with entertainment, tourism, leisure and non-economic cultural value, which when harnessed then leads to economic spillovers due to the increased value of the place or space as a destination. But when viewed in terms of creative industries these effects are mostly incidental to the central relevance of the cluster to the growth of knowledge and innovation process. These industries are thus recognized as providing creative innovation services (Potts and Morrison 2009) with cultural services as spillover (externality) benefits.

Cluster policy of all forms seeks to work by development of targeted spaces and places rather than directly in terms of particular firms or broad industry support. This is especially relevant for creative industries clusters due to the alchemy that seems necessary to create the agglomeration benefits in terms of creative frisson, intellectual stimulation, knowledge exchange and experimental learning that have characterized the clustered creative milieus of past epochs (Hall 1998). The key issue is not whether to advance these, but how. We have made several key observations.

First, the growth of knowledge always involves clusters, and in the absence of public fostering and direction, creative clusters will occur naturally and spontaneously simply because of the collective benefits that stand to accrue to a variety of stakeholders. However, the extent to which these form and where they form depend upon the ability of the stakeholders to coordinate both resources and actions. There is a clear role for local and regional policy actors to facilitate this process, or at least not to inhibit this process as it may spontaneously emerge from the actions of private individuals, firms or coalitions. A cluster may thus emerge as a kind of creative commons or common pool resource (Ostrom 1990). Unlike cultural clusters, which can plausibly be created *ab nihilo* through government planning and spending, when done with sufficient commitment and necessary scale, creative clusters can rarely be achieved by this means. At best they can be assisted or at worst not discouraged by government policy. Thus a pragmatic creative cluster policy will not start by deciding what sort of clusters it wants in a particular region, but rather by seeking to discover what clusters are already gathering and emerging and then seeking to be a force-multiplier for this naturally occurring process of economic evolution.

Second, creative cluster formation is a competitive process. While many interests may align within a 'cluster coalition', this is not necessarily so with respect to alternative uses of the space (for example for housing, public space, or other industries), and with respect to competing clusters in other districts within a city or between regions. The increasing returns inherent in clusters means a tendency toward winner-takes-all outcomes, again highlighting the important strategic role of political cooperation.

Yet, this also means that some cluster coalitions and initiatives will invariably fail. While extraneous factors and luck will play a role in this, global evidence points to the importance of sustained first-mover advantages (Storper 1997, Porter 2000, Rowen 2007).

Third, the impact of such clusters may be expected to extend beyond increased rents for councils and landowners, but also to have perhaps significant spillover effects into the regional economy through the dynamic implications of new ideas, capabilities and improved innovation services. These dynamic benefits are difficult to quantify because they lead to structural changes in the workforces, the composition of businesses and markets, and so on. These are more than simply cultural or even economic spillovers, but are improvements in the competitive advantages of not just the cultural and creative sector, but potentially many other industries through their effect on innovation through improved access to design services, architecture, media and communications, and so on (Bakhshi et al. 2008). While often diffuse and inherently difficult to measure, it is these dynamic innovation benefits of clusters that can be expected to have the greatest sustained and long-run impact on economic growth and development.

Fourth, there are important differences between cultural clusters and creative industries clusters. While cultural clusters often come first, it is a far from trivial exercise to transition from a cultural to a creative cluster. In essence, creative clusters are much freer spaces, much more open to networked cooperation and experimental business models, and to new firms, new ideas and new markets. In contrast, cultural clusters, while often culturally vibrant and particularly so with respect to retail, entertainment and tourism, often tend to be more conservative in respect of regulation, business and innovation. Start-up businesses for example are rare in a cultural cluster while common in a creative industries cluster. Venture finance and accountancy may be key support services in a creative cluster in the same way that hotels and restaurants are key support services in a cultural cluster. These differences in support industries matter.

Fifth, creative clusters require creative space. This can literally mean creative workshops and studios, as well as market space (for example, 798 in Beijing). But it also implies a creative mental and entrepreneurial space, in the sense of willingness to experiment with new ideas, to engage in competitive cooperation across networks of businesses, and to learn quickly in the adoption and adaptation of successful ideas. This further combines with an outwardly focused sense of value creation toward other industries and regions, and toward global markets. All historically successful 'creative clusters' have fostered and developed an outward and open focus that broadly seeks to engage with open competition, not to avoid it. Yet this is almost the opposite of the cultural cluster model, which is largely self-contained – producing within the cluster for consumers who come to the cluster, and with little deep connection or engagement with other sectors. Furthermore, cultural clusters tend to explicitly engage in rent-seeking behaviours to protect the cultural assets (often publically supplied or supported, as in the case of museums or galleries for example) that form the basis of the local cluster economy. A cultural cluster that is relabelled under a progressive new policy agenda as a creative cluster, but which yet retains its inward focus and conservatism toward experimentation, is still only a cultural cluster: it cannot be expected to have dynamic economic benefits beyond those of increased consumer traffic and property rents. Ergo, if it is not contributing to innovation through competitively incentivized co-location and emergent cooperation and knowledge-sharing then it is not a creative cluster.

Finally, what strategic management and policy implications follow? The central lesson, we think, is to make a clear distinction between cultural clusters and creative clusters. For businesses engaged in such coalitions, there are different expectations and strategic responses associated with each. A cultural cluster presents opportunities for gains through asset holdings associated with the cluster, if successful. This, in essence, is no different to land speculation where there is a known quantum of public investment with expected gains in demand for scarce resources. Furthermore, there would be expected to be limited benefits to other businesses in the area beyond the effect of increased consumer traffic. Most rents will accrue to consumers, developers and landowners (and in turn the government agencies that can levy taxes on these agents). So cultural clusters represent a mostly known and familiar strategic opportunity set, for both private agents and public agencies.

A creative cluster is different because it focuses about the development of ideas, technologies, innovations, businesses and markets. It is here that new opportunities lie, and thus potential benefits are more likely to accrue to those entrepreneurs and competitive firms who seek to start or to grow businesses within such a cluster, and who are much more committed to the cluster development and the institutions that govern its functioning and stability. These agents, in other words, are much less speculatively oriented toward viewing participation in the cluster as a tradable asset and more deeply orientated to its possibilities and opportunities as a knowledge generating and sharing community. Benefits to landowners and consumers will in turn be a secondary effect. The reasons for entering a cluster or backing a cluster coalition are thus different in each case and involve different time horizons for commitment and different incentives for engagement in governance. There is a strong incentive to be involved in governance of a cultural cluster for short-term rent-seeking reasons (namely protection of a shared ownership of a known asset), whereas there is an equally strong incentive to be engaged in the governance of a creative cluster for long-term profit-seeking reasons (namely coordination of shared participation of a dynamic process). These differences obviously imply different strategic responses for firms within the respective clusters.

For local and regional government, the same point applies. The extent and distribution of the benefits differ between cultural and creative clusters. Both create the opportunity for rents through various mechanisms (licenses, taxes, and so on, as well as political capital) and there will be many instances when a cultural cluster will yield higher returns at a point in time than a creative cluster. Cultural clusters also yield clear and manifestly visible public goods in the form of cultural goods. Yet it is the creative cluster that ultimately has the most to contribute to ongoing public revenue and economic growth and development through its role in the creation and development of new ideas and its contribution to the innovation services that drive many sectors of the economy (Swedberg 2006, Bakhshi et al. 2008). This is the prime difference between public investments in cultural space versus creative space.

Clusters are a crucial and important aspect of creative industries' structure and dynamics. There are strong forces that tend creative industries' economic activities toward co-location, and these forces are part of the evolutionary market process driving firms to rationally co-locate and gain from the knowledge, learning and innovation benefits that a cluster provides. Clusters also provide static efficiency and productivity gains. But it is important to recognize two classes of benefits from clusters: (1) static benefits through efficiency and productivity through market specialization and scale; and (2) dynamic benefits through the growth of knowledge and innovation through competitive learning and cooperative exchange. This difference highlights the distinction between cultural and creative clusters.

Clusters are rational outcomes of economic incentives and natural outcomes of economic evolution. This chapter has argued that these two rationales are often confused and that this confusion sets up the live possibility of strategic management and policy mistakes. Cultural clusters have a different economic logic to creative clusters at the point of innovation. Cultural clusters are explicitly focused on external market economies, whereas creative clusters are implicitly focused on the gains from co-location and competitive collaboration in the growth of knowledge or innovation process. This basic difference is not widely recognized in academic analysis and policy advocacy of clusters. But it should be. The point of a cultural cluster is to facilitate market externalities on the consumer side but the point of a creative cluster is to facilitate innovation on the supply side.

NOTES

1. Rodríguez-Clare (2007: 43) argues that 'rather than distorting prices to promote clusters in "advanced sectors" that may exhibit strong clustering possibilities, countries should focus instead on promoting clustering in current sectors, which have been revealed to have the strongest comparative advantage.'
2. For instance, this is an explicit policy of China's government at present, particularly in Beijing and Shanghai where extant cultural quarters are being transformed by various policy initiatives into cultural-creative clusters (Keane 2007, Keane and Hartley 2006).

14. Novelty bundling markets

14.1 CHOICE UNDER ABUNDANT NOVELTY: A SERIOUS CONSUMER PROBLEM

The problem of consumer choice over novelty is not often taken seriously – as if, for example, it were somehow a generalization of the problem of how very rich people choose new yachts. Yacht choice among rich people is of course a serious economic problem for the dedicated microeconomist, involving all manner of uncertainties and signalling challenges. But what I want to examine here is the broader problem of how any person chooses amongst novel consumer goods in a context of abundant novelty in a social context, and with the market institutions that facilitate that choice. My hypothesis in this chapter points to the intermediating role of what I call 'novelty bundling markets' as emergent market forms that intermediate novelty choice and adoption as key institutions of a creative economy.

Choice under abundant novelty in social contexts is a much under-examined aspect of modern economics that affects a lot more people than those choosing new yachts; for one, it affects those engaging in choice in the output of the creative industries, which is most of us (see also Karpik 2010). My argument here is that we may make sense of this evolutionary process via the construct of novelty bundling markets as emergent market forms that intermediate the production and consumption of novelty and which evolve from consumer specialization turned professional.

Our starting point is that the economics of choice over new goods or novelty consumption remains a surprisingly sparse domain of economic theory (Earl 1986, Witt 2001, Bianchi 2002). Of course the production of novelty and new goods (Romer 1990b, Bresnahan and Gordon 1997, Galenson 2007, Magee 2005, Becker et al. 2006, Witt 2009a, 2009b) is extensively analysed and well grounded in Schumpeterian and evolutionary economic analysis. Yet much less attention has been devoted to the consumer side of this same problem (cf. Veblen 1899). The problem is what Witt (2001) calls 'learning to consume' new or novel goods. The problem, specifically, is that the consumer of novelty has by definition no comparable experience and must proceed with substantial uncertainties over expected value due to incomplete preferences and missing information. Consumers may not know what they want; they may not know the domain and range of new consumption possibilities; and they may not know how to evaluate the new goods and the potential opportunities they provide. They may know the price of the new good, but yet have no idea of what it is worth. The consumer challenge is thus search in the context of abundant novelty when you don't actually know what you are looking for. This chapter seeks to unpack the evolutionary economics of this common situation.

New or novel goods challenge the standard (neoclassical) microeconomic framework of rational choice theory. The problem is with how these new goods fit into consumers' preference sets and utility functions and with what organizational and institutional prostheses are required for their integration. The default analytic stratagem employed in general equilibrium theory is to assume that preference sets or utility functions already contain these as potentials so that new goods simply map to preferences unrealized. More sophisticated treatments decompose novelty into characteristic components assessed with existing preferences (Lancaster 1966) or otherwise suppose that consumers arrive at preferences over novel goods by experimental learning or by observing other agents' consumption experiences and feedback (Earl and Potts 2004). When faced with novel goods and services, agents therefore either already know what to do (assuming complete and sovereign preferences), or they individually learn what to do (assuming preference decomposition and experimentation), or they socially learn what to do (by the presumption of intelligent social observation and learning from other people's choices and outcomes). Latent rationality, experimentation or social learning thus seemingly exhaust the microeconomic analysis of the economics of consumer interaction with novel goods.

Yet note some hidden assumptions. First, these models all implicitly assume that novel goods arrive individually and sequentially. Novelty is assumed to be scarce, not abundant. It is assumed that novelty presents singularly, not in multiples, and that analysis of singular novelty scales monotonically to multiple novelty. (This assumption carries over from the producer side of innovation studies.) Multiple novelties are thus, by definition, more costly to evaluate than singular novelties. There is, therefore, no reason to suppose that multiple novelties may actually represent a consumption solution in itself.

Second, these standard models assume that the discovery or learning process is costly and not a good in itself. Discovery, learning and experimental processes are all assumed to contribute nothing in themselves to individual utility. The problem with novelty is the cost of dealing with the unknown, requiring trial and experimentation (a point trivially true on the producer side, but not necessarily true on the consumer side). This assumes that the consumer experience of novelty evaluation and choice has no end in itself. No learning aspect to novelty consumption is supposed. There is no social dimension to that learning, and no positive externalities that individually accrue to this process of engagement. The consumer engaging with novelty is not assumed to be learning anything about themselves in the process of learning about new goods; this model thus assumes the complete absence of reflexivity.

Third, this framework assumes that producers play no role in this process. Business models thus treat novelty as a cost of 'informing' consumers and with no value created in the process of consumers acquiring this information and learning. This represents the additional production cost of advertising and marketing as another input expense (or from a political economy perspective, as some manner of exploitation). Novelty production and consumption are thus distinct events with separable costs and pay-offs. This generalizes the classic industrial innovation model of R&D labs on one side and grateful expectant consumers on the other. Consumers themselves play no important or value-creating role in this process and do not contribute through their experimental consumption endeavours to the production and meaning of newness. This presumes that the provision of information about choice over novelty extends exclusively from the producer side and not from the consumer side.

Fourth, and most strikingly, it assumes that a basic principle of economics does not apply; namely emergent specialization. Firms produce novelty (at a cost of developing it) and consumers consume novelty (at a cost of learning about it). If there are other agents involved, these are agents for the producers (for example advertisers) or for the consumers (for example consumer advice). But missing is a further class of agents that specializes on both sides of the market to bundle multiple novelties from producers into a single experience good (an intermediate production over novelty) for consumers who value social learning as a good in itself and who value the experience of multiple simultaneous novelty. In turn, individual producers of novelty may value the institutions such bundling agents can produce as effective ways to interact with consumers, while consumers may simultaneously value the expert bundling of high-quality novelty assembled by these intermediating agents.

This intermediating role between the production and consumption of novelty is often diffused as special cases in existing markets (for example advertising, trade events, and so on), with each treated as a special case of market imperfections in respect of its own production market. But taken together and viewed through the lens of emergent specialization about abundant novelty, a distinct class of economic organization and institutions is suggested, that I shall call 'novelty bundling markets'. When seen thus, all manner of other organizations and markets fold into this domain. For example, internet dating markets have this character, as do social network sites, but also the fashion industry, the festival and events industries, many aspects of tourism and sports, significant parts of the education industries, and much of the media industries and the myriad of other entire markets and industries devoted to the experience of social consumption of bundled novelty.

The purpose of this chapter is thus twofold. The first is to introduce the class of market forms that I call novelty bundling markets. Like the concept of a 'market for preferences' (Earl and Potts 2004) and 'social network markets' (Potts et al. 2008a) novelty bundling markets arise under the particular context of consumer choice over uncertainty and novelty in cases where it is costly or difficult to make a good choice because these are experience goods, or due to these goods being sufficiently novel that consumers lack effective rules for choice. In these circumstances consumers often look to other consumers or agents to furnish missing information, recommendations or even decision rules.

Potts et al. (2008a) argued that much of the creative industries can effectively be classified as social network markets, an insight suggesting a switch from an industrial production-based definition to a market or consumer-based definition of the creative economy. The concept of novelty bundling markets extends this method to define a further class of market forms that meet the following criteria:

1. Abundant flows of novelty on the producer side (novelty is in effect a 'free good').
2. An expert and often reputation branded market form that intermediates and organizes (bundles) the flow of novelty production to a reduced form for consumption of novelty. Producers and consumers of novelty do not interact directly but via the agency of the novelty bundling market.
3. The novelties are subject to multiple evaluative criteria. Often they are 'boundary objects' (Star and Griesemer 1989) that are of conflicting, ambiguous or uncertain value. Social interaction to resolve these uncertainties of value and worth (Stark 2009) is thus instrumental in novelty bundling markets.
4. In novelty bundling markets, consumers are typically engaged in a process of search in which they don't necessarily know what they are looking for, yet will know it when they find it (Stark 2009: 1–3).

A paradigmatic example of a novelty bundling market (hereafter, NBM) is an arts-music festival such as Burning Man (US), Glastonbury (UK), or Woodford (Australia). These are expertly bundled suites of novelty that are socially consumed, and from which consumers expect to be surprised and challenged by a bundle that presents reflexive opportunities for experience and discovery (Sundbo and Darmer 2008, Hutter 2010). Other examples include fashion magazines such as *Vogue* or technology magazines such as *Wired*. Many think-tanks are well construed as novelty bundling markets, as are many blogs. There is an abundance of creative acts and styles that could be in these festivals, magazines or think-tanks, but only some are chosen for the bundle. They are chosen by experts in the field, typically with substantial reputation. The elements of these bundles are rarely simple to evaluate, containing multiple criteria of worth. Consumers search in festivals, magazines and blogs looking for exciting new things or opportunities without necessarily having a specific search target in mind; yet they nevertheless expect to find something that is both surprising and valuable, even if it requires some effort at eliciting value or estimates of worth through reflexive engagement. While such instances (festivals and magazines, among other examples of NMBs) are clearly not major sectors of the economy, the argument here is that NBMs play a significant role in facilitating the demand side of the innovation process in many sectors and particularly so in the creative industries.

The second purpose of this chapter, beyond introducing and outlining the analytic concept of a NBM, is to contrast three analytic explanations of NBMs: (1) a neoclassical economic explanation, centered on market failure and bounded rationality; (2) an evolutionary economic explanation, centered on the emergence of professional consumers and resultant endogenous transformation of preferences and market structure; and (3) an economic sociology account, centered on the dissonance of multiple evaluative criteria. I will argue that while the economic frameworks shed considerable light on NBMs, it is the economic sociology approach that provides the deepest insight into the nature of the entrepreneurial opportunities that NBMs afford.

A final introductory remark concerns the origin and nature of the demand for novelty. In that novel goods are just more goods, then there is a trivial explanation of demand in terms of expected value: consumers demand novel goods for the same reason they demand extant goods, namely the expectation of utility or consumer surplus. But this needs to be set against the costs and uncertainties associated with novel goods, costs and uncertainties that are not present in the class of known consumption possibilities. The question therefore arises as to what motivations exist for consumers to engage in this more risky and potentially costly extension of consumption sets. The hypothesis I suggest here turns on the supposition that consumers are not simply individually maximizing utility in a socially isolated context (cf. Veblen 1898) but are further engaged in various degrees of social competition (cf. Veblen 1899). In such domains, consumers can signal their ability to make good, interesting choices over novel goods as a play in the ongoing game of social competition.[1] Notably, the underlying assumption of abundant novelty seems to be precisely most evident in domains where social competition is strongest and most readily observable, for example over choice in music, fashion, media consumption and political ideas. Interestingly, this significantly overlaps with the output of the creative industries. The social competition hypothesis of novelty adoption underscores why the demand for novelty remains strong in the face of substantial costs and risks associated with its consumption, why the emergence of organizations and institutions that facilitate this consumption provide a valuable service, and also to explain why NMBs tend to be clustered about particular forms of abundant novelty, specifically those associated with creative industries' output.

14.2   WHAT ARE NOVELTY BUNDLING MARKETS?

A novelty bundling market is a market form that arises in a particular context characterized by situations in which there is abundant novelty issuing from the producer side and substantial search costs and evaluation difficulties on the consumer side, and where moreover consumers don't necessarily know what they're searching for (Stark 2009). These difficulties on the demand side are specifically caused by the fact that novel goods, which are in most cases experience goods (Hutter, forthcoming), often require new 'rules for choice' or new suites of evaluative criteria (Earl and Potts 2004). While NBMs tend to concentrate about the creative industries (Potts et al. 2008), they potentially extend throughout the economy wherever these specific conditions in novelty supply and demand arise.

Consider four examples of NBMs: (1) a branded music festival such as Glastonbury; (2) a branded garment retailer such as Zara; (3) a fashion magazine such as *Vogue*; and (4) a think tank such as the Cato Institute. In each case, these are ostensible bundles of novel goods – new music; new ready-to-wear fashion; new fashion concepts; new policy ideas. These are assembled by experts (typically experts with substantial reputational assets) that have selected from the cornucopia of novelty flows in these domains to present a narrowed set of consumption prospects (often a complex mix of the more familiar and the more exotic) but also, and

---

BOX 14.1   SOME NOVELTY BUNDLING MARKETS

Branded garment retailers	Policy think tanks
Fashion magazines, new technology magazines	Dating and introduction agencies
Arts festivals, music festivals, film festivals	Holiday tour packaging (some)
Degustation experiences	Boutique stores
Blogs (some)	Media channels, particular types of 'shows'
Trade fairs	Showrooms (especially in consumer electronics)

---

crucially, organizing the space and form of the presentation of this novelty to embed implicit references, contrasts, tensions and navigation cues (for example in the organization of the line-up, the display, the spread, the layout, the position). In each case these bundles are finite in the sense of not presenting an assemblage of all possible new things minimally sufficient, but rather presenting a suite of novelties that may be plausibly visited in a single experience. These bundles are also typically complex in the sense that the consumer can expect a gradient of familiar, partially familiar and unfamiliar arranged in a form that can be navigated but yet equally contains predictable surprises. Novelty bundling markets are not just lists or samples but are highly organized assemblies in which content may vary yet the principles of organization will persist and indeed become known by consumers as a form of 'literacy'. Box 14.1 offers a list of novelty bundling markets.

An NBM has the following features. First, it intermediates production and consumption of novelty. Consumers interact with novel goods via the NBM, and producers of novelty interact with consumers also via the NBM. Producers and consumers no longer meet in an unmediated manner.

Second, an NBM is a specialist domain organized by experts who are experienced and skilled in the particular domain of novelty abundantly produced. They are experts in the sense of knowledge and access of the range of novelty produced and also in the rules for choosing or the evaluative principles applied in mapping novelty to consumer lifestyles and dimensions of social competition. For this reason, this specialization and experience may issue from experience and specialization in consumption. Novelty bundling markets are thus competitive between rivalrous experts who compete by accumulating or investing in reputational capital as the outcome of their ability to assemble and organize high-quality bundles that meet consumer demands.

Third, NMBs present organized complex structures of display or forms of presentation, often embedding the implicit rules for choice in the physical, spatial or temporal organization of the bundle. An NBM is thus more than an indexed searchable list of new novelties (for example the early days of the Yahoo portal or as exemplified in the infinite possibility of Google search-bar, which presumes that you know what you're looking for) but is substantially embodied in an organized market design. The difference is that this design is not intended to promote efficient search or shopping – it is not intended to create maximal efficiencies and minimize transaction costs; rather the design is deliberately intended to be somewhat challenging by contextualizing the frictions, tensions and uncertainties inherent in the novelty and presenting these so as to make the multiple evaluative criteria over value or 'orders of worth' (Boltanski and Thévenot 2006) able to be actively engaged with and navigated by the consumer. For this reason, NBMs tend to be more complex and challenging than an 'efficient search and shopping' model would suggest. This is the difference between a boutique store and a supermarket (where the former is not necessarily designed for ease of use), or between a fashion magazine such as *Vogue* and a mail-order catalogue (where the former is not necessarily intended for ease of search). This additional complexity serves a purpose, as we will see later when we consider how NMBs promote deliberate contexts of dissonance to provide effective contexts for creative discovery and evaluation of worth.

Fourth, consumers participate in NBMs not only for the filtered choice set but also for both the social opportunities afforded and to exploit the generative possibilities this harnesses. NBMs are social spaces as well as market spaces. This is of particular salience because of the ambiguity, uncertainty and multiplicity of evaluative judgements that are commonly required over novel goods. An organized and inviting social context facilitates such local feedback mechanisms that are often instrumental to such consumption opportunities. Clearly, not all markets involving novel goods require strong forms of social feedback. In markets for new construction materials, for example, or industrial polymers, technical functionality requirements and price considerations dominate. But where novel goods do present in multiple registers of worth (economic, cultural, political, industrial, civic, spiritual, and so on; Boltanski and Thévenot 2006) and thus where value criteria are themselves part of what must be chosen, the social space of a NBM becomes a critical part of the value that is created.

14.3   DEMAND FOR BUNDLING MARKETS

We have already considered the demand for novelty and we now turn to the specific demand for the particular organizational and institutional form of 'bundling markets'. The following factors are suggested to differentiate individual novelty experiences from multiple or bundled novelty experiences.

First, a multiple or bundled novelty context differs from single novelty by reframing the experience from a search context that will likely be focused on in terms of downside risk of failure (or loss aversion), due to the binary nature of the search being either successful or not, to a context in which failure is actually expected, in the sense that some and perhaps many of the novelties bundled will not be desired. Yet this is expected before the experience and is not a salient focus. Instead, focus shifts to the prospect of good, useful or interesting novelties, thus reframing the context to an upside rather than downside focus. This reframing or shift in focus is well known in behavioural and experimental psychology and provides a plausible mechanism to explain the demand for multiple bundled novelties where this same set experienced in a disaggregated sequential context would be less valued. Novelty bundling shifts the risk function from downside loss aversion (a powerful behavioural inhibitor) to one that already expects that loss and has discounted it, so that it no longer functions as a behavioural inhibitor, allowing attention to be refocused on the possibility of discovery. This reframing of the experience of novelty is suggested as a cognitive mechanism to explain the superiority of bundled novelties over sequential single novelties.

Second, the search and information acquisition and processing costs associated with novelty will have fixed and variable cost aspects. Novelty bundling allows the fixed cost (associated perhaps with organizing time to think about the novelty or travel and opportunity costs to experience it) to be spread over a larger number of novelties, thus lowering the marginal cost of each novelty experience. This induces a higher quantity of consumption, in turn increasing the likelihood of discovery of novelties for adoption. Bundling distributes fixed costs more widely, lowering the marginal cost of each novelty experience and increasing the demand for novel experiences.

Third, novelty bundling markets enable consumers to access the specialized selection services of the experts who assemble the bundle (for example the editors of a fashion magazine, or the producer of a music festival) – services that they would not be able to afford in respect of an individual choice over a specific novelty. That this quasi consultancy service is also accessed by many others does not necessarily diminish the value of that access to expertise. This induces the emergent possibility of market-based outsourcing of initial selection over an abundance of novelties to experts or specialists in a way that few individual consumers would normally find feasible. Multiple novelties thus facilitate a greater division of labour in the novelty selection process, offering a direct consumer benefit (consumer surplus, in the language of neoclassical demand theory). Consumers of novelty in a bundling market will be presented with a greater range of viable options, including many they had not considered before due to their limited knowledge of the full range of possibilities. These options are known to specialists and experts who would commonly be prohibitively expensive for any individual to contract for advice on selection of an individual novelty experience. The value of the expert selected bundle lies less with high profile novelties, which may already be well known to the consumers, but rather with those on the periphery that may now enter due to the imprimatur of expert suggestion. Thus while nominally offering a reduced form of selection, novelty bundling markets may simultaneously widen the space of novelty selection, legitimating solutions not previously entertained. This may thus improve the efficiency of novelty consumption.

Fourth, novelty bundling markets are commonly socially consumed experience goods (Hutter, forthcoming). This brings the consumer of novelty into contact with other consumers of novelty, facilitating the exchange of information, rules for choice, frameworks for understanding, and possibly the positive externality of acquired social connections and access to social networks that would be more costly to assess and access in the context of individual novelty search. This acquired social network capital acts in effect to cross-subsidize the fixed costs of the novelty search and is revealed in the simple willingness to pay of consumers to enter such markets.

A fifth point concerns the nature of the bundle assembled in an NBM. These do not necessarily or even generally map to producer definitions of markets (for example for every X industry there is an associated X NBM), nor to consumer definitions of search problems (I'm searching for X, so I'll go to the X NBM). Rather, each NBM is an entrepreneurial conjecture by the NBM agent as to what novelties go together. These may not be from the same market *per se*. This can be seen in the case of fashion magazines and new technology magazines, which bundle together an often significant variety of sources of novelty into a single bundle. Similarly music festivals often mix very different genres of performance, along with things having at first sight little to do with new music (such as new political ideas, or new social technologies). So the bundles are very much more than just 'what's new' catalogues of a particular industry's latest output, but rather are conjectures of what novelties fit together in interesting and valuable ways that will often be drawn from many different sources. Note that the focus here is on solving consumer problems (and not in representing producer output) and that NBMs compete with each other by the extent to which consumers come to trust and rely on the complex bundles they assemble. This is why NBMs are both infinitely contestable, in the sense of the myriad of permutations of possible bundles that may be assembled, but also monopolistically competitive, in the sense of the futility of an exact imitation of another NBM.

By these factors alone we may appreciate that there is reason to expect that multiple novelties (that is, bundles) offer a superior consumer experience to singular novelties, and that the added value here will induce entrepreneurial supply of such novelty bundling markets. We now turn to consider specific economic and sociological analysis of NBMs. We will see that different economic frameworks offer rather different explanations for their nature and existence and that a critical analytical insight issues from economic sociology.

14.4 ANALYSIS OF NOVELTY BUNDLING MARKETS

Microeconomics of Novelty Bundling Markets

A standard microeconomic account of the existence of an NBM turns on the presumption of market failure or imperfect competition. This would assume that an NBM can exist where it is able to exclude competition to capture rents through various means. How might this happen? Perhaps the agents of the NBM may have preferential access to a key resource, for example a festival site, or to artistic talent, or to a distribution channel. By exclusive control over this key resource, an NBM may exclude both direct access to producers as well as competition in bundling markets, and thus function as a monopolist. A further account of imperfect competition may be due to reputation or brand capital (as a result of accumulated investment, say) that new entrants may find very difficult to compete with. Longstanding festivals or widely known fashion brands are suitable examples. By capturing key resources or creating exclusive assets on the supply side, an NBM may provide consumers with a monopolized or otherwise imperfectly competitive access to a particular novelty. The NBM agent thus exists to create and capture consumer rents. The standard policy response to such market failure would therefore be to regulate the NBM. This may involve for example limiting the prices it can charge (as in festivals), or legislating shared access to channels of distribution or sites of access, or in seeking antitrust action against monopoly brands and seeking to limit their holdings.

Note that the standard microeconomic approach has nothing to say about the consumer side; indeed, the imperfect competition hypothesis presumes that NBMs exist to capture consumer rents and that there is no consumer value to their existence. This is because of the assumption that more choice is always preferred to less, hence bundling or any other choice reduction mechanism is implicitly harmful to consumer interests. Underpinning this is a critical assumption about novelty: by treating any new good as 'just another good' there is no prima facie reason to suppose that the particular situation of abundant novelty ever presents a consumer problem. Note also that the standard microeconomic framework assumes that new goods arrive 'fully labelled' as it were; they are unambiguous as to their functional value as defined by producers and their expected value as they interact with consumer preferences. Complementary and substitution relations to other goods are assumed to be well defined and marginal utility will have a clear expected value that maps to price. In essence, there is no consumer choice problem, only the risk of producer rent-seeking. The novel good is most definitely not socially constructed, and NBMs cannot by definition add to consumer value (but only subtract from consumer surplus as NBM-captured rents). Each individual consumer has no role for other consumers in figuring out what the new good is, what it means, what its value is, and whether or not it is worth experiencing.

The upshot of this hypothetical standard economic analysis of NBMs is as a form of imperfect competition that subtracts from consumer surplus. Consumers have no need for them, and enter only when better alternatives are foreclosed. The incomes of NBM agents are rents, not entrepreneurial profits. While I want to argue that in general this is wrong, there are of course certain instances where this analysis is useful. This occurs where NBMs are subject to regulatory capture (some festivals, for example) or sustained first-mover advantages that lock in critical inputs or complementary resources (for example exclusivity contracts, preferential access to sites, ownership of critical distribution channels or licences, and so on). This opens a path to a welfare-theoretic and public choice analysis of NBMs. This formulation allows us to run NBMs through standard analytic set pieces in applied microeconomics, yet that does not imply that these are *ipso facto* important analytic concerns. The limit is that this formulation implicitly sets the problem up as a supply-side problem. But our framing intuition is that the interesting questions are instead on the demand side. So how do we arrive at an economic analysis of the consumer side of NBMs?

Departures from the model of imperfect competition begin when we introduce bounded rationality. This means that search is no longer a free good and that agents are not assumed to already possess effective rules for choice over the domains of novelty they encounter. This affects the consumer side because, now, each additional novelty imposes a further cost to learning about the expected and experiential value of the good. Novelty abundance no longer simply means a larger commodity space but is now manifestly a problem, and a direct cost, for the consumer who must survey and evaluate that larger space. Obviously, one way to avoid this cost is simply not to engage with any novelty. With unknown expected values (maybe they are all negative, for example) consumer disengagement and retreat is a legitimate and indeed common option. Novelty bundling markets can thus offer consumers pathways into this space, potentially bringing them back into the market and thus facilitating innovation.

By assuming bounded rationality we can explain the existence of NBMs without reference to imperfect competition. The rationale of NBMs is due to the value-added to consumers (not to producers) by filtering abundant novelty down to a reduced set of high average quality novelty that is less risky and costly for consumers than any attempt they might otherwise make to sample from the unfiltered and mass flow themselves. From the consumer perspective, an NBM is thus an extension of the production process that operates at the market level rather than that of the individual firm or novelty producer. Introducing bounded rationality does not negate the prospect of imperfect competition where there is monopolized access to key input resources, but it does however suggest a very different explanation of branding or reputational capital. Rather than viewing these as further mechanisms of rent extraction, branding and reputational capital now function as 'information shorthand' for consumers, signalling the particular attributes of particular bundles. Brands (including branded bundles) in other words are not further instances of imperfect competition (specifically monopolistic competition) but rather add value for consumers by further simplifying their search and choice process (Earl 2002). That all NBMs are observed to be heavily branded is thus neither an incidental nor accidental aspect of their function but is instead integral to the way in which they create value for consumers.

Evolutionary Economics of Novelty Bundling Markets

An evolutionary approach to NBMs builds on the behavioural approach, but shifts the focus from a simple 'lowering of the costs of search' explanation to an unpacking of how it does this in terms of decision rules and their evolution in a market space. This process is driven by entrepreneurial agents. This seeks to explain the emergence of an NBM as a result of entrepreneurial behaviour of increasingly specialized consumers, or increasingly diverse producers, moving further into bundling and distribution niches. An evolutionary economic analysis of NBMs seeks to trace the pathways of their emergence and development from an initial state of abundant production of novelty and the varieties of consumer experience in facing this abundant novelty.

The hypothesis I propose is that NBMs are (most often) an evolutionary consequence of consumer specialization with feedback as expert consumers turn from amateur to professional with the entrepreneurial adoption of business models to create and occupy a new intermediating market space. The rationale for this is in part attributable to the previous explanation of the prospect of producer rents and the creation of consumer value-added (as profit). NBMs are thus explained as entrepreneurial conjectures about the value of particular combinations of novelty and particular organizational forms of presenting this. They will succeed and replicate, drawing imitation, or fail and exit by open-market selection processes. If NBMs exist, it is because they add value for consumers, and the particular form in which they exist tells us what value they add.

An evolutionary account of an NBM can be stylized as follows. In the beginning there are many consumers facing an abundant flow of novelty. Because of heterogeneity in taste and experience, some consumers soon become better than others at making good choices over this domain. These are the emerging experts that while still amateur are nevertheless distinguished from peers by demonstrated success and emergent recognition in a socially competitive context. The motive driving this emergent specialization at this stage need not be due to financial incentives. The social competition hypothesis may underpin this, as too may intrinsic motivations with respect to aesthetic enjoyment, hobbies, social or reputational status, or the expression of native talent in the construction of such consumption as an art form. But whatever the motivating factor, other consumers in turn will come to notice this expertise and the choices it involves and, for bounded rationality reasons, they will begin to orient their own choices with respect to the choices made by these emerging specialists. This gives rise to a social network market (Potts et al. 2008a). The next step is the entrepreneurial decision by the amateur but specialized consumer to turn professional by developing a business model about their specialized niche and extant reputation.

Thus a novelty bundling market emerges from a social network market fitted with a business model attached to a particular reputation and expressed as a market offering. Consumers of novelty are free to choose whether to delimit their choices to those suggested by the NBM, and producers of novelty are free to solicit the brokerage of the NBM as an indirect channel to consumers. What particular configurations of NBM will be successful cannot be known in advance but will be revealed by market experimentation and consumer selection. NBMs thus emerge out of consumer specialization, perhaps beginning with an enthusiastic, loyal or even cult following. They emerge as intermediaries into an open market ecology with reputational capital and connection to consumers already established, making these agents attractive channels for novelty producers, who would otherwise seek to make these connections themselves but without operating from a position of credibility. Both producers and consumers of novelty can potentially gain from their existence.

What we also observe is that the 'professional consumers' who enter this space are not entering a predefined latent space of NBMs. This was a tacit assumption in the neoclassical and behavioural models above, where there was a predefined opportunity for rent extraction and a predefined opportunity for reducing consumer search costs. Rather, from the evolutionary perspective, the emergent NBMs are creating and occupying a new market space that previously did not exist but instead represents a value conjecture about particular configurations of novelty and ways of organizing and presenting it. NBMs are suggested by the attention that specialist amateur consumers may receive and in turn recognize, but the emergence of an NBM is then an entrepreneurial conjecture about how to create temporary or sustained profits by creating a new and specific organizational form that bundles particular novelties in particular ways. This may of course then attract imitators who seek to occupy slightly different points in this dynamic market ecology. This will give rise to the emergence of monopolistic competition in NBM space. Thus NBMs evolve.

Formally considered, the first professional consumer establishes a monopoly position that will eventually tend towards a competitive state as imitators of the strategy enter the niche. Yet this is a somewhat misleading description of the emergence and evolution of a NBM because exact imitation is largely impossible (remember, we are dealing with novelty bundling, not commodity bundling). What is instead occurring is the development and unfolding of new market niches, enabling and facilitating further specialization on both consumer and producer sides. So where does this end? In an important sense, there is no end to this process and no final equilibrium. Some NBMs will continue to evolve into more general arbiters of taste and increasingly to function as gatekeepers of new ideas. This will commonly occur as reputation is increasingly developed and leveraged. Others will increasingly specialize in particular niches, while others may exit. While this is happening, new amateur consumers may develop their skills and turn professional to contest the market space. It may happen that a domain of novelty production expands, supplying an ever richer market ecology of NBMs. Or the domain may normalize, devaluing the contribution of NBMs. Or the domain may cease to produce a sufficiently abundant flow of novelty, rendering little value to be added by NBMs. NBMs may thus unfold as a rich and flourishing ecology, or they may collapse. These are, after all, derivative markets; if there is reduced flow of novelty, or reduced problems for consumers in processing it, they will cease to provide functional value. For example, consider the current difficulties faced by packaged holiday tour bundlers, who had more monopolistic power prior to the advent of internet search facilities that enable consumers to search, evaluate and bundle holidays themselves. Previously it was difficult for consumers to assemble these, or even to know what options were available, due to the abundance of new possibilities. This is an instance of a once-successful NBM that is now a less rich ecology. Yet within this, for example in relation to high-end adventure tours focusing on unique experiences, a new NBM has emerged and is flourishing.

Novelty bundling markets are not an industry *per se*, as a distinct and stable subset of economic production. Rather they are an evolutionary outcome that emerges under certain conditions associated with sufficient producer flows of novelty and consumer problems in dealing with these. They are a feature of an evolving economy. An evolutionary economic analysis emphasizes how NBMs create further opportunities for producers and consumers by furnishing not just a selected bundle of novelty but, as importantly, in furnishing rules for choice for consumers facing such novelty (Earl and Potts 2004), thus enabling individual consumers to develop more sophisticated choices over this domain. Novelty bundling markets thus facilitate an increase in the complexity of consumers' choices, thus driving preference evolution. The effect of NBMs is thus not neutral on the forward development of other markets, as the very existence of an NBM shapes consumer preferences – indeed, its ability and consequence in doing so is a basic test of whether any hypothesized intermediary is an NBM or simply a retail aggregation: if preferences are not affected, then it is not an NBM.

Thus NBMs shape the pathways of economic evolution, just as do new technologies and other business models. But NBMs do so specifically by their effect on consumer preferences, effectively enabling them to attain a higher degree of complexity than would otherwise be possible. Thus unlike the neoclassical account, which views NBMs as rent extractions, or even the bounded rationality account which saw NBMs as efficiency improvements, an evolutionary account emphasizes that NBMs actually change the underlying structure of preferences in an economic order. If so, this will feed back to producers who may now also increase the complexity of their creative offerings (see Chapter 5 above), thus further fuelling the process of economic evolution. Novelty bundling markets may thus be understood as a further mechanism within the creative industries (in significant part) for driving economic evolution and the innovation process.

Economic Sociology of Novelty Bundling Markets

From the perspective of an evolutionary economics of creative industries, that would seem to be the end of the analytic story, namely novelty bundling markets are also drivers of economic evolution on the demand side by facilitating the uptake of creativity. But there remain some unanswered questions: particularly with respect to why NBMs have the particular characteristic forms they do, tending to be smallish, boutique, niche-orientated and often confronting or challenging to mainstream consumer sensibilities. Not everyone will be comfortable at Glastonbury. Not everyone will be *au fait* with the ideas pitched by certain think tanks. Not everyone can enter a boutique fashion store and confidently consume. All examples of NBMs I have suggested are somewhat elite or challenging consumption environments, inviting a certain measure of consumer courage to enter and an expectation of a certain frisson in experience. Why? Our economic analysis has shed no light on this overarching aspect. For this, we turn to economic sociology.

What can economic sociology add to our economic explanations of NBMs? The obvious answer is an elaboration of the social dimension of novelty choice. This is legitimate from the behavioural economic introduction of bounded rationality that drove agents to look to others for useful information as an input to choice. Social network markets are of course social as well as network markets, so some unpacking of this social aspect would surely help. And the evolutionary account turned on a social transformation from amateur to professional consumer. It seems obvious that an economic sociology can build on the economic foundations of novelty bundling market analysis to elaborate and refine these identified mechanisms and processes. Both cases offer space for an economic sociological account of how the social is constructed in social network markets or how social structures facilitate the transformation from amateur to professional consumers (see Chapter 6 above). But I want to argue a different line in which an economic sociology account returns to the original question of what an NBM is and what value it adds. From the economic sociology perspective, what is a novelty bundling market?

Economic sociology is a branch of modern sociology that has developed over several distinct yet overlapping schools of thought. There is an institutional approach, a social network approach, and an organizational ecology approach (in overview, see Swedberg 2007). The approach

I pursue here draws on a recent contribution by Columbia University economic sociologist David Stark, drawing in particular on his *Sense of Dissonance: Accounts of worth in economic life* (2009), in which Stark builds on Boltanski and Thévenot's (2006) *On Justification: The economies of worth*.[2] Stark proposes a new definition of entrepreneurship in heterarchical organizations based on the dissonance or frictions of multiple evaluative criteria of worth: 'Entrepreneurship is the ability to keep multiple evaluative principles in play and to exploit the resulting friction of their interplay' (Stark 2009: 15). Stark conducts ethnographic analysis of organizational contexts in three situations of organizational heterarchy (a socialist factory, a new media start-up and an arbitrage trading room), in each case finding that the key drivers of entrepreneurial discovery are the tensions and frictions or the dissonance created by the interplay of different evaluative criteria of worth.

Stark offers an account of how such spatially and structurally organized dissonance, which is often but not always deliberately engineered, can contribute to the discovery and realization of entrepreneurial opportunities. He models this with the concept of 'structural folds' (Balazs and Stark 2010), contrasting it with Ronald Burt's (1995) entrepreneurial brokerage concept of 'structural holes'. Stark's analysis of knowledge creation in three different heterarchical contexts is offered as a new framework for the study of entrepreneurship and innovation in organizations. But the underlying theoretical idea and insight of Stark's structural folds analysis as spaces of overlapping, diverse and ultimately dissonance-creating evaluative criteria of worth can, I suggest, be extended to account for the value created by novelty bundling markets. Where Stark focuses on producer organization for knowledge creation by exploiting 'the ability to keep multiple evaluative criteria in play', we may recognize that a similar generative entrepreneurial process may also be at work on the consumer side, and particularly in the context of consumer adoption of novelty as a space of entrepreneurial knowledge creation.

Novelty bundling markets would seem to be paradigmatic instances of 'structural folds'. They are institutional spaces characterized by deep uncertainty in which multiple evaluative criteria of worth intersect and are socially processed about an endeavour to figure out what counts, and to assess what values and criteria of value are relevantly applied (see also Karpik 2010). As testimony to this, it is rare in a novelty bundling market that a particular offering is singled out and valorized as to its obvious choice context. Novelty bundling markets don't tend to do this. Rather NBMs work best and are seemingly most viable and valuable when they perform the more equivocal task of presenting and organizing multiple novelties across a well-constructed 'structural fold'; in effect deliberately creating tensions and frictions and contrasting criteria (sometimes subtly, sometimes forcefully) of evaluative worth in which entrepreneurial consumers can meet with ambiguous possibilities and possibly arrive at consumption choices that will work as strategic plays in further rounds of social competition.

The result is a social space in which such measures of value can be explored and revealed, and in which consumer entrepreneurial action can therefore flourish. Searching consumers, who already know what they want, will therefore by definition have no need for NBMs; they will be frustrated by their complexity and forced engagement and find them wasteful in their deliberate inefficiencies. But for consumers who are searching for things they don't yet understand, these heterarchic forms and structural folds in NBMs highlight differences like those between pulp fiction and avant garde literature, or Hollywood and art-house cinema: the challenge is the point, when deliberately designed to lead you to a place that you would not otherwise easily go by your own evaluative criteria. NBMs are thus sites of consumer entrepreneurship by way of creating complex spaces (structural folds) that enable consumers to engage with novelty and to process it in a complex social space where other consumers are similarly attempting to do so (see also Moeran and Strandgaard, forthcoming, who touch on this same theme). Obviously, this requires constraints and boundaries, which is what NBM agents furnish, selecting this particular set of novelties and arranging them in this particular organizational form.

Stark's framework of organizational dissonance as the mechanism underpinning how creative friction yields organizational reflexivity thus suggests a model of entrepreneurship that may be further extended to consumer choice over novelty. Moreover, this offers a compelling explanation for the emergence and properties of novelty bundling markets that intermediate the production and consumption of novelty. The dissonance model of overlapping and conflicting accounts of worth explains why it is a 'bundling' market in the first place: why consumer choice and adoption is facilitated by the creation of a structured environment of multiple novelties.

Furthermore, Stark's model explains the entrepreneurial content of novelty bundling markets. This has two aspects: first in the entrepreneurial role of the expert 'bundler' of novelty who both filters the abundant flows of novelty as a select set and organizes the experience of this in particular ways; and second, in the consumer who enters as an entrepreneurial agent, not passively consuming from a commodified set but as engaged in a complex process of navigating the tensions and dissonance in the different orders of worth that are set up in the novelty bundling market. Consumers are not just consuming another good (as in the neoclassical explanation), but are engaged by the specific organization of the novelty bundling market in 'reconstructions of the self' (that is, identity dynamics, Hermann-Pillath 2010) through their novel choices. NBMs are a space that creates an 'ecology of knowledge' of evaluative principles in which multiple and potentially conflicting evaluative principles and criteria of worth are in play and are entrepreneurially resolved (Stark 2009: 142).

The efficacy of novelty bundling markets does not turn on an efficient filtering of novelty, as the standard microeconomic explanation would have it, but rather in their ability to create organized spaces in which novelty with multiple registers of worth can enter and be effectively evaluated by the tensioned social interaction of agents with differing criteria and perspectives on that worth. In this way, abundant flows of novelty are transformed by the social interactions interior to novelty bundling markets into assessments of newness and value. NBMs do not cause economic evolution, in that they are not creative generators *per se*, they facilitate and ultimately shape the uptake of novelty by resolving multiple criteria of worth into singular assessments of value.

14.5 CONCLUSION

A novelty bundling market is an extension of the concept of a social network market to incorporate two further special conditions: (1) multiple novelties experienced at once in a context of search where consumers don't necessarily know what they're looking for but know it when they find it; and (2) an emergent market form that intermediates between producers and consumers of novelty. This intermediating form is typically the product of amateur (but expert) consumers turned professional. This may seem a rather minor subset of the broader economy, perhaps barely worth the designation of a special class of market. I am certainly not arguing here that arts and music festivals, eisteddfods, fashion and technology magazines, blogs and think tanks, among other instances of NBMs, constitute in any sense a 'significant' part of total economic activity, jobs, exports, and so on. I'm certainly not making a new creative industries case here. But I have sought to draw out the implications of several stylized observations on novelty and innovation in the creative industries and to connect this to a generalized analytic framework. These points are salient because in many respects they are the almost exact opposite of standard assumptions of innovation theory that are realized by a consumer focus on the problem of innovation.

The first was the supposition of abundant novelty. This is the opposite assumption to most innovation studies where new ideas are scarce and valuable things that are the product of significant investment. But in the context of art, music, fashion and intellectual ideas, for example, the consumer experience is closer to a regular downpour of novelty. The 'novelty problem' is not that of incentivizing production but rather that of dealing with its abundance. NBMs thus address the consumer problem of novelty abundance.

A second aspect is the consumer problem of search amidst such abundant novelty. Consumers will not necessarily know what they are looking for, although they may recognize it when they find it. Compounding this problem is that such novelties often present in multiple registers of value, making novelty difficult to evaluate individually and in isolation. NBMs facilitate the resolution of this problem by bundling novelties and preparing a context of comparative choice that is often built into the organizational or spatial composition of the bundle (for example in the program, the lay-out, and so on). Furthermore, NBMs are often highly social spaces that facilitate the sorts of interactions that bring the multiple evaluative criteria of value or worth to a level of consumer engagement. Unlike 'standard' consumer markets that aim to minimize transactions costs in shopping, NBMs commonly deliberately induce frictions, tensions and sources of dissonance into the market experience in order to provide the generative edge that enables consumers to engage with the novel goods in an entrepreneurial manner, and to discover their own sense of value and worth within.

Novelty bundling markets are important not because they are a significant part of the economy. Rather, the particular context and needs they serve – abundant novelty, the sort of search beyond the capabilities of search engines, novelty in multiple registers of value and with multiple criteria of worth – are all contexts that we can expect to become more common in an evolving economy in which the service economy and the experience economy continue to grow as an increasingly dominant share of economic activity.

Epilogue

I have thus far not sought to locate novelty bundling markets in historical context, or to ask what ancestral forms they might have developed from. While we may certainly trace back fairs and festivals, as well as fashion magazines and other such media, I nevertheless suggest that these are not necessarily the most pertinent historical origins. Rather, following Hayek (1960, Chapter 3) I would draw attention to the role of social inequality and those at the forefront of knowledge and wealth in any social milieu. The place of NBMs in pre-capitalist and early capitalist times was not in magazines or festivals, but rather among a wealthy, leisured class of agents engaged in intense social competition that played out over novelty consumption. This was infamously satirized by Veblen (1899) and others, but maybe Veblen (and subsequent sociologists) missed a key point here, viewing this behaviour through the lens of class, rather than noting its contribution to innovation (on the demand side). Novelty bundling markets are in many respects this same thing, but because of the enormous growth in material standards of living and wealth and its distribution through economic society, they are now open to far more consumers than ever before (that is, not only the idle rich choosing between yachts).

NOTES

1. This also predicts that those most engaged in NBMs will be those who are new entrants to the game of social competition (e.g. the young), or those who have been less successful in previous rounds (e.g. those seeking to 'reinvent themselves' for whatever reason.)
2. They elaborate a sociological theory of value framework of six 'orders of worth' — civic, market, inspired, fame, industrial and domestic — that applies in all calculative economic situations.

15. Creative industries and economic development

Prolegomena

This chapter arose from projects on cultural and creative industries in developing nations (including China and Papua New Guinea). The question was whether creative industries as a policy framework applies only to advanced nations. I present the case here that from the evolutionary/ adaptation perspective, creative industries may actually be more important in the process of economic development than as a driver of economic growth.

15.1 INTRODUCTION

Economic growth is the increase in gross domestic product or some market-based measure of economic output. Economic development is a broader topic by its additional concern with the social, cultural, industrial and institutional conditions underlying the economic progress of a nation, thus referring to a broader composite of indicators that also include factors such as poverty, sanitation, literacy and education, unemployment, underground economy and income distribution, along with other political, social and environmental indicators. Growth theory concerns the dynamics of an economy, and development theory concerns the dynamics of a socio-political–cultural–environmental economic order.

Apart from greater attention to welfare, structural and institutional factors in development theory, a further distinction is that where economic growth theory is largely a positive analysis, development economics has a strong normative and teleological dimension relating to the scope for public, government or non-governmental intervention. Development theory focuses on the institutional changes in socio-cultural, legal and political as well as economic institutions to promote goals of economic development. The significance of this to creative industries is that many of the received notions of industry significance and policy frameworks currently being advanced derive from a development economics mode of thinking and analysis, with their implicit emphasis on: (a) broader socio-cultural objectives than just economic growth in value-added; (b) a sense that different industries are more or less important at different 'stages of economic development'; and (c) that government intervention in this process can help (Oakley 2004). It will be useful, therefore, to begin with a brief review of the theory of economic development.

15.2   THEORY OF ECONOMIC DEVELOPMENT

Economic development theory recognizes that economic growth is not simply an expansion of economic activity driven by capital accumulation and new technology (as in neoclassical growth models), but involves change in the institutions that coordinate the economy, along with structural change in the composition of economic activities. This work was largely motivated by realization of the extent to which the socio-cultural and institutional conditions of less-developed nations differed from those of more-developed nations. Implicit in development theory is an evolutionary hierarchy through which nations can be ranked in terms of their current stage of development.

Early development theory was proposed by economic historians, notably Alex Gerschenkron and Walt Rostow, in terms of five stages of development that countries pass through to modernity: (1) traditional society; (2) pre-take-off; (3) take-off; (4) drive to maturity; and (5) high mass consumption. This line of analysis connected to statistical work on the composition of economic activities pioneered by Colin Clark and Simon Kuznets, who emphasized the relative distribution of economic activities between primary (agriculture and extractive industries), secondary (manufacturing) and tertiary industries (the service sector).[1] Chenery (1975) developed a structural change model to represent the 'sequential process through which the economic, industrial and institutional structure of an underdeveloped economy is transformed over time to permit new industries to replace traditional agriculture as the engine of economic growth'. A key idea is the notion of objective phases of industrialization through which countries pass as they 'climb the ladder' of economic development. This is associated with stations marked by the adoption of more advanced institutions and changed industrial structures along the way.

A traditional (autarkic) society enters the path to modern institutions by developing its agricultural base and deploying its surplus to invest in other sectors. Primary industries will thus dominate a less-developed nation, but this will reduce as a share of economic activity as manufacturing begins to rise. This requires a shift from rural to urban production and from a simple trading economy to investment in capital equipment. The education system, labour market and financial markets must then adapt appropriately. Countries proceed at different speeds along this path, even backwards if afflicted by events such as war or rogue governance. The logic of how primary industries provide the surplus for the development of secondary industries and so on means that all development roads follow the same path. There is no possibility of leaping ahead. Further along this path of development a similar process happens again, but this time with manufacturing declining as a share of economic activity and the service sector rising as the major source of value added, employment and exports. Daniel Bell (1973) labelled this phase the post-industrial economy, in which industries such as tourism, finance and creative industries now fit as the leading edge. Various models have more recently been proposed about what comes after these stages, including the notions of an *experience economy* at the higher reaches of the post-industrial service-based economy (Pine and Gilmour 1999, Sundbo and Darmer 2008).

An implication of the sequential model is that development can be planned by government. Indeed, the case was often made more strongly: namely that development is a process *best* planned by a strong central government. By implication, market forces were not widely regarded as significant mechanisms in the coordination of economic development and were often seen as structural problems to be overcome through regulations, price controls, tariffs and other instruments. This led to a significant focus on government-led development processes in much of Eastern Europe, Asia and Africa in the post-colonial era. These are now widely regarded to have been abject failures (Easterly 2002).

Modern development economics has mostly jettisoned command and control models in favour of market-based approaches to economic development, in which the mix of economic activities and therefore patterns of trade and structures of industries emerge through market-based trial and error. Amartya Sen (1999a) and Deepak Lal (1998) provide comprehensive statements of this new conception of economic development and its connection to the market order. Although economic development remains a complex, contingent and emergent process, fewer development economists accept the notion that development is a serial, sequential process that can be managed by government leadership and intervention. Indeed, 'public choice' economics reverses this statement to argue that government intervention actively retards the process of economic development.

This profound shift in economic development theory over the past 30 or so years has immediate bearing on thinking about the creative industries, both in the current context of developing nations such as India or China, and also in relation to the role of government in fostering these industries in developed nations such as the UK or Australia. It will thus be instructive to unpack the meaning of an industry, the relation of different industries to each other, and their relation to the process of economic development.

15.3   INDUSTRIES

The concept of an industry is neither as clear nor as obvious as is commonly supposed. The core problem is that industries do not actually exist but are an artifact of classification.[2] What do exist are firms, markets, commodities, technologies, producers and consumers (see Chapter 8). An industry is a way of classifying sets of related economic activities associated with specific commodities, technologies or markets.[3] These are usually taken to refer to the activities of a set (or ecology) of firms engaged in the production of these commodities or that are cooperating or competing in the same markets. This set of firms composes the industry supply schedule.

The concept of an industry is useful for analysing macroeconomic governance, as it offers a convenient framework for decomposing the supply side of the economy into a set of identifiable components (the industries). This provides a basis for monitoring the relative performance of each industry and developing strategies and programs to influence their production. The concept of an industry (in this 'national accounts' sense) provides a model for conceptualizing and measuring the activities of a large number of individual firms variously engaged in cooperation and competition as if they were just one big firm. Indeed, this concept was developed as a tool for planning and managing a socialist economy – via the use of input–output tables that track the flow of goods between industrial sectors – and not for operational use in a market-capitalism economic order. This distinction between the socialist planning (industrial policy) sense of an industry and the concept of an industry in an evolving market-capitalist economic order has caused much confusion about the industrial nature of the economic order.

First, there is no ideal set of industries that each nation should aspire to, nor are there ideal proportions between sets. The optimal set of industries for each nation depends upon the prevailing vector of prices for inputs and outputs; on the relative abundance of resources and the set of capabilities of each nation; on the transaction costs of coordinating production and moving goods about; on the regulatory, political and environmental conditions of each nation; and on the choices made by other nations in their matrix of economic activities. There is no ideal level of primary industries or manufacturing industries for that matter, irrespective of whether a nation is developing or developed. The distribution of industries and the patterns of international trade depend on the distribution of resources (of all kinds) and prevailing relative prices. Economists have long understood this, yet they perpetually run up against arguments decreeing that an economy must develop a manufacturing base, or must develop a strategic industry X, where X can be anything at all. Any argument that 'economy Y must develop industry X for the sake of economic development' is bad economic logic. Instead, this is invariably social, cultural or even environmental policy masquerading as economic policy. Kate Oakley (2006) has written about this effect in recent creative industries policy in the UK.

Second, there is no intrinsic ranking of industries from most to least important by any measure other than value added, which will constantly change under competitive pressure (Rodrik 2007). There is of course a panoply of possible measures of industrial significance that further include employment, exports, location in a network of other industries, security, and so on. And while these factors may all have socio-cultural or political significance, they have little economic significance. It is important to be clear about this because of the fallacies that result when we are not. The notion that the steel industry, for example, is intrinsically more important than the video-games industry is wrong on *a priori* grounds. This may well be true *a posteriori* when value added is compared, but the notion that some industries are inherently 'more important' than others has no basis in economic logic (other than in a purely autarkic economy). This is of particular significance to the creative industries (and the service industries in general) owing to the widespread but manifestly false presumption that primary or manufacturing industries are inherently more important and deserving of special policy attention.

Third, there is no universally optimal set of industries or an *a priori* invariant ranking of industry significance. The set of industries in an economy continuously evolves. Industries, like species in the Darwinian framework, are not fixed and immutable categories of economic activity. Rather, they emerge, grow, fragment, become embedded or go extinct. Industries are rarely static but always growing or shrinking in their relative significance in the industrial population (Metcalfe 1998). The key implication is that static measures of significance, such as the relative share of value added, are less interesting than dynamic measures of relative growth rates (including negative growth). So although there has been much effort to measure the 'economic significance' of the creative industries through the myriad of mapping documents (starting with DCMS 1998), there remains little economic theory justification for doing so (other than as a way to get at estimates of relative growth rates). That does not mean that growth and development just happen, such that there is no point either way in inquiring about particular technologies or industries, but rather that this is ultimately analysis of a matrix of economic variables not of timeless parameters. Different industries will be differentially important in promoting growth at different stages of each economy's history.

Still, it is important to distinguish between the creation of new wealth and the maintenance of existing wealth. Agriculture, for example, was a major driver of economic growth in Australia from colonial times through to the 1960s. It has since shrunk significantly as a percentage of economic activity (although it continues to grow in absolute terms). But that most emphatically does not mean that it is no longer a source of wealth and no longer 'important'; rather, in absolute terms, it has never produced more. This industry has achieved sustained productivity growth and is now able to produce ever greater output with fewer and fewer inputs, and that's a good thing. For Australians to feed themselves (and others too) now requires only 3 per cent of the workforce, not 40 per cent as earlier. Note the implication: as a simple matter of accounting, the growth of the service sector (including the creative industries) is only possible *because* of the increased productivity (or relative decline as a percentage of economic activity) of primary and secondary industries. The same is true of manufacturing, where job losses and relative decline in the share of economic output are a reflection of its success in productivity improvement, not evidence of being a drag on the economy or of increasing insignificance to modern wealth. We need to look deeper into the ways an industry adds value across the entire economy to assess its significance to economic growth. Industries are far more complex, protean and dynamic structures and systems than is often conventionally represented.

This point goes to the heart of the difficulty of defining the 'creative industries' in any static industrial framework. This in turn underscores the line developed in this book of the role of creative industries in the process of economic evolution, which is ultimately an evolution of industries, and of institutions too (as below). That is how creative industries link to economic development.

15.4   INSTITUTIONS

Modern economic growth and development theory highlights the significance of institutions. This is not surprising, as institutions refer to the 'coordination technology' that connects individual behaviour to the social context. Institutions have several definitions in economic theory. Veblen (1919: 239) defined them as 'settled habits and thoughts common to the generality of men'. For Schotter (1981: 11) they are 'a regularity in social behaviour that is agreed to by all members of society, [and which] specifies behaviour in specific recurrent situations'. For North (1990: 3) institutions refer to 'the rules of the game in society, as the humanly devised constraints that shape human interaction'. Institutions are the process and structural regularities that constrain behaviour and provide the stability and predictability that makes social behaviour possible in the first place (Loasby 1999).

Institutions have long been a central feature of economic analysis as either: (1) the rules that structure coordination; or (2) as the self-organized outcomes of distributed but correlated individual behaviour. The modern revival of institutional analysis began with the work of the economic historians Douglass North and Robert Fogel who re-analysed the growth history of many nations and concluded that 'good' institutions were the dominant explanation because of the role they played in facilitating trade, capital accumulation and the growth of knowledge (North 2005). In consequence, getting the 'right' institutions as appropriate to market-led coordination (De Soto 2000) is central to modern economic growth and development policy.

Institutions have differential value owing to their performance as coordinating technologies. Nelson and Sampat (2001) develop a similar conception of institutions as 'social technologies'. Institutions are not simply social structures in the sociological sense, or habits and routines in the behavioural sense, but mechanisms for the production of coordination. The more effectively these mechanisms function, the better the coordination outcome; and the better the coordination outcome, the greater value is created from a given set of inputs. Institutional evolution, in the form of continual improvements to the coordinating rules, is a major cause of economic growth and development. The modern consensus of theory and evidence points to the general superiority of market-based institutions of decentralized coordination over planned forms of economic coordination. Nations that develop institutions that support this mechanism (such as property rights, rule of law, and so on) have, on the whole, superior growth and development outcomes to nations that do not.

Two points follow (with a similar theme to our discussion of industries). First, the economic order is not composed of one big institution (namely 'the market') but of a great many particular institutions (that is, markets). Furthermore, these institutions function as a complex co-evolving socio-cultural and socio-economic system. This recognizes institutions as evolving social technologies. It is of course nonsensical to speak of 'the technology' when considering the knowledge-base of the industries that constitute a particular economy instead of a vast network of particular physical technologies (Arthur 2009). The same is true of social technologies of coordination, or institutions.

Second, institutions as social technologies are not given (except in the short run) and evolve through an institutional trajectory (Potts 2007a). Institutions can be exogenously given or imposed. They are more often the result of a process that begins like all new technologies with individual origination (a new behavioural or social rule) that develops through a social, self-organizing process of adoption and retention. Institutional evolution, like technological and industrial evolution, is a normal and indeed necessary dimension of economic growth and development.

A connection between institutional evolution, economic growth and development, and the creative industries thus emerges. The economic value of the creative industries is due not only to their production of cultural goods and services, but also to their role in the evolution of institutions through the origination, adoption and retention of novel 'social technologies' or coordinating rules. The creative industries contribute to institutional innovation. This is why they matter for economic development.

15.5 CREATIVE INDUSTRIES AND ECONOMIC DEVELOPMENT

The creative industries are significant for economic growth and development not just in the sense of adding jobs or expanding economic activity but also for their role in facilitating economic evolution by their contribution to behavioural, social and institutional evolution. In the modern account of economic growth, institutions and development, economic growth drives the process of economic development as the demand from newly created wealth induces political mobilization to secure effective protection of property and other rights. This, in turn, facilitates further economic growth, through the effect of these evolved and adapted institutions. Chapter 11 discussed the idea that the rise of the creative industries may be a function of adaptation to market-capitalist institutions, yet we have the reverse flow here: from creative industries to market-capitalist development by facilitating institutional change in the form of socio-cultural adaptation to a new economic order.

It is easy to think of the creative industries as a vanguard of advanced civilizations (Hall 1998) and in particular to associate them with the powerhouses of modernity, in for example New York, London, Paris, and so forth (Florida 2002, Currid 2007). Thus the cultural and creative industries provide information content to the masses produced by the elite, in elite places. But that may not be entirely so, and a basic test of this proposition is whether the creative industries can also play a role in the process of economic development. The same urban feedback will surely occur, such that the creative industries in China, for example, will probably tend to be largely a product of operations in Beijing, Shanghai or Guangzhou. But that is to be expected, given the importance of co-location in production and the aggregation or clustering process this implies (see Chapter 13). But we might also expect a broader transformation in socio-cultural norms and expectations toward a more open, experimental and adaptive cultural and economic order. The creative industries may thus be key parts in this co-evolutionary process of economic and socio-cultural adaptation, a process that is, technically, development.

The case for technological development in developing economies is elucidated in the national systems of innovation literature (Freeman 2002, OECD 2002). But the arts, cultural and broader creative industries may be a much overlooked yet crucial part of a national innovation system. This idea was presented in Chapter 9 in relation to the role of creative industries in facilitating an innovation trajectory, mostly on the demand side. But this same argument extends to an institutional trajectory too. This may ultimately be a more significant component of growth in developing countries than in developed countries owing to the effect of the creative industries on behavioural, social and institutional evolution.

In many developing economies, and particularly those with a recent history of centralized economic control, the problem is not that the creative industries were insufficiently supported – as in the arts council type refrain in developed economies, *á la* Baumol and Bowen (1966) – but rather that they were actively repressed. Lifting that repression, along with the implications for personal freedom and institutional experimentation that that implies, may be a major spur to economic development by freeing the creative mechanisms that facilitate the sorts of institutional dynamics that are a necessary concomitant of economic development (Coyne and Leeson 2009). This highlights the importance of entrepreneurship, support services, clusters, and the overall institutional system of the cultural and creative economy and its connection with the innovation system.

Yet for most nations and regions, and arguably especially developing nations, this is not the standard or received cultural policy setting. Instead, policy tends to go in the opposite direction, favouring bureaucratic management, centralized allocation and equity based distribution, a focus on preservation and maintenance, and separateness from the rest of the economy. The UNESCO model is a suitable example. Yet the findings and framework of the evolutionary economics of creative industries point in a different direction: specifically toward increased openness and market-based institutions that may facilitate not only a sustainable cultural and creative economy but possibly even a thriving one (Cowen 2002).

Creative industries contribute to the process of economic development by their contribution to the co-evolutionary process of economic and socio-cultural adaptation. Economic development requires institutional change, which requires cultural and behavioural change. The creative industries contribute to this aspect of the 'national innovation system' mostly on the demand side, as explained in Chapter 9 above in relation to market goods, but it can also be seen at deeper levels of change in the behavioural, socio-cultural and institutional prerequisites of economic development.

15.6 CONCLUSION

The modern theory connecting economic development to economic growth has been reviewed, along with the role of economic institutions. We have highlighted the role of creative industries in institutional evolution, and thus as a driver of economic development. This connection is suggestive. It implies that the creative industries may actually play a more significant role in the process of economic development than previously appreciated. This occurs by their role in facilitating the institutional dynamics that are a necessary condition of the economic development (that is, institutional change) that in turn underpins economic growth.

Consider John Hartley (2009b) on this same theme of co-evolutionary adaptation (although his focus is just on 'media studies'):

> The place where this rethink seems to have progressed most energetically in recent years is in the new field of 'creative industries'. The issues raised in the attempt to identify and explain the creative industries are of significance to 'media industry studies', because the creative industries are located at the very place where new values, both economic and cultural, new knowledge and new forms of social relationship are emergent, and where they are in the process of society-wide adoption and retention, often through market mechanisms. It may even be argued that the 'creative industries' are the empirical form taken by innovation in advanced knowledge-based economies, in which case their importance – like that of the media – exceeds their scale as a sector of the economy. It extends to their role as a general enabling social technology. This would place *creative innovation* on a par with other enabling social technologies like the law, science, and markets. Where the media (in the guise of 'cultural industries') were regarded as the social technology of ideological control in the modern industrial era, the creative industries may be regarded as the social technology of distributed innovation in the era of knowledge-based complex systems.

In 'advanced knowledge-based economies' creative industries are the driving form of innovation. This argument applies to developing nations too and for the same reasons: namely that 'it extends to their role as a general enabling social technology'. Creative industries shape the new social technologies that co-evolve with economic evolution. This can be a critical factor in developing as well as advanced economic orders.

I have sought here to highlight and critique the often all-too-implicit model of economic development in terms of stages of industrial development. I have also argued against the idea that the cultural and creative industries and the service industries in general, represent a latter or penultimate phase of development that arrives only after industrial modernity is achieved. Instead, I have suggested that creative industries are involved whenever there is evolutionary economic development. The problem with the stages of development model is that it makes little economic sense from the evolutionary perspective of a market economy (that is, it is a planning model). Furthermore, it utterly negates the role of institutions and institutional dynamics in the process of economic development. It is therefore important to reject the stages of development model if one is to have a clear view of the role of creative industries in economic development. Once recognized, the cultural and creative industries can be seen to play a more central role in the process of economic development through their role in the process of economic evolution and its co-evolutionary behavioural and socio-cultural correlates.

The significance of institutions in economic growth and development is a relatively recent finding in modern economics. This is based on the role of institutions in facilitating economic coordination and re-coordination in the face of ever-changing opportunities and constraints. Institutions are thus coordinating technologies, or 'social technologies' in the model of Nelson and Sampat (2001). In itself, this highlights the role of 'good' institutions (or social technologies) in facilitating economic development. But it also raises the question of what then coordinates the coordinating technologies, or facilitates the dynamics and evolution of institutions themselves. Many development models still hew to an exogenous explanation, supposing that institutions are historical givens or imposed from above (by the government, or the IMF, say). But as social technologies, institutions also evolve within a socio-cultural and socio-political system; they can be modelled over an innovation trajectory (Potts 2007a, 2007b).

My argument continues the core thesis of this book on the role of creative industries in the innovation system. But I have extended this now to the evolution of institutional structure itself as a theory of how creative industries affect economic development. The creative industries contribute to the process of institutional origination and dynamics, which connects them to the process of economic development that in turn facilitates evolutionary economic growth. In this theory, the creative industries may actually be more important for developing economies than for already developed economies because the potential gains from institutional change will have greater marginal benefits in the former. Creative industries' policy in this way presents a possible development strategy.

This in turn highlights a fundamental weakness of standard models of cultural industries in developing nations; in particular the line developed by organizations such as UNESCO that focus on maintaining and preserving cultural heritage and the institutions that support it. (This is of course itself based on recognition that in poorer developing nations there will often be insufficient public resources to protect and maintain such cultural heritage.) Yet the unintended consequence of such policy is often to isolate the cultural and creative industries from their role in social and institutional transformation. Instead, it often works to reinforce their role in preserving and maintaining existing socio-cultural institutions and ways of life which, in turn, weakens their role in facilitating the institutional change that economic development requires.

This presents a difficult trade-off between the values of tradition and the value of modernity. But it is equally important to recognize that this trade-off exists and that an overemphasis on preservation of cultural heritage and institutions may come at the cost of the very economic development that eventually provides resources for such maintenance. Recognizing the role of cultural and creative industries in facilitating institutional adaptation and change may move them, rightfully, closer to the core of economic development policy.

NOTES

1. This is sometimes extended to include the quaternary industries, consisting of intellectual services.
2. Originally, see Alfred Marshall's discussion of this in *Principles of Economics*.
3. For a discussion of the mess that results from treating 'the media' as an industry, see Hartley (2009b).

16. Conclusion

16.1 SUMMARY AND IMPLICATIONS

This book has sought to present the outlines of an evolutionary economics of the creative industries. The overarching theme has been that of the contribution of the creative industries to evolutionary economic dynamics. My line has been that they play an important role in the innovation process; both an under-appreciated role and a widely misunderstood role. The creative industries have been under-appreciated as drivers of innovation because they have been over-represented as a welfare problem. Their role has been misunderstood because we have not taken enough notice of the deep similarity of artists and entrepreneurs. To address these issues I have sought to present and in part develop in this book an evolutionary economics of creative industries. In this world, the creative industries matter because of their significance to economic change: they are part of the mechanism of economic evolution. That's what makes them economically valuable: they make change.

Yet this is not the standard line in cultural economics, nor a particularly confident line in modern creative industries analysis. What I have argued instead is that the economics of creative industries is properly based on an evolutionary economics organized in terms of the micro–meso–macro framework (Dopfer and Potts 2008). This suggests three distinct levels of analytic focus for the dynamic contribution of the creative industries.

First, the creative industries have micro dynamic effects. This recognizes that the process of economic evolution involves agents reacting to novelty and becoming different. This is an entrepreneurial action in that it is an imaginative creative leap based on perceptions of economic opportunity within the constraints of economic institutions. The creative industries play a key role in these micro dynamics.

Second, the creative industries have meso dynamic effects. These are the contribution of the creative industries to the innovation process. A meso or innovation trajectory is modelled in evolutionary economics as following a three-phase process of origination, adoption and retention. The creative industries are instrumentally involved, on both the demand and supply side, in all three phases, making the creative industries manifestly part of the innovation system.

Third, the creative industries have macro dynamic effects. These are the industrial and institutional dynamics in the context of economic growth and development. Again, the creative industries contribute to institutional dynamics (and therefore economic development) through their role in the co-evolution of cultural, political and social economic systems.

This gathers into an open market policy perspective on the creative industries. The open market focus of this evolutionary economic approach is because mechanisms of creativity and the process of origination, adoption and retention of new ideas is something that occurs best and most effectively in a free market system that is behaviourally, organizationally and institutionally geared to evolutionary change. The creative industries are an important part of the innovation system at the micro, meso and macro levels through their contribution to the evolutionary economic process. That connection between contribution to innovation systems and (co-evolving) contribution to economic evolution has been the central theme of this book.

Obviously, I have not developed a rigorous analytic framework or a mathematical suite of models. My more modest goal has been to open some pathways by working through the development of evolutionary economics to creative industries analysis. I have sought to present here a coherent overarching framework that sufficiently illuminates the various aspects of an evolutionary economic approach to the study of creative industries as a legitimate element of innovation studies and innovation policy, and also to economic growth and development theory and policy. This has been based on a combination of evolutionary economics, complexity theory, and cultural and media studies. What comes next is cultural science, which is this hybrid manifest.

16.2 TOWARD CULTURAL SCIENCE

I have charted in this book a path from the neoclassical economics of the cultural industries to the evolutionary economics of the creative industries. But after that, what's next? Many lines of conceptual and theoretical speculation were advanced here, some maybe even deserving further theoretical inquiry and empirical analysis. Yet if we will follow these lines, the next step is to further augment the evolutionary economics integration into cultural studies with a broader integration of evolutionary theory and complexity science (Lee 2007, Potts 2008, Hartley 2009a, Herrmann-Pillath 2010). This emergent hybrid is cultural science.[1]

Cultural science is an interdisciplinary and perhaps transdisciplinary science that combines the analytic core of cultural studies (cultural emergence and cultural systems) with the analytic core of evolutionary economics (economic dynamics in open systems). The result is a new framework and a new dialogue for the study of cultural dynamics. This is exemplified in the study of the creative industries as presented here from an evolutionary and complexity perspective. The research program of cultural science is based on bringing the analytic insights of evolutionary economics and complexity theory into the study of cultural dynamics. In practice this means the study of the creative industries from the innovation perspective. This is not the same as from the economic perspective, or from the cultural and media studies perspective, or even from the humanities perspective. Cultural science seeks a methodological and analytic–and indeed ontological–middle ground of cultural dynamics as co-evolving with economic dynamics. This forms a complex emergent and open system that can be approached with an amalgam of methods and tools drawn from cultural studies, evolutionary economics and complexity science.

So, what's next? The major key of this book has been the role of the creative industries in the process of economic evolution. The core analytic and policy argument has been for dynamic economic efficacy of the creative industries vis-à-vis economic evolution, rather than their static economic significance vis-à-vis jobs and value added. Cultural science offers a way to further explore the mechanisms by which this evolutionary process operates, as well as how it changes. Throughout this book, I have sought to highlight some important complex systems and evolutionary processes that have been misunderstood or overlooked in previous analysis of the creative industries because they deal with social and cultural systems, including interactions between market and non-market systems. A cultural science approach enables us to go deeper into these mechanisms and dynamic processes. It extends the evolutionary economics of creative industries by connecting it to the methodologies and analytic focus of cultural studies and then linking these together back to the mainstream of scientific inquiry. This moves beyond the 'ideology-critique' stance built into cultural and media studies from the beginning and reifying a deep-set suspicion of market mechanisms and preference for political solutions over market solutions. Instead, the cultural science model seeks to reconnect with those market mechanisms as evolutionary mechanisms. Cultural science seeks to study how people adapt to new 'market' circumstances and through whatever these markets may be.

This book has been about economic and cultural co-evolution. We have examined how cultural evolution is a facilitating mechanism of economic evolution. Creative industries are properly part of innovation systems analysis, in particular on the demand side. This book has sought to elaborate several aspects of that mechanism.

NOTE

1. See http://www.cultural-science.org/.

References

Adorno, T., Horkheimer, M. (1979) *Dialectics of Enlightenment*. Verso: London.

Aghion, P., Howitt, P. (1992) 'A model of growth through creative destruction' *Econometrica*, 60: 323–51.

Akerlof, G., Kranton, R. (2000) 'Economics and identity' *Quarterly Journal of Economics*, 105(3): 715–53.

Akerlof, G., Kranton, R. (2002) 'Identity and schooling: Some lessons for the economics of education' *Journal of Economic Literature*, 40(4): 1167–201

Akerlof, G., Kranton, R. (2005) 'Identity and the economics of organizations' *Journal of Economic Perspectives*, 19(1): 9–32.

Akerlof, G., Kranton, R. (2010) *Identity Economics*. Princeton University Press: Princeton.

Akerlof, G., Shiller, R. (2009) *Animal Spirits*. Princeton University Press: Princeton.

Andersson, D.E., Andersson, A.E. (2006) *The Economics of Experiences, the Arts and Entertainment*. Edward Elgar: Cheltenham, UK and Northampton, MA, USA.

Arthur, W.B. (1989) 'Competing technologies, increasing returns and lock-in by historical events' *Economic Journal*, 99: 116–31.

Arthur, W.B. (2009) *The Nature of Technology*. Free Press: New York.

Bakhshi, H., McVittie, E., Simmie, J. (2008) 'Creating innovation: Do the creative industries support innovation in the wider economy?' NESTA: London.

Balazs, V., Stark, D. (2010) 'Structural folds: Generative disruption in overlapping groups' *American Journal of Sociology,* 115(4): 1150–90.

Banks, M., Hesmondhalgh, D. (2009) 'Looking for work in creative industries policy' *International Journal of Cultural Policy*, 15(4): 415–30.

Banks, J., Humphreys, S. (2008) 'The labour of user co-creators: Emergent social network markets?' *Convergence: The International Journal of Research into New Media Technologies*, 14(4): 401–18.

Banks, J., Potts, J. (2010) 'Consumer co-creation in online games' *New Media and Society*, 12(2): 253–70.

Barabasi, A.L. (2002) *Linked: The new science of networks*. Perseus Publishing: Cambridge, MA.

Baumol, W. (1982) 'Contestable markets: An uprising in the theory of industry structure' *American Economic Review*, 72: 1–15.

Baumol, W. (2002) *The Free-market Innovation Machine*. Princeton University Press: Princeton.

Baumol, W. (2004) 'Entrepreneurial cultures and countercultures' *Academy of Management Learning and Education*, 3(3): 316–26.

Baumol, W., Bowen, W. (1966) *Performing Arts: The economic dilemma*. Twentieth Century Fund: New York.

Baumol, W., Blackman, S., Wolff, E. (1989) *Productivity and American Leadership*. MIT Press: Cambridge, MA.

Beck, J. (2007) 'The sale effect of word of mouth: A model for creative goods and estimation for novels' *Journal of Cultural Economics*, 31(1): 5–23.

Becker, M., Knudsen, T., March, J. (2006) 'Schumpeter, Winter and the source of novelty' *Industrial and Corporate Change*, 15(2): 353–71.

Beinhocker, E. (2006) *The Origin of Wealth: Evolution, complexity and the radical remaking of economics*. Harvard Business School Press: Cambridge, MA.

Bell, D. (1973) *The Coming of Post-Industrial Society*. Basic Books: New York.

Belleflamme, P., Picard, P., Thisse, J. (2000) 'An economic theory of regional clusters' *Journal of Urban Economics*, 48(1): 158–84.

Benkler, Y. (2001) 'Coase's penguin, or Linux and the nature of the firm' *Yale Law Review*, 112: 369–98.

Benkler, Y. (2006) *The Wealth of Networks*. Yale University Press: New Haven.

Bentley, R.A. (2009) 'Fashion versus reason in the creative industries', in M. O'Brien and S. Shennan (eds) *Innovation in Cultural Systems: Contributions from evolutionary anthropology*. MIT Press: Cambridge, MA, pp. 121–6.

Bentley, R.A., Lipo, C., Herzog, H., Hahn, M. (2007) 'Regular rates of popular culture change reflect random copying' *Evolution and Human Behavior*, 28(3): 151–8.

Bianchi, M. (2002) 'Novelty, preferences and fashion: when goods are unsettling' *Journal of Economic Behaviour and Organization*, 47: 1–18.

Blaug, M. (2001) 'Where are we now on cultural economics?' *Journal of Economic Surveys*, 15: 123–43.

Blaug, M. (ed.) (1976) *The Economics of the Arts*. Martin Robinson: London.

Blien, U., Maier, G. (eds) (2008) *The Economics of Regional Clusters: Networks, technology and policy*. Edward Elgar: Cheltenham, UK and Northampton, MA, USA.

Boden, M. (1990) *The Creative Mind*. Weidenfeld & Nicolson: London.

Boden, M. (ed.) (1994) *Dimensions of Creativity*. MIT Press: Cambridge, MA.

Boldrin, M., Levine, K. (2008) *Against Intellectual Monopoly*. Cambridge University Press: Cambridge.

Boltanski, L., Thévenot, L. (2006) *On Justification: The economies of worth*. Princeton University Press: Princeton.

Bowles, S., Gintis, H. (1986) *Democracy and Capitalism*. Basic Books: New York.

Boyd, T. (2003) *Young Black Rich and Famous*. Doubleday/Random House: New York.

Boyd, B. (2009) *The Origin of Stories: Evolution, cognition and fiction*. Harvard/Belknap Press: Cambridge (MA).

Boyd, R., Richerson, P. (2004) *The Origin and Evolution of Cultures*. Oxford University Press: Oxford.

Breger, L. (1974) *From Instinct to Identity*. Prentice-Hall: New York.

Bresnahan, T., Gordon, R. (eds) (1997) *The Economics of New Goods*. Chicago: University of Chicago Press.

Brooks, A. (2001) 'Who opposes government arts funding?' *Public Choice*, 108: 355–67.

Bruns, A. (2008) *Blogs, Wikipedia, Second Life and Beyond: From production to produsage*. Peter Lang: New York.

Burgess, J., Green, J. (2008) *Youtube: Online video and the politics of participatory culture*. Polity Press: London.

Burt, R. (1995) *Structural Holes: The social structure of competition*. Harvard University Press: Cambridge, MA.

Caballero, R., Hammour, M. (1994) 'The cleansing effect of recessions' *American Economic Review*, 84: 1350–68.

Campbell, D. (1960) 'Blind variation and selective retention in creative thought as in other knowledge processes' *Psychological Review*, 67: 380–400.

Castañer, X., Campos, L. (2002) 'Determinants of artistic innovation: Bringing in the role of organizations' *Journal of Cultural Economics*, 26(1): 29–52.

Castells, M. (1996) *The Rise of the Network Society*. Blackwell: Boston.

Castronova, E. (2005) *Synthetic Worlds: The business and culture of online games*. University of Chicago Press: Chicago.

Castronova, E. (2006) 'On the research value of large games' *Games and Culture*, 1(2): 163–86.

Caves, R. (2000) *Creative Industries: Contracts between art and commerce*. Harvard University Press: Harvard.

Chai, A., Earl, P.E., Potts, J. (2007) 'Fashion, growth and welfare: An evolutionary approach', in M. Bianchi (ed.), *The Evolution of*

Consumption – Advances in Austrian Economics, 10, JAI/Elsevier: Oxford, pp. 187–207.

Chenery, H. (1975) 'A structuralist approach to development policy' *American Economic Review*, 65: 310–16.

Christakis, N., Fowler, J. (2009) *Connected*. Little Brown: New York.

Christensen, C. (1997) *The Innovator's Dilemma*. Harvard Business School Press: Cambridge, MA.

Coelho, P., Klein, D., McClure, J. (2004) 'Fashion cycles in economics' *Economic Journal Watch*, 1(3): 437–54.

Conlisk, J. (1996) 'Why bounded rationality?' *Journal of Economic Literature*, 34(2): 669–700.

Cooke, P., Lazzaretti, L. (eds) (2007) *Creative Cities, Cultural Clusters and Local Economic Development*. Edward Elgar: Cheltenham, UK and Northampton, MA, USA.

Cooley, T., Greenwood, J., Mehmet, Y. (1997) 'The replacement problem' *Journal of Monetary Economics*, 40: 457–99.

Cooper, R., Haltiwanger, J. (1993) 'The aggregate implications of machine replacement' *American Economic Review*, 83: 360–82.

Cowen, T. (1996) 'Why I do not believe in the cost-disease' *Journal of Cultural Economics*, 20(3): 207–14.

Cowen, T. (1998) *In Praise of Commercial Culture*. Harvard University Press: Cambridge, MA.

Cowen, T. (2002) *Creative Destruction: How globalization is changing the world's cultures*. Princeton University Press: Princeton.

Cowen, T. (2006) *Good and Plenty*. Princeton University Press: Princeton.

Cowen, T. (2009) *Create Your Own Economy*. Penguin: New York.

Cowen, T., Kaplan, B. (2004) 'Why do people underestimate the benefits of cultural competition?' *American Economic Review*, 94: 402–7.

Cowen, T., Tabarrok, A. (2000) 'An economic theory of avant-garde and popular art, or high and low culture' *Southern Economic Journal*, 67: 232–53.

Coyne, C., Leeson, P. (2009) *Media, Development and Institutional Change*. Edward Elgar: Cheltenham, UK and Northampton, MA, USA.

Croteau, D. (2006) 'The growth of self-produced media content and the challenge to media studies' *Critical Studies in Media Communication*, 23(4): 340–44.

Csikszentmihalyi, M. (1996) *Creativity*. New York: Harper.

Cunningham, S. (2002) 'From cultural to creative industries: Theory, industry, and policy implications' *Media International Australia*, 102: 54–65.

Cunningham, S. (2004) 'The creative industries after cultural policy' *International Journal of Cultural Studies*, 7: 105–15.

Cunningham, S. (2006) 'What price a creative economy?' *Platform Papers #9*. Currency House: Sydney.

Cunningham, S. (2009) 'Trojan horse or Rorschach blot? Creative industries discourse around the world' *International Journal of Cultural Policy*, 15(4): 375–86.

Cunningham, S., Potts, J. (2010) 'National Cultural Policy submission by ARC Centre of Excellence in Creative Industries and Innovation', Submission to National Cultural Policy: Canberra, Australia.

Currid, E. (2007) *The Warhol Economy: How fashion, art, and music drive New York city*. Princeton University Press: Princeton.

Curruthers, P. (2002) 'Human creativity: Its evolution, cognitive basis, and connection with childhood pretence' *British Journal for the Philosophy of Science*, 53(2): 225–49.

Davis, J. (1995) 'Personal identity and standard economic theory' *Journal of Economic Methodology* 2(1): 35–52.

Davis, J. (2003) *The Theory of the Individual in Economics*. London: Routledge.

Davis, J. (2007) 'Akerlof and Kranton on identity in economics: inverting the analysis' *Cambridge Journal of Economics*, 31(3): 349–62.

Dawkins, R. (1982) *The Extended Phenotype*. Freeman: Oxford.

DCMS (1998) *Creative Industries Mapping Document*. DCMS (Department of Culture, Media and Sport of the UK Government): London.

DCMS (2001) *Creative Industries Mapping Document*. HMSO: London.

De Soto, H. (2000) *The Mystery of Capital*. Bantam Press: London.

De Vany, A. (2004) *Hollywood Economics*. Routledge: London.

De Vany, A., Walls, W. (1996) 'Bose-Einstein dynamics and adaptive contracting in the motion picture industry' *Economic Journal*, 106: 1493–514.

DEMOS (2007) 'So, what do you do? A new question for policy in a creative age'. Green Paper. DEMOS: London.

Department of Communications and the Arts (Australian Government) (1994) *Creative Nation: Commonwealth Cultural Policy*. DCA: Canberra.

Dissanayake, E. (1992) *Homo Aestheticus*. Free Press: New York.

Dodgson, M., Gann, M., Salter, A. (2005) *Think, Play, Do*. Cambridge University Press: Cambridge.

Dopfer, K. (2004) 'The economic agent as rule maker and rule user: Homo sapiens oeconomicus' *Journal of Evolutionary Economics*, 14(2): 177–95.

Dopfer, K. (2005) 'Evolutionary economics: a theoretical framework' in K. Dopfer (ed.) *The Evolutionary Foundations of Economics*. Cambridge University Press: Cambridge, pp. 3–55.

Dopfer, K., Potts, J. (2008) *The General Theory of Economic Evolution*. Routledge: London.

Dopfer, K., Foster, J., Potts, J. (2004) 'Micro–meso–macro' *Journal of Evolutionary Economics*, 14: 263–79.

Dosi, G. (1982) 'Technological paradigms and technological trajectories: A suggested interpretation of the determinants and direction of technological change' *Research Policy*, 11(3): 147–62.

Dosi, G. (1988) 'Sources, procedures and microeconomic effects of innovation' *Journal of Economic Literature*, 26(3): 1120–71.

Dosi, G., Marengo, L., Fagioli, G. (2005) 'Learning in evolutionary environments', in K. Dopfer (ed.) *The Evolutionary Foundations of Economics*. Cambridge University Press: Cambridge, pp. 255–334.

Du Gay, P., Pryke, M. (eds) (2002) *Cultural Economy: Cultural analysis and commercial economy*. Sage: London.

Dutton, D. (2009) *The Art Instinct: Beauty, pleasure and human evolution*. Oxford University Press: Oxford.

Earl, P.E. (1986) *Lifestyle Economics: Consumer behaviour in a turbulent world*. Wheatsheaf: Brighton.

Earl, P.E. (2002) *Information, Opportunism and Economic Coordination*, Edward Elgar: Cheltenham, UK and Northampton, MA, USA.

Earl, P.E. (2003) 'The entrepreneur as a constructor of connections' in R. Koppl (ed.) *Austrian Economics and Entrepreneurial Studies – Advances in Austrian Economics*, 6, JAI/Elsevier: Oxford, pp. 117–34.

Earl, P.E. (2010) 'The Sensory Order, the economic imagination and the tacit dimension', in R. Koppl and S. Horwitz (eds) *The Social Science of Hayek's 'The Sensory Order' (Advances in Austrian Economics, Volume 13)*, Emerald Group Publishing Limited, pp. 211–36.

Earl, P.E., Potts, J. (2001) 'Latent demand and the browsing shopper' *Managerial and Decision Economics*, 21: 111–22.

Earl, P.E., Potts, J. (2004) 'The market for preferences' *Cambridge Journal of Economics,* 28: 619–33.

Earl, P.E., Wakeley, T. (2010) 'Alternative perspectives on connections in economic systems' *Journal of Evolutionary Economics* (forthcoming).

Earl, P.E., Peng, T.C., Potts, J. (2007) 'Decision-rule cascades and the dynamics of speculative bubbles' *Journal of Economic Psychology*, 28: 351–64.

Easterly, W. (2002) *The Elusive Quest for Growth*. MIT Press: Cambridge, MA.

Ebner, A. (2006) 'Institutions, entrepreneurship, and the rationale of government' *Journal of Economic Behavior and Organization*, 59: 497–515.

Edquist, C. (1997) *Systems of Innovation: Technologies, institutions and organizations*. Pinter: Washington.

Eisenstein, E. (1980) *The Printing Press as an Agent of Change*. Cambridge University Press: Cambridge.

Findlay, C., Lumsden, C. (1988) 'The creative mind: Toward an evolutionary theory of discovery and innovation' *Journal of Social and Biological Structures*, 11: 3–55.

Florida, R. (2002) *The Rise of the Creative Class*. Basic Books: New York.

Florida, R. (2005) *Cities and the Creative Class*. Routledge: London.

Foster, J. (2006) 'From simplistic to complex systems in economics' *Cambridge Journal of Economics*, 29: 873–92.

Foster, J., Potts, J. (2006) 'Complexity, networks and the importance of demand and consumption in economic evolution', in M. McKelvey and M. Holman (eds) *Flexibility and Stability in Economic Transformation*. Oxford: Oxford University Press, pp. 99–120.

Freeman, C. (1995) 'The national system of innovation in historical perspective' *Cambridge Journal of Economics*, 19: 5–24.

Freeman, C. (2002) 'Continental, national and sub-national innovation systems: complementarity and economic growth' *Research Policy*, 31(2): 191–212.

Freeman, C., Soete, L. (1997) *Economics of Industrial Innovation*. Pinter: London.

Freeman, R. (1976) *The Overeducated American*. New York: Academic.

Frey, B. (2000) *Arts and Economics: Analysis and cultural policy*. Springer: New York.

Frey, B., Pommerehne, W. (1989) *Muses and Markets: Explorations in the economics of arts and culture*. Blackwell: Oxford.

Friedman, B. (2005) *The Moral Consequences of Economic Growth*. Knopf: New York.

Gabora, L. (2005) 'Creative thought as a non-Darwinian evolutionary process' *Journal of Creative Behavior*, 39(4): 65–87.

Galbraith, J. (1960) *The Liberal Hour*. Houghton Mifflin: New York.

Galenson, D. (2007) *Old Masters and Young Geniuses*. Princeton University Press: Princeton.

Galenson, D. (2009) *Conceptual Revolutions in Twentieth-Century Art*. Cambridge University Press: Cambridge.

Gallouj, F. (2002) *Innovation in the Service Economy*. Edward Elgar: Cheltenham, UK and Northampton, MA, USA.

Galloway, S., Dunlop, S. (2007) 'A critique of definition of the cultural and creative industries in public policy' *International Journal of Cultural Policy*, 13(1): 17–31.

Garnham, N. (2005) 'From cultural to creative industries: An analysis of the implications of the "creative industries" approach to arts and media policy making in the United Kingdom' *International Journal of Cultural Policy*, 11: 15–29.

Gill, R., Pratt, A. (2008) 'In the social factory? Immaterial labour, precariousness and cultural work' *Theory, Culture and Society Annual Review*, 25(7–8): 1–30.

Godfray, H. (1991) 'Signalling of need by off-spring to parents' *Nature*, 352: 328–30.

Grafen, A. (1990) 'Biological signals as handicaps' *Journal of Theoretical Biology*, 144: 517–46.

Grammp, W. (1989) *Pricing the Priceless: Art, artists and economics*. Basic Books: New York.

Green, J., Jenkins, H. (2009) 'The moral economy of Web 2.0: Audience research and convergence culture', in J. Holt and A. Perren (eds) *Media Industries: History, theory and method*. Wiley-Blackwell: New York.

Greenfield, S. (2008) *ID: The quest for identity in the 21st century*. Sceptre: London.

Greif, A. (1994) 'Cultural beliefs and the organization of society: A historical and theoretical reflection on collectivist and individualist societies' *Journal of Political Economy*, 102(5): 912–50.

Griliches, Z. (1957) 'Hybrid corn: An exploration in the economics of technological change' *Econometrica*, 25(4): 501–52.

Groot, W., Maassen van den Brink, H. (2000) 'Overeducation in labour markets: A meta-analysis' *Economics of Education Review*, 19: 131–47.

Gwee, J. (2009) 'Innovation and the creative industries cluster: A case study of Singapore's creative industries' *Innovation: Management, Practice and Policy*, 11(2): 240–52.

Haan, M., Dijkstra, G., Dijkstra, P. (2005) 'Expert judgment versus public opinion' *Journal of Cultural Economics*, 29: 59–72.

Hall, P. (1998) *Cities in Civilization*. Pantheon Books: New York.

Handke, C. (2006) *Surveying Innovation in the Creative Industries*. Humboldt University: Berlin; and Erasmus University: Rotterdam.

Hanusch, H., Pyka, A. (eds) (2007) *Elgar Companion to Neo-Schumpeterian Economics*. Edward Elgar: Cheltenham, UK and Northampton, MA, USA.

Hartley, J. (1996) *Popular Reality: Journalism, modernity, popular culture*. Arnold: London.

Hartley, J. (ed.) (2005) *Creative Industries*. Blackwell: Carlton.

Hartley, J. (2008) *Television Truths: Forms of knowledge in popular culture*. Blackwell: Oxford.

Hartley, J. (2009a) *The Uses of Digital Literacy*. University of Queensland Press: Brisbane.

Hartley, J. (2009b) 'From the consciousness industry to creative industries: Consumer-created content, social network markets and the growth of knowledge', in J. Holt and A. Perren (eds) *Media Industries: History, theory and methods*. Malden, MA and Oxford: Wiley-Blackwell, pp. 231–44.

Hartley, J., Cunningham, S. (2001) 'Creative industries: from *Blue Poles* to fat pipes', in M. Gillies (ed.) *Papers from the National Humanities Summit*. DETYA: Canberra.

Hartley, J., Montgomery, L. (2009) 'Fashion as consumer entrepreneurship: Emergent risk culture, social network markets, and the launch of Vogue in China' *Chinese Journal of Communication*, 2(1): 61–76.

Hartog, J. (2000) 'Over-education and earnings' *Economics of Education Review*, 19(2): 131–47.

Hayek, F. (1931) *Prices and Production*. Routledge: London.

Hayek, F. (1945) 'The use of knowledge in society' *American Economic Review*, 35: 519–30.

Hayek, F. (1952) *The Sensory Order*. University of Chicago Press: Chicago.

Hayek, F. (1960) *The Constitution of Liberty*. University of Chicago Press: Chicago.

Hayek, F. (1973/1976) *Law, Legislation, and Liberty: Rules and order*. University of Chicago Press: Chicago.

Hazledine, T., Siegfried, J. (1997) 'How did the wealthiest New Zealanders get so rich?' *New Zealand Economic Papers* 31: 35–47.

Heilbrun, J. (1991) 'Innovation in arts, innovation in technology and the future of the high arts' *Journal of Cultural Economics*, 17: 89–98.

Heilbrun, J., Gray, C. (2001) *The Economics of Art and Culture*. Cambridge University Press: Cambridge.

Herrmann-Pillath, C. (2006) 'Cultural species and institutional change in China' *Journal of Economic Issues*, 40(3): 539–74.

Herrmann-Pillath, C. (2008) 'Identity economics and the creative economy' *Cultural Science* 1(1).

Herrmann-Pillath, C. (2010) *The Economics of Identity and Creativity: A cultural science approach*. University of Queensland Press: Brisbane.

Hesmondhalgh, D. (2002) *The Cultural Industries*. Sage: London.

Hesmondhalgh, D., Pratt, A. (2005) 'Cultural industries and cultural policy' *International Journal of Cultural Policy*, 11: 1–13.

Higgs, P., Cunningham, S., Bakhshi, H. (2008) 'Beyond the creative industries: Mapping the creative economy in the UK', Policy Briefing, NESTA: London.

Higgs, P., Cunningham, S., Pagan, J. (2007) 'Australia's creative economy: Definitions of the segments and sectors', Technical Report,

Faculty Research Office, CCI. http://eprints.qut.edu.au/archive/0000 8242/.

Hodgson, G. (1988) *Economics and Institutions*. Polity Press: Cambridge.

Hodgson, G. (1997) 'The ubiquity of habits and rules' *Cambridge Journal of Economics*, 21: 663–84.

Hodgson, G. (2004) *The Evolution of Institutional Economics*. Routledge: London.

Holbrook, M. (1995) *Consumer Research*. Sage: Thousand Oaks, CA.

Howkins, J. (2001) *The Creative Economy*. Penguin: London.

Howkins, J. (2009) *Creative Ecologies*. University of Queensland Press: Brisbane.

Hutter, M. (2008) 'Creating artistic from economic value: Changing input prices and new art', in M. Hutter and D. Throsby (eds) *Beyond Price*. Cambridge University Press: Cambridge, pp. 60–74.

Hutter, M. (2010) 'Familiar surprises: Creating value in the creative industries', in P. Aspers and J. Beckert (eds) *The Worth of Goods*. Cambridge University Press: Cambridge.

Hutter, M. (forthcoming) 'Experience goods', in R.Towse (ed.) *Handbook of Cultural Economics* (2nd edn). Edward Elgar: Cheltenham, UK and Northampton, MA, USA.

Jacobs, J. (1969) *The Economy of Cities*. Penguin: London.

Jayne, M. (2005) 'Creative industries: The regional dimension' *Environment & Planning C: Government & Policy*, 23: 537–56.

Jenkins, H. (2006a) *Convergence Culture: Where old and new media collide*. New York University Press: New York.

Jenkins, H. (2006b) *Fans, Bloggers, and Gamers: Exploring participatory culture*. New York University Press: New York.

Johnson, J.P. (2002) 'Open source software: Private provision of a public good' *Journal of Economic and Management Strategy*, 11: 637–62.

Jones, C. (2002) 'Signalling expertise: How signals shape careers in creative industries', in M. Peiperl, M. Arthur, N. Anand (eds) *Career Creativity: Explorations in the remaking of work*. Oxford University Press: Oxford.

Jones, E. (1995) 'Culture and its relationship to economic change' *Journal of Institutional and Theoretical Economics*, 151: 269–85.

Jones, E. (2006) *Cultures Merging: A historical and economic critique of culture*. Princeton University Press: Princeton.

Kahneman, D., Tversky, A., Slovic, P. (1982) *Judgment Under Uncertainty*. Cambridge University Press: Cambridge.

Karpik, L. (2010) *Valuing the Unique: The economics of singularities*. Princeton University Press: Princeton.

Keane, M. (2007) *Created in China: The great new leap forward.* Routledge: London.

Keane, M., Hartley, J. (2006) 'Creative industries and innovation in China' *International Journal of Cultural Studies*, 9(3): 259–64.

Keane, M., Potts, J. (2010) 'China's new creative space' *International Journal of Chinese Culture and Management* (in press).

Keat, R. (2000) *Cultural Goods and the Limits of the Market: Beyond commercial modeling.* Macmillan: Basingstoke.

Kesenne, S. (1994) 'Can a basic income cure Baumol's cost disease?' *Journal of Cultural Economics*, 18: 93–100.

Keynes, J.M. (1930) *Treatise on Money.* McMillan: London.

Kirman, A. (1993) 'Ants, rationality and recruitment' *Quarterly Journal of Economics*, 108: 137–56.

Kirman, A. (2005) 'Demand theory and general equilibrium. From observation to introspection,' Paper presented for the HOPE conference, Duke University, April 2005.

Kirman, A., Teschl, M. (2004) 'On the emergence of economic identity' *Revue de philosophi économique*, 9(1): 59–86.

Kirzner, I. (1973) *Competition and Entrepreneurship.* University of Chicago Press: Chicago.

Kirzner, I. (1997) 'Entrepreneurial discovery and the competitive market process: An Austrian approach' *Journal of Economic Literature*, 35: 60–85.

Kler, P. (2007) 'A panel data investigation into over-education among tertiary educated Australian immigrants' *Journal of Economic Studies*, 34(3): 179–93.

Konner, M. (2010) *The Evolution of Childhood.* Belknap Press: Cambridge, MA.

Kretschmer, M., Klimis, G., Choi, C. (1999) 'Increasing returns and social contagion in cultural industries' *British Journal of Management*, 10(1): 61–72.

Krugman, P. (1991) 'Increasing returns and economic geography' *Journal of Political Economy*, 99: 483–99.

Kücklich, J. (2005) 'Precarious Playbour: Modders and the digital games industry' *Fibreculture Journal*, 3(5).

Lakhani, K., von Hippel, E. (2000) 'How OS software works: "free" user to user assistance' MIT Sloan Working paper #4117.

Lal, D. (1998) *Unintended Consequences.* MIT Press: Cambridge, MA.

Lancaster, K. (1966) 'A new approach to consumer theory' *Journal of Political Economy*, 74: 132–57.

Landry, C. (2000) *The Creative City.* Comedia: London.

Lanham, R. (2006) *The Economics of Attention.* University of Chicago Press: Chicago.

Lash, S., Urry, J. (1994) *Economies of Signs and Space*. Sage: London.

Lazzeretti, L., Boix, R., Capone, F. (2008) 'Do creative industries cluster? Mapping creative local production systems in Italy and Spain' *Industry and Innovation*, 15(5): 549–67.

Leadbeater, C. (2000) *Living on Thin Air: The new economy*. Penguin: London.

Leadbeater, C. (2008) *We Think: Mass innovation, not mass production*. Profile Books: London.

Leadbeater, C., Miller, T. (2004) *The Pro-Am Revolution: How enthusiasts are changing our economy and society*. Demos: London.

Lee, R. (2007) 'Cultural studies, complexity studies and the transformation of the structures of knowledge' *International Journal of Cultural Studies*, 10(1): 11–20.

Lee, S., Miosa, N., Weiss, M. (2003) 'Open-source as a signalling device' (available at: http://www.econbiz.de/archiv/f/uf/finanzierung/open_source.pdf).

Lerner, J., Tirole, J. (2002) 'Some simple economics of open source' *Journal of Industrial Economics*, 50: 197–234.

Lessig, L. (2004) *Free Culture: How big media uses technology and the law to lock down culture and control creativity*, Penguin Books: New York.

Lewis, D. (1969) *Convention: A philosophical study*. Harvard University Press: Cambridge, MA.

Lie, M., Sørensen, K. (eds) (1996) *Making Technology Our Own? Domesticating technology into everyday life*. Scandinavian University Press: Oslo.

Lindsay, I. (2005) 'Causes of overeducation in the Australian labour market' Department of Economics discussion paper #940, University of Melbourne.

Lipsey, R., Carlaw, K., Bekar, C. (2006) *Economic Transformations: General purpose technologies and long run economic growth*. Oxford University Press: Oxford.

Livet, P. (2006) 'Identities, capabilities and revisions' *Journal of Economic Methodology*, 13(3): 327–48.

Llanes, G. (2007) 'Technology sharing in open source' mimeo, Universidad Carlos III de Madrid: Madrid.

Loasby, B. (1999) *Knowledge, Institutions, and Evolution in Economics*. Routledge: London.

Loasby, B. (2002) 'The evolution of knowledge: Beyond the biological model' *Research Policy*, 31: 1227–39.

Long, N. (1958) 'The local community as an ecology of games' *American Journal of Sociology*, 64(3): 251–61.

Lumsden, C. (1999) 'Evolving creative minds: Stories and mechanisms', in

R. Sternberg (ed.) *Handbook of Creativity*. Cambridge University Press: New York, pp. 153–68.

Lundvall, B.Å. (1992). *National Systems of Innovation: Towards a theory of innovation and interactive learning*. Pinter: New York.

Magee, G. (2005) 'Rethinking invention: cognition and the economics of technological creativity' *Journal of Economic Behavior and Organization*, 57: 29–48.

Malaby, T. (2006) 'Parlaying value: Capital in and beyond virtual worlds' *Games and Culture*, 1(2): 141–62.

Martin, R., Sunley, P. (2002) 'Deconstructing clusters: Chaotic concept or policy panacea?' *Journal of Economic Geography*, 3(1): 5–35.

Mas-Colell, A. (1999) 'Should cultural goods be treated differently?' *Journal of Cultural Economics*, 23: 87–93.

Mavromaras, K., McGuinness, S., Wooden, M. (2007) 'Overskilling in the Australian labour market' *Australian Economic Review*, 40(6): 307–12.

Maynard-Smith, J. (1972) *On Evolution*. Edinburgh University Press: Edinburgh.

McCloskey, D. (2006) *The Bourgeois Virtues*. University of Chicago Press: Chicago.

McCraw, T. (2007) *Profit of Innovation: Joseph Schumpeter and Creative Destruction*. Harvard University Press: Cambridge (MA).

Menger, P.M. (1999) 'Artistic labour markets and careers' *Annual Review of Sociology*, 25: 541–74.

Menger, P.M. (2006) 'Artistic labour markets: contingent work, excess supply and occupational risk', in V. Ginsberg and D. Throsby (eds) *Handbook of Economics of Art and Culture*. North-Holland: Amsterdam, pp. 765–806.

Metcalfe, J.S. (1998) *Evolutionary Economics and Creative Destruction*. Routledge: London.

Metcalfe, J.S. (2001) 'Consumption, preferences and the evolutionary agenda' *Journal of Evolutionary Economics*, 11: 37–58.

Miller, G. (2000) *The Mating Mind*. Doubleday: New York.

Miller, G. (2009) *Spent: Sex, evolution and consumer behaviour*. Viking: New York.

Miller, G., Haselton, M. (2002) 'Fertile women prefer poor, creative men to wealthy, uncreative men as short-term sexual partners', Human Behavioural and Evolutionary Society Conference.

Miller, J.H., Page, S.E. (2007) *Complex Adaptive Systems: An introduction to computational models of social life*. Princeton University Press: Princeton.

Minsky, H. (1974) 'The modelling of financial instability: An introduction' *Modelling and Simulation*, 5: 267–72.

Minsky, H. (1975) *John Maynard Keynes*. Columbia University Press: New York.

Minsky, H. (1986) *Stabilizing an Unstable Economy*. McGraw-Hill: New York.

Mithen, S. (1996) *The Prehistory of the Mind*. Phoenix: London.

Moeran, B., Strandgaard, J. (eds) (forthcoming) *The Negotiation of Values in the Creative Industries: Fairs, festivals and competitive events*. Cambridge University Press: Cambridge.

Mokyr, J. (2004) *The Gifts of Athena: The historical origins of the knowledge economy*. Princeton University Press: Princeton.

Mommaas, H. (2004) 'Cultural clusters and the post-industrial city: Towards the remapping of urban cultural policy' *Urban Studies*, 41(3): 507–32.

Mustonen, M. (2003) 'Copyleft: Economics of Linux and other open source software' *Information Economics & Policy*, 15: 99–121.

Neff, G. (2005) 'The changing place of cultural production: The location of social networks in a digital media industry' *Annals of the American Academy of Political and Social Science*, 597: 134–52.

Nelson, R. (2002) 'Technology, institutions and innovation systems' *Research Policy*, 31: 265–72.

Nelson, R. (ed.) (1993) *National Innovation Systems*. Oxford University Press: New York.

Nelson, R., Consoli, D. (2010) 'An evolutionary theory of household consumption behavior' *Journal of Evolutionary Economics* (forthcoming).

Nelson, R., Sampat, B. (2001) 'Making sense of institutions as a factor shaping economic performance' *Journal of Economic Behaviour and Organization*, 44: 31–54.

Netzer, R. (1978) *The Subsidized Muse: Public support for the arts in the US*. Cambridge University Press: New York.

Newman, M.E. (2003) 'The structure and function of complex networks' *SIAM Review*, 45: 167–256.

North, D. (1990) *Institutions, Institutional Change and Economic Performance*. Cambridge University Press: Cambridge.

North, D. (2005) *Understanding the Process of Economic Change*. Princeton University Press: Princeton.

Oakley, K. (2004) 'Not so cool Britannia: The role of creative industries in economic development' *International Journal of Cultural Studies*, 7: 67–77.

Oakley, K. (2006) 'Include us out: Economic development and social policy in the creative industries' *Cultural Trends*, 15(4): 255–73.

Oakley, K. (2009) 'Art works – cultural labour markets: A literature review' *Creativity, Culture and Education Literature Reviews*. http://

www.creativitycultureeducation.org/data/files/cce-lit-review-8-a5-web-130.pdf.

OECD (2002) *Dynamising National Innovation Systems*. OECD: Paris.

OECD (2007) 'Participative Web: User-created content', Working Party on the Information Economy, OECD: Paris. http://www.oecd.org/dataoecd/57/14/38393115.pdf.

Orians, G. (2001) 'An evolutionary perspective on aesthetics' *Bulletin of Psychology and the Arts*, 2(1): 20–25.

Ormerod, P. (1998) *Butterfly Economics*. Faber & Faber: London.

Ormerod, P. (2005) *Why Most Things Fail: Evolution, extinction and economics*. Faber & Faber: London.

Ormerod, P. (2006) 'Extracting deep knowledge from limited information on evolved social networks' *Physica A*, 378: 48–52.

Ormerod, P., Roach, A. (2004) 'The medieval inquisition: scale-free networks and the suppression of heresy' *Physica A*, 339: 645–52.

Ostrom, E. (1990) *Governing the Commons*. Cambridge University Press: Cambridge.

Ostrom, E. (2006) *Understanding Institutional Diversity*. Princeton University Press: Princeton.

Page, S., Bednar, S. (2007) 'Can game(s) theory explain culture? The emergence of cultural behavior within multiple games' *Rationality and Society*, 19(1): 65–97.

Peacock, A. (1969) 'Welfare economics and public subsidies to the arts' *Manchester School of Economics and Social Studies*, 37: 323–35.

Peacock, A. (1993) *Paying the Piper: Culture, music and money*. Edinburgh University Press: Edinburgh.

Peacock, A. (2006) 'The arts and economic policy', in V. Ginsurgh and D. Throsby (eds) *Handbook of the Economics of Art and Culture*. North-Holland: Amsterdam, pp. 1123–40.

Pesendorfer, W. (1995) 'Design innovations and fashion cycles' *American Economic Review*, 85(4): 771–92.

Pine, B.J., Gilmour, J. (1999) *The Experience Economy*. Harvard Business School Press: Boston.

Pinker, S. (1997) *How the Mind Works*. WW Norton: New York.

Pinnock, A. (2006) 'Public value or intrinsic value: The arts–economics consequences of Mr Keynes' *Public Money & Management*, 26(3): 173–80.

Popper, K. (1945) *The Open Society and its Enemies*. Routledge: London.

Popper, K. (1968) *Conjectures and Refutations*. Harper & Row: New York.

Porter, M. (1990) *The Competitive Advantage of Nations*. Free Press: New York.

Porter, M. (1996) 'Competitive advantage, agglomeration economies and regional policy' *International Regional Science Review*, 19(1): 85–94.

Porter, M. (1998) 'Clusters and the new economics of competition' *Harvard Business Review*, Nov–Dec: 77–90.

Porter, M. (2000) 'Location, competition and economic development: Local clusters in a global economy' *Economic Development Quarterly*, 14(1): 15–34.

Postrel, V. (2005) *The Substance of Style*. Harper Collins: New York.

Potts, J. (2000) *The New Evolutionary Microeconomics: Complexity, competence and adaptive behaviour*. Edward Elgar: Cheltenham, UK and Northampton, MA, USA

Potts, J. (2001) 'Knowledge and markets' *Journal of Evolutionary Economics*, 11: 413–31.

Potts, J. (2003) 'Toward an evolutionary theory of homo economicus: The concept of universal nomadism', in J. Laurent (ed.) *Evolutionary Economics and Human Nature*. Edward Elgar: Cheltenham, UK and Northampton, MA, USA, pp. 195–216.

Potts, J. (2004) 'Liberty bubbles', *Policy*, 20: 15–21.

Potts, J. (2006) 'How creative are the super rich?' *Agenda*, 13(4): 339–50.

Potts, J. (2007a) 'Evolutionary institutional economics' *Journal of Economic Issues*, 41(2): 341–51.

Potts, J. (2007b) 'Art and innovation: An evolutionary view of the creative industries' *UNESCO Observatory e-journal*, 1(1).

Potts, J. (2008) 'Creative industries & cultural science' *Cultural Science*, 1(1), e-journal.

Potts, J. (2009a) 'Why the creative industries matter to economic evolution' *Economics of Innovation and New Technology*, 18(7): 663–73.

Potts, J. (2009b) 'Creative industries and innovation policy' *Innovation: Management, Practice and Policy*, 11(2): 138–47 (Special Issue on 'Creative Industries and Innovation Policy').

Potts, J. (2009c) 'Do developing economies require creative industries? Some old theory about new China' *Chinese Journal of Communication*, 2(1): 92–108.

Potts, J. (2009d) 'The innovation deficit in public services' *Innovation: Management, Policy and Practice*, 11(1): 34–43.

Potts, J. (2009e) 'Open occupations: Why work should be free' *Economic Affairs*, 29(1): 71–76.

Potts, J. (2010) 'Toward behavioural innovation economics: Heuristics and biases in choice under novelty' *Prometheus* (forthcoming).

Potts, J., Cunningham, S. (2008) 'Four models of the creative industries' *International Journal of Cultural Policy* 14(3): 233–47.

Potts, J., Mandeville, T. (2007) 'Toward an evolutionary theory of innovation and growth in the service economy' *Prometheus*, 25(2): 147–60.

Potts, J., Montgomery, L. (2009) 'Does weaker copyright mean stronger creative industries? Some lessons from China' *Creative Industries Journal*, 1(3): 245–61.

Potts, J., Morrison, K. (2009) 'Nudging innovation: fifth generation innovation, behavioural constraints and the role of creative business' Discussion Paper, NESTA: London.

Potts, J., Cunningham, S., Hartley, J., Ormerod, P. (2008a) 'Social network markets: A new definition of creative industries' *Journal of Cultural Economics*, 32: 167–85.

Potts, J., Hartley, J., Banks, J., Burgess, J., Cobcroft, R., Cunningham, S., Montgomery, L. (2008b) 'Consumer co-creation and situated creativity' *Industry & Innovation*, 15(5): 459–74.

Pratt, A. (2004) 'Creative clusters: Towards the governance of the creative industries production system?' *Media International Australia*, 112: 50–66.

Pratt, A. (2005) 'Cultural industries and cultural policy: an oxymoron?' *International Journal of Cultural Policy*, 11(1): 31–44.

Quah, D. (1999) 'The weightless economy in economic development' CEP Discussion Paper; CEPDP0417, 417. Centre for Economic Performance, London School of Economics and Political Science, London.

Quiggin, J. (2006) 'Blogs, wikis and creative innovation' *International Journal of Cultural Studies*, 9(4): 481–96.

Quiggin, J., Potts, J. (2008) 'Economics of non-market innovation & digital literacy' *Media International Australia*, 128: 144–50.

Raustiala, K., Sprigman, C. (2006) 'The piracy paradox: Innovation and intellectual property in fashion design' *Virginia Law Review*, 92(8): 1687–777.

Richardson, G.B. (1960) *Information and Investment*. Oxford University Press: Oxford.

Ridley, M. (2010) *The Rational Optimist: How prosperity evolves*. Harper: New York.

Robbins, L. (1963) 'Art and the state', in *Politics and Economics: Papers in Political Economy*. Macmillan: London, pp. 53–72.

Rodríguez-Clare, A. (2007) 'Clusters and comparative advantage: Implications for industrial policy' *Journal of Development Economics*, 82(1): 43–57.

Rodrik, D. (2007) *One Economics, Many Recipes*. Princeton University Press: Princeton.

Rogers, E. (1995) *Diffusion of Innovations*. The Free Press: New York.

Romer, P. (1990a) 'Human capital and economic growth: Theory and evidence', Carnegie-Rochester Conference Series on Public Policy, Elsevier, 32(1): 251–86.

Romer, P. (1990b) 'Endogenous technological change' *Journal of Political Economy*, 98(5): 71–102.

Roodhouse, S. (2006) *Cultural Quarters: Principles and practice*. Intellect Books: Bristol.

Rosen, S. (1981) 'The economics of superstars' *American Economic Review*, 71: 845–58.

Ross, A. (2009) *Nice Work If You Can Get It: Life and labor in precarious times*. New York University Press: New York.

Rothenberg, A. (1990) *Creativity and Madness*. Johns Hopkins University Press: Baltimore.

Rothwell, R. (1994) 'Towards the fifth-generation innovation process' *International Marketing Review*, 11(1): 7–31.

Rowen, M. (2007) 'The curious life of clusters' *Far Eastern Economic Review*, 170(6): 51–4.

Runciman, W. (2009) *The Theory of Cultural and Social Selection*. Cambridge University Press: Cambridge.

Ruskin, J. (1880) *'A Joy Forever' and its Price in the Market, or the Political Economy of Art*. http://www.gutenberg.org/catalog/world/readfile?fk_files=274196.

Schelling, T. (1973) 'Hockey helmets, concealed weapons, and daylight saving: A study of binary choices with externalities' *Journal of Conflict Resolution*, 17(3): 381–428.

Schotter, A. (1981) *The Economic Theory of Social Institutions*. Cambridge University Press: Cambridge.

Schubert, C. (forthcoming) 'Is novelty always a good thing? Towards an evolutionary welfare economics' *Journal of Evolutionary Economics*.

Schultz, T. (1961) 'Investment in human capital' *American Economic Review*, 51(1): 1–17.

Schumpeter, J. (1939) *Business Cycles*. McGraw Hill: New York.

Schumpeter, J. (1942) *Capitalism, Socialism and Democracy*. George Allen & Unwin: London.

Schumpeter, J. (1943) 'Capitalism in the postwar years', in S. Harris (ed.) *Postwar Economic Problems*. McGraw-Hill: New York, pp. 113–26.

Scitovsky, T. (1981) 'The desire for excitement in modern society' *Kyklos*, 34: 3–13.

Scott, A. (2002) 'A new map of Hollywood: The production and distribution of American motion pictures' *Regional Studies*, 36(9): 957–75.

Scott, A. (2006) 'Entrepreneurship, innovation and industrial development: Geography and the creative field revisited' *Small Business Economics*, 26(1): 1–24.

Seaman, B. (1987) 'Arts impact studies: A fashionable excess' *Economic Impact of the Arts: A sourcebook*, Chapter 2 (reprinted in Towse (ed.) 1997, Vol II, pp. 723–56).

Sen, A. (1985) 'Goals, commitment and identity' *Journal of Law, Economics & Organization*, 1(2): 341–55.

Sen, A. (1999a) *Development as Freedom*. Knopf: New York.

Sen, A. (1999b) *Reason before Identity*. Oxford University Press: Oxford.

Sen, A. (2004) 'Social identity' *Revue de philosophi économique*, 9(1): 7–27.

Sen, A. (2007) *Identity and Violence*. WW Norton: New York.

Shackle, G.L.S. (1972) *Epistemics and Economics: A critique of economic doctrines*. Cambridge: Cambridge University Press.

Shackle, G.L.S. (1979) *Imagination and the Nature of Choice*. Edinburgh University Press: Edinburgh.

Shirky, C. (2008) *Here Comes Everybody*. Allen Lane: New York.

Shirky, C. (2010) *Cognitive Surplus*. Penguin: New York.

Siegfried, J., Roberts, A. (1991) 'How did the wealthiest Britons get so rich?' *Review of Industrial Organization*, 6: 19–32.

Siegfried, J., Round, A. (1994) 'How did the wealthiest Australians get so rich?' *Review of Income and Wealth*, 40: 191–204.

Siegfried, J., Blitz, R., Round, D. (1995) 'The limited role of market power in generating great fortunes in Great Britain, the United States and Australia' *Journal of Industrial Economics*, 43: 277–86.

Silverstone, R., Hirsch, E. (eds) (1992) *Consuming Technologies: Media and information in domestic spaces*. Routledge: London.

Simmel, G. ([1904] 1957) 'Fashion' *American Journal of Sociology*, 62(6): 541–58.

Simon, H.A. (1978) 'Rationality and product and process of thought' *American Economic Review*, 68: 1–16.

Simonton, D.K. (1999) *Origins of Genius*. Oxford University Press: Oxford.

Smith, A. ([1795] 1980) 'The principles which lead and direct philosophical enquiries: Illustrated by the history of astronomy', in W. Wightman (ed.) *Essays on Philosophical Subjects*. Oxford University Press: Oxford, pp. 33–109.

Spence, M. (1973) 'Job market signalling' *Quarterly Journal of Economics*, 87: 355–74.

Star, S., Griesemer, J. (1989) 'Institutional ecology, translations and boundary objects' *Studies of Social Science*, 19: 387–420.

Stark, D. (2009) *Sense of Dissonance: Accounts of worth in economic life*. Princeton University Press: Princeton.

Sternberg, R. (ed.) (1999) *Handbook of Creativity*. Cambridge University Press: Cambridge.

Stilwell, F., Ansari, M. (2003) 'Wealthy Australians' *Journal of Australian Political Economy*, 52: 143–57.

Storper, M. (1997) *The Regional World: Territorial development in a global economy*. Guilford: New York.

Strogatz, S. (2001) 'Exploring complex networks' *Nature*, 410: 268–76.

Sundbo, J., Darmer, P. (eds) (2008) *Creating Experiences in the Experience Economy*. Edward Elgar: Cheltenham, UK and Northampton, MA, USA.

Swedberg, G. (2006) 'The cultural entrepreneur and the creative industries: beginning in Vienna' *Journal of Cultural Economics*, 30: 243–61.

Swedberg, R. (2007) *Principles of Economic Sociology*. Princeton University Press: Princeton.

Tabarrok, A. (2002) 'Patent theory versus patent law' *B.E. Journal of Economic Analysis and Policy*, 1(1).

Taylor, T. (2006) *Play Between Worlds: Exploring online game culture*. MIT Press: Boston.

Tether, B. (2003) 'The sources and aims of innovation in services: Variety between and within sectors' *Economics of Innovation and New Technology*, 12: 481–505.

Tether, B., Metcalfe, J.S. (2004) 'Systems of innovation in services' in F. Malerba (ed.) *Sectoral Systems of Innovation*. Cambridge University Press: Cambridge.

Thaler, R. (1980) 'Toward a positive theory of consumer choice' *Journal of Economic Behavior and Organization*, 1: 39–60.

Throsby, D. (1994) 'The production and consumption of the arts' *Journal of Economic Literature*, 32: 1–29.

Throsby, D. (2001) *Economics and Culture*. Cambridge University Press: Cambridge.

Throsby, D. (2006) *Does Australia need a Cultural Policy?* Platform Papers #7, Currency House: Sydney.

Throsby, D., Hollister, V. (2003) 'Don't give up your day job: An economic study of professional artists in Australia', Australia Council for the Arts: Canberra.

Throsby, D., Withers, G. (1979) *Economics of the Performing Arts*. Edward Arnold: London.

Tidd, J., Hull, F. (eds) (2003) *Service Innovation*. Imperial College Press: London.

Towse, R. (1996) *The Economics of Artists' Labour Markets*. Arts Council of England: London.

Towse, R. (ed.) (1997) *Cultural Economics*. Edward Elgar: Cheltenham, UK and Northampton, MA, USA.

Towse, R. (ed.) (2003) *A Handbook of Cultural Economics*. Edward Elgar: Cheltenham, UK and Northampton, MA, USA.

Towse, R. (2006) 'Human capital and artists' labour markets', in V. Ginsburgh and D. Throsby (eds), *Handbook of the Economics of Art and Culture*. North-Holland: Amsterdam, pp. 865–94.

Turok, I. (2003) 'Cities, clusters and creative industries: The case of film and television in Scotland' *European Planning Studies*, 11(5): 549–65.

Vang, J., Zellner, C. (eds) (2005) *Industry and Innovation*, Special issue on 'Innovation in services', 12(2): 141–301.

Veblen, T. (1898) 'Why is economics not an evolutionary science?' *Quarterly Journal of Economics*, 12(4): 373–97.

Veblen, T. (1899) *The Theory of the Leisure Class*. Macmillan: New York (reprinted Penguin: London, 1994).

Veblen, T. (1919) *The Place of Science in Modern Civilization and Other Essays*. Viking Press: New York.

Vega-Redondo, F. (2007) *Complex Social Networks*. Cambridge University Press: Cambridge.

von Hippel, E. (1988) *The Sources of Innovation*. Oxford University Press, New York.

von Hippel, E. (2006) *Democratizing Innovation*. Boston: MIT Press.

Wallas, G. (1926) *The Art of Thought*. Harcourt Brace: New York.

Wang, J. (2004) 'The global reach of new discourses: How far can creative industries travel?' *International Journal of Cultural Studies*, 7 (1): 9–19.

Wang, J. (2007) 'Industrial clusters in China: the low road versus the high road in cluster development', in A. Scott and G. Garofoli (eds) *Development on the Ground: Clusters, networks and regions in emerging economies*. London: Routledge, pp. 145–64.

Watson, N., Wooden, M. (2004) 'The HILDA survey: A summary' *Australian Journal of Labour Economics*, 7: 117–24.

Watts, D. (1999) *Small Worlds*. Princeton University Press: Princeton.

Williams, D. (2006) 'Why game studies now: Gamers don't bowl alone' *Games and Culture*, 1(1): 13–16.

Williams, R., Stewart, J., Slack, R. (2004) *Social Learning in Technological Innovation*. Edward Elgar: Cheltenham, UK and Northampton, MA, USA.

Winter, S. (1975) 'Optimization and evolution in the theory of the firm' in R. Day and T. Groves (eds) *Adaptive Economic Models*, pp. 73–118.

Witt, U. (2001) 'Learning to consume: A theory of wants and the growth of demand' *Journal of Evolutionary Economics*, 11: 23–36.

Witt, U. (2009a) 'Novelty and the bounds of unknowledge in economics' *Journal of Economic Methodology*, 16(4): 361–75.

Witt, U. (2009b) 'Propositions about novelty' *Journal of Economic Behavior and Organization*, 70(1–2): 311–20.

Woodman, R., J. Sawyer, R. Griffin (1993) 'Toward a theory of organizational creativity' *Academy of Management Review*, 18(2): 293–321.

Work Foundation (2007) *Staying Ahead: The economic performance of the UK's creative industries*. Work Foundation: London.

Yachi, S. (1995) 'How can honest signalling evolve?' *Proceedings of Royal Society of London*, B262: 283–8.

Young, H.P. (1998) *Individual Strategy and Social Structure: An evolutionary theory of institutions*. Princeton: Princeton University Press.

Zahavi, A., Zahavi, A. (1997) *The Handicap Principle*. Oxford University Press: Oxford.

Zeitlyn, D. (2003) 'Gift economies in the development of open source software: anthropological reflections' *Research Policy*, 32(7): 1287–91.

Index